Spirit Wars

Spirit Wars

*Native North American Religions
in the Age of Nation Building*

Ronald Niezen

WITH CONTRIBUTIONS BY

Manley Begay Jr.
Kim Burgess
Phyllis Fast
Valerie Long Lambert
Bernard C. Perley
Michael Wilcox

4/07

UNIVERSITY OF CALIFORNIA PRESS
Berkeley · Los Angeles · London

University of California Press
Berkeley and Los Angeles, California

University of California Press, Ltd.
London, England

© 2000 by the Regents of the
University of California

Library of Congress Cataloging-in-Publication Data

Niezen, Ronald.
    Spirit wars : Native North American religions in
the age of nation building / Ronald Niezen ; with
contributions by Kim Burgess . . . [et al.].

        p.   cm.
    Includes bibliographical references and index.
    ISBN 0-520-20985-0 (alk. paper).—
ISBN 0-520-21987-2 (pbk. : alk paper)
    1. Indians of North America—Canada—
Religion.   2. Indians of North America—
Canada—Government relations.   3. Indians of
North America—Cultural assimilation—
Canada.   4. Evangelistic work—Canada.
5. Genocide—Canada.   6. Canada—Race rela-
tions.   7. Canada—Politics and government.
I. Burgess, Kim.   II. Title.
E78.C2 N55   2000
299'.7—dc21   99-053116
                                            CIP

Manufactured in the United States of America

09   08   07   06   05   04   03   02   01   00
        10   9   8   7   6   5   4   3   2   1

To Doug and Beverly

Do but behold yon poor and starved band,
And your fair show shall suck away their souls,
Leaving them but the shales and husks of men.
    William Shakespeare, King Henry V

Contents

Figures

Preface

This book began as an effort to go beyond the limitations of general surveys of indigenous religions in North America. The native traditions of North America are tremendously varied, yet some culture areas are unified by common themes and practices; and in general these native traditions are pervaded by an orientation toward the land and the spirit world that could, for some, provide the basis for "pan-Indianism" and intertribal religious movements. The challenges of writing a general study of this kind are therefore almost overwhelming. Two surveys that stand out are Ake Hultkrantz's *The Religions of the American Indians* (1967), which does not limit its scope to the indigenous religions of North America but incorporates those of the South American continent as well, and Ruth Underhill's atavistically titled *Red Man's Religion* (1965). The main problem with these and other general treatments of indigenous religions is that the discussion too often hearkens back to a time when the traditions were "untarnished" or "undiminished" by colonial encounters—loss of land, missionary endeavors, schools, and so on—creating a false sense of permanence, as though spiritual traditions described at the time of contact were fixed, in a state of fragile harmony with the even more fragile political and economic systems, and incapable of adapting to the tumultuous changes brought about by settlement and "civilization." Underhill, it is true, devotes one of twenty-three chapters to "modern religions," mainly the Ghost Dance and Peyote religions, but overall she describes the religions of North America as picturesque, frozen in time, as that which occurred "before the white man's coming" (1965, 254). At best, such surveys can tell only part of the story. My intention in starting this book was to use the tools of ethnohistory and ethnography to write another kind of survey of indigenous North American religions, one that considers the dynamic uses and responses of spiritual traditions in the contexts of colonization and nation building.

Several recent experiences added significance to what would otherwise have been a largely pedagogical exercise. In the summer of 1996 I was invited by the Nishnawbe-Aski Nation, a political organization of forty-eight Cree and Anishinawbe (Ojibwa) communities in northern Ontario, Canada, to conduct interviews with social-service workers, native health professionals, elders, and other members of six villages in order to provide decision makers with research material for mental health policy development. I had made many trips to northern Québec, which varied in length from a week to three months, usually to do similar research for the Cree Board of Health and Social Services of James Bay; but I had never seen the western side of James Bay, and, looking forward to the experience of visiting a number of communities accessible only by airplane, I accepted the invitation.

I had, or so I thought, a certain familiarity with life in native villages in which things had somehow gone wrong. In an earlier research tour of the (then) eight Cree communities of northern Québec in 1987, the social consequences of rapid change—in this case following massive hydroelectric construction—were evident. Events that struck me as sad, compelling, and extraordinary were described by witnesses almost casually, as though they were normal occurrences. Deaths from suicide and reckless behavior, I was later to learn, paralyzed the communities in mute grief, but the near misses could be openly talked about, fueling a gossip network that reached even a visiting stranger.

Nothing prepared me, however, for the pervasive sorrow and emotional confusion prevalent in some of the villages of northern Ontario. Interviews with counselors sometimes became impromptu counseling sessions; the anonymity of an interview with someone outside the community provided an opportunity to unshoulder the burden of professional responsibility for clients who were sometimes friends and family members, of seeing them descend into an irreversible sense of selfloathing, of seeing some of them even commit suicide after an apparent, but evidently fragile, movement toward recovery. If I had chosen to do so, I could have filled the pages of this book with such material, but there seemed an obvious, if intangible, connection between such events and a wider spiritual crisis, so I decided to stay with a more inclusive topic.

Another recent experience provided more hope and informed the writing of this book in a different way. In 1997 the Grand Council of the Crees assigned me status as a delegate to meetings of the United Nations Working Group on Indigenous Populations and the Working Group on the Draft Declaration on the Rights of Indigenous Peoples. Since its creation in 1982, the Working Group on Indigenous Populations has became the largest United Nations forum dealing with human rights issues, sending some thirty participants to its first annual meeting in 1982 and over seven hundred in 1999. Indigenous delegations span the continents, with speakers from not only the widely known indigenous groups of North and South America, Australia, and New Zealand but also from groups with less well-known origins, such as the Sami of Finland, Norway, and Sweden; the Ainu of Japan; the Tuareg of Niger; and a growing number of emerging groups previously unrecognized as a result of suppression of both peoples and information in the former Soviet Union. At this one-week- or two-week-long forum, indigenous speakers report on conditions faced by their people, often making reference to states' violations of treaties and existing international standards of human rights and fundamental freedoms. The forum also gives states, nongovernmental organizations, and indigenous peoples' organizations the opportunity to state their positions on efforts by the United Nations to set permanent standards for the rights of indigenous peoples.

Setting human rights standards for indigenous peoples has taken the issues of religious freedom and protection against cultural genocide a step closer to international law. From 1985 to 1993 the Working Group of the Sub-Commission on the Prevention of Discrimination and Protection of Minorities developed a draft Declaration on the Rights of Indigenous Peoples, produced by a body of five independent international experts who faced the almost insurmountable task of collating and assessing a massive collection of living and historical testimony of indigenous peoples from around the world. This draft U.N. declaration makes a number of very straightforward and reasonable requests, such as its call for protection against genocide and other state-orchestrated campaigns of violence. It recognizes the distinctive and profound relationship that indigenous peoples have with their lands and the importance of their right to own, control, and use their lands and territories; and it requires states to obtain their consent before beginning development projects such as mining, hydroelectric construction, logging, and ranching, which often permanently destroy indigenous lands and result in forced relocation of communities. From the perspective of this book, the most relevant provisions of the draft U.N. declaration identify forced assimilation, or deprivation of indigenous peoples' distinct cultural characteristics, as "cultural genocide" and specifically recognize the right to protection against such actions. The right to defend against assimilation is reinforced by the right to preserve cultural, religious, and linguistic identity, which includes the right to protect sacred sites, to expect restitution of cultural property (including human remains), and to enable reestablishment of indigenous languages and cultural traditions.

Hearing indigenous delegates from around the world describe strikingly similar experiences of state-sponsored violence, loss of land, and assimilation policies, combined with what can be described as the invasion of cultural privacy, reinforced in my mind the importance of maintaining a broad coverage of native North American religions in the age of nation building. My attention was, above all, drawn to article 13 of the draft U.N. declaration, which states, "Indigenous peoples have the right to manifest, practice, develop, and teach their spiritual and religious traditions, customs and ceremonies" (United Nations 1995). Some indigenous representatives I spoke with believe the words "spiritual" and "religious" in this article are intended to describe distinct phenomena: *spirituality* describes indigenous traditions and conceptions of sacred power with potential moral implications for all aspects of life, while *religion* refers to organized worship brought to indigenous communities by colonizers. Both are deemed important and worthy of protection by international law. I have loosely adhered to this distinction, with one major exception: the word *religions* in the title of this book is meant to cover the entire range of polyvalent spiritual and religious beliefs and practices.

A third influence on this book made itself felt only in the final stages of revision. In July 1998, I moved with my family to Cross Lake, Manitoba, a large Cree community, having been invited to witness and document the community's struggle following the construction of a hydroelectric megaproject and the subsequent treaty violations that left the community in a state of dependency without alternative economic strategies, and to observe their innovative use of local lawmaking as a strategy of resistance. Material about Cross Lake has found its way into the text in a few places and has indirectly informed the revision of other parts of the text, though the name does not appear there.

Of the many people who assisted in the writing of this volume, I thank first those who contributed the original essays appended to each of the six main chapters. Part of my strategy for developing the cultural and geographic scope of this book has been to invite members of the Harvard community who have recently conducted fieldwork with native peoples of the United States or Canada to contribute short essays that provide contemporary perspectives on the historical material and a range of case explorations informed by personal experience and recent scholarly research. Taken together, this collection of essays, while integrated by a central narrative, goes beyond what I, or anyone else, would be able to do as sole author. Kim Burgess brings the account of Protestant evangelism in New England up-to-date with new material; Manley Begay Jr. writes from his and his family's perspective on boarding school experience among the Diné; Phyllis Fast considers Gwich'in Athabaskan approaches to spiritual crisis and formal systems of healing; Valerie Long Lambert presents a case of political resistance to traditional spirituality among the Choctaws of Oklahoma; Mike Wilcox addresses the repatriation controversy from the point of view of a Native American archaeologist; and Bernard C. Perley recalls several of his personal encounters with followers of the New Age movement. I thank each of these authors for their important contributions to this work.

Going back several years, I owe thanks to Stanley Holwitz for the original impetus to begin this project, the result of his suggestion that many of the important themes in anthropology and Native American studies are not being adequately summarized in broadly accessible formats. I also thank him for his patience in seeing this project progress slowly through the diversions of fieldwork and other writing projects, and for his advice on the fundamentals of presentation. Readers of my original proposal, Robert Brightman and Joseph Jorgensen, also provided useful guidance. Jennifer Brown read the manuscript at a later stage and made many helpful comments on the Canadian material (or lack of it).

The people of northern Canada gave me my starting point: the Cree Board of Health and Social Services of James Bay, the Grand Council of the Crees, the Nishnawbe-Aski Nation, the Cross Lake First Nation, Cross Lake Education Authority, and the Pimicikamak Cree Nation are the formal organizations that offered me the community support and personal relationships so important for acquiring an understanding of indigenous approaches to spirituality. Each of these organizations also provided financial support for the research projects that brought me to the reserve communities, sometimes on short notice, and always with the kind of commitment I felt comfortable with. Other support for my work in the James Bay area came from the Milton Fund of the Harvard Medical School.

At Harvard University Arthur Kleinman stands out, a compassionate mentor who read and astutely commented on an early draft of the manuscript. To Michael Herzfeld I owe the buoyant effect of an unflagging enthusiasm for academe in general and my career in particular, and to David Maybury-Lewis the benefit of a steady reminder that a broad approach to the issues surrounding indigenous peoples is not only interesting but necessary for an understanding of particular situations. Aside from the contributing authors, many students approached the teaching relationship with a measure of intellectual reciprocity, from which this book benefited. Kimberly Arkin, Galit Sarfaty, and Jeremy Saum took the initiative to contribute to the archival and library research. Sarah Pearsall, a graduate student in the Department of History, uncovered a great deal of useful material as a research assistant in the Work Study Program.

To my wife, Barbro, and sons, Erik and Alexander, I offer gratitude for their patience and willingness to live with uncertainty in the pursuit of a greater measure of hope.

CHAPTER I

Introduction

Tolerance is a social rather than a religious virtue. A broad-minded view of the private belief of others undoubtedly makes for the happiness of society; but it is an attitude impossible for those whose personal religion is strong. For if we know that we have found the key and guiding principle of Life, we cannot allow our friends to flounder blindly in the darkness. . . . Opinions may vary as to the nature of the help that should be given, whether peaceful persuasion and a shining example, or the sword and the *auto da fé*. But no really religious man can pass the unbeliever by and do nothing.

Steven Runciman, The Medieval Manichee

Rituals are often mistakenly perceived as permanent and unchangeable, usually by those who are looking for stability in their own lives through contact with an essential aspect of humanity. The emotionally charged atmosphere of almost any native ceremony is often enough to convince amateur enthusiasts of a timeless quality, fulfilling a need for contact with an archaic, simple form of human spirituality. But the wider social context of ritual is rarely given the same attention, probably because this shift in perception makes the sense of timelessness vanish. The social forces behind spiritual change are much more complex—and much more violent—than is often assumed. Hidden from view in today's sweat lodge ceremonies or in the drumming and dancing of powwows are histories of religiously motivated massacres and atrocities, Christian proselytizing, state policies of assimilation, and, among Indian peoples themselves, forgetting, reinvention, and renewal. The appeal of ritual to the senses and imagination gives a false impression of permanence that belies tumultuous histories of suppression, defiance, and religious creativity.

Some native spiritual leaders, responding to the pace of change and the intrusion of non-native enthusiasts, have turned inward, closing off ceremonies to outsiders. But secrecy only reinforces the sense of permanence. If the protected ceremonies did not have a major point of contact with ancestral powers, what would be the point in closing them off to strangers?

Others see religious change as tacitly consensual and having few social consequences outside of reconfigured belief systems and ritual practices. Indian religion can be manipulated by evangelical persuasion, made obsolete by a rapidly changing lifestyle, even suppressed by the powers of the state, and it will find its way through, altered but unscathed, giving a new form to the human search for meaning.

On the surface, there appears to be some validity to the view that stresses spiritual resilience. Missionaries have filled churches and trained native religious leaders, facilitating the willing conversion of new Christians. Sacred places have been mined, logged, or submerged by hydroelectric reservoirs to apparently temporary grief, while the essence of native spirituality survives elsewhere. In both the United States and Canada in the late nineteenth century and early twentieth, native leaders were fined or arrested and imprisoned for conducting ceremonies deemed by the state to be destructive of soul and character. In response to many such pressures, practices were taken underground and were cautiously renewed when prohibitions and sanctions were lifted. The willing conversion to various denominations of Christianity by many native people throughout North America has coexisted with a variety of surprisingly resilient forms of traditional spirituality, despite concerted efforts at suppression and cultural assimilation.

While miracles of continuity among Native American practices are common, it is important to also be attentive to changes in the meaning and context of renewed traditions. An elder who lived long enough to experience periods of both suppression and revival might see similarities of style in "neotraditional" ritual and recognize the words to some of the songs. The social context of the performance, however, would in most cases have been transformed completely, the needs and perceptions of the participants would not be the same, and often, in order to maintain a connection to social reality, the ritual itself would have been creatively adapted. Ironically, it is in the revival of traditions that we find the clearest evidence of ritual transformation.

But, as in all human societies, so long as spiritual practices continue to exist their outward appearances will usually be characterized by stability, consensus, and sincerity. Only in moments of conflict as a result of missionary zeal, the enthusiasm of millenarian expectation, or the appearance of a new prophecy does the world turn upside down, revealing the true tensions in people's lives, the real obstacles in their search for meaning, and the main rivals for their control of spiritual power.

Under normal circumstances, the tensions associated with religious change are hidden from view. This makes it easy for an outside observer to come away with an incomplete picture, especially given the natural tendency of human beings to "totalize" from an experience that is always, to some degree, restricted. Elders, the usual source of information on all aspects of "tradition," are likely to have a fund of knowledge and experience that is very different from that of young people, whose course in life is undecided. Catechists in a Christian church will offer views on native spirituality that are different from those of a "Road Man" who leads sweat lodge or peyote ceremonies. Female elders may have perceptions and sympathies different from those of male elders. Most experienced researchers are aware of such differences, yet the lure of totalization persists. The narratives and opinions of "expert informants" often take precedence, obscuring barriers to communication that may exist between generations or between local religious leaders, politicians, and administrators and the people they serve.

Outside researchers are not the only ones who often miss the significance of spiritual dispossession and conflict. Those actively attempting to improve Indian lives—whether volunteers or employees serving in charitable organizations, administrators in government agencies, or members of local band councils—are often without an explanation for the self-destruction of native communities through addiction, violence, and suicide, and are even more perplexed by the negative outcomes of their efforts. Or, if they have explanations, these take the form of clichés, such as the supposed genetic predisposition of Indians to alcohol dependency[1] or supposed inability to deal with sudden "affluence" following a change in their economic fortune.

The spiritual history of a community is often overlooked or misread by those trying to understand the causes of "social pathology." The spiritual legacy is often embedded in the distant past, sometimes changing only through slow accretions—nothing that would help explain a social disaster. It is far easier and more logical to look at events in the imme-

1. Mancall (1995, 6–7) provides a summary of theories and evidence concerning Indian alcohol abuse, and finds that "genetics alone does not determine how or why individual Indians choose to drink. . . . American Indians' sensitivity to alcohol resembles that of the general American population" (ibid., 7), and there is wide variation in native peoples' responses to alcohol, in which we can see that "many Indians do not drink and not all who do suffer as a result" (ibid., 6).

diate past: the destruction of a habitat, relocation of a village, a sudden economic reversal; but even these events cannot be adequately understood without considering their impact upon spiritual relationships. For those who once lived on the land (and may continue to do so), spirituality is all-pervasive. In hunting societies, the relationship between humans and hunted animals is mediated by spirits, while the living animals themselves have knowledge of human attitudes and intentions. In the agricultural societies of the Southwest the seasonal cycles of sowing, caring for crops, and harvesting, and the climatic conditions that make it all possible, are governed by spiritual agencies. Ecological destruction, the social consequences of formal education, the movement to reservations and greater participation in a formal economy—all the major transitions in native communities that are considered to explain current social problems also have important implications for the continuity of spiritual practices. The historical background of "social pathology" in native communities often reveals radical instability in the human relationship with the spirit world; and there is an enduring relevance to this history, not just a reason to grieve at grievances foregone.

It is easy to assume that missionaries, those who consider themselves in possession of the guiding principles of life and able to use this knowledge to transform the lives of others, are the sole culprits behind the loss or radical transformation of native spiritual traditions. Evangelical enterprises, after all, were usually forthright in their rejection of a wide range of cultural practices and beliefs and ingenious in their efforts to eradicate them; their practitioners usually saw these efforts as a struggle of good against evil. Missionary propagandists told their supporters that the Indians had been lost or neglected and had given themselves over to evil. It was a Christian duty to rid them of their flagrant satanism and bring them closer to the truth and salvation. To their credit, missionaries usually saw Indians as human and worth the effort of improvement; others in competition with Indians for resources and sovereignty would sooner have settled the "Indian problem" with tracking dogs and rifles—and sometimes did.

Evangelical persuasion, however, is by no means the only source of spiritual disjuncture in Native American societies. The missions themselves, despite a deep commitment to religious transformation, were not the only purveyors of new ideas, nor the only source of change in patterns of ritual observance. It is important to also consider the relationships between indigenous traditions and non-native institutions and belief systems not often considered exclusively "religious": formal education, biomedicine, and social research, each supported in various ways by legislation and other forms of political intervention.

Residential schools were a significant and direct attempt at cultural transformation, intended to assimilate Indians or, as Richard Pratt, founder of Indian residential schools in the United States, put it, to "kill the Indian in him, and save the man" (Prucha 1973, 260–61), to eliminate the differences seen as standing in the way of settlement, administration, and progress. Schools, especially off-reservation boarding schools, have been one of the most powerful tools for the resocialization of native children. Rules forbidding use of native languages or contact with family were the starting point for rigorous programs of relearning intended to make "useful citizens" of Indian children. In many instances, especially in Canada, residential schools were run by the Christian missions and had a broad mandate to implement programs of religious instruction. This included instilling a disregard for values and traditions considered "sinful" while instructing children in the habits, beliefs, and even occupational preferences of their teachers and supervisors.

Medicine is not usually thought of as an institutional appendage to missionary programs. Nevertheless, it is associated with selective intolerance of indigenous healing practices, and it complemented the goals of Christian evangelism. In some ways biomedicine acts as a rival belief system when compared to native practices, much as Christianity is, but one that is able to build upon the advantages of a powerful technology. Medicine, like Christianity, tolerates few obstacles to its influence. In pursuing its basic goal of improving and extending human life it often overlooks, or strives to eliminate, local rivals. Its influence, also like that of Christianity, is often highly valued, inadequate only in the sense that its services are not fully developed. There is at the same time a growing recognition that biomedicine's competition with indigenous practices, especially in the treatment of mental illness, does not always lead to the desired results. Loss of local medical knowledge and counseling strategies can lead to loss of autonomy, often with important consequences for the ability to heal.

It is useful to consider the campaigns against native spiritual practices as having developed not only from evangelical ambitions but also from, and at the same time as, territorial and ideological ambitions of the state. The use of the term "nation building" in the title of this book could in some ways be misleading. It does not correspond with a specific historical period, although Benedict Anderson (1991, 46) points to the period from 1776 to 1838 (without including Canadian confederation in 1867) as the time when self-consciously national political entities sprang up in the Western Hemisphere. It is not possible, however, to pin a date on the consciousness of national identity, which can be a powerful force in a new nation well before a constitution is drawn up and sometimes before blood is shed. Nor does the nation-building urge entirely disappear after the creation of independent states; it pushes on to conquer new frontiers long after states are established as secure entities.

The first perceptions of Native American religion occurred in the context of a large-scale ethnic conflict in which a dominant society's ambitions for territory and nation building were obstructed by visibly different, virtually ungovernable groups of people with justifiable claims to sovereignty, land, and maintenance of cultural differences. In the drive to eliminate these differences, the new national governments of North America favored programs of cultural assimilation; or, as McGarry and O'Leary put it, "If one community's language, culture, religion, and national myths are given precedence then we are not talking of assimilation or integration but of annexation" (1993, 19).

Cultural annexation involved legal prohibition of practices deemed especially harmful to Indian morality, temperament, and social progress. Under various administrations, the Potlatch, Sun Dance, and Peyote religions were all subject to official prohibition, and most legal freedoms of their adherents were not reinstated until as late as the 1950s. More recently there have been lobbying efforts on behalf of imprisoned Native Americans, whose religious freedom, despite the high proportion of incarcerated Indians, remains incomplete in comparison with rights granted to adherents of major denominations.

Even those agencies usually considered the strongest supporters of indigenous spirituality engaged in cultural annexation. At the same time that some government agencies took steps to alter native cultures, others supported efforts to preserve them. This was not the kind of preservation that involves support of cultural continuity, but a collector's preservation that sees an evanescent phenomenon on the verge of disappearance and, in a race against time, attempts to capture everything about it on camera and in notes, drawings, and artifacts. But these early anthropologists sometimes obstructed ritual practice, either by their intrusive presence as "observers" or by collecting the paraphernalia used in ceremonies and storing it in museums. Some archaeologists desecrated native burial sites by removing human remains for osteological research, an action that is now the focus of repatriation initiatives and controversies between native leaders and bioarchaeologists.

It is often assumed that tribal governments will inevitably act in support of local or "pan-Indian" traditions, but this is not always the case. It is useful to recognize in this context that there have existed not one but two ages of nation building in North America: the commonly recognized congruence of nationalist consciousness with strivings toward statehood, and the more fragile "belated nation building" of indigenous peoples. The indigenous nation building that has gained strength in recent decades usually aspires to recognition of self-determination and implementation of regional autonomy within existing states. But the connections between spiritual and political reemergence are often less well-defined; and the process of redefining indigenous spiritual traditions in the context of this most recent process of tribal nation building is an increasingly common source of conflict within indigenous communities.

More recently, practitioners of "New Age" religion have attracted the notice and censure of native activists who see the misinterpretation, decontextualization, and popularization of native ceremonies as the source of serious disruptions in local practice. Some "traditionalists" see such popularization as breaking the chain of knowledge, replacing personal relationships between elders and initiates with simplified and impersonal literature, and replacing long and sometimes arduous preparation for visionary revelation with "weekend retreats." A few argue further that those who engage in destructive popularization are aware of what they are doing and are motivated by profit. The defense of religious freedom claimed by New Age popularizers is seen by their opponents as a guise for the plundering of ritual knowledge that is "owned" and passed on through careful instruction and initiation. The New Age movement, in this view, becomes one more form of spiritual intrusion, one more process of ritual desecration, of self-conscious appropriation and alteration of the spiritual lives of native peoples.

Social researchers and legal scholars use several terms to describe acts that involve intentionally altering the ways of life of distinct peoples. The mildest, in terms of moral resonance, is *acculturation,* used in a general sense to refer to the process of change in a people's way of life as they encounter another, usually dominant, society. An element of intention may be involved in the acculturative process—a law or policy, for example, directed at indigenous fostering or marriage practices—but changes can as well be incidental to the cultural encounter, as in the pervasive influence of television and other popular media. Sometimes "reverse acculturation" occurs, when ideas, technology, or practices of a distinct people are taken up with enthusiasm by a dominant society. Acculturation is therefore not always overwhelming but can refer to the piece-meal changes that occur through cultural exchange.

Assimilation is somewhat less benign, though it is sometimes presented by governments as a solution to the "Indian problem" or masked as a process of cultural awareness and "improvement." Often it is used in conjunction with the word "policy," linking it much more firmly with formal efforts to alter the ways of life of distinct peoples. It is almost unlimited in the scope of changes that are intended. An assimilationist policy is one that attempts to integrate a distinct people into a mainstream society, to make them disappear—not through massacre but a bloodless process of education and "development," often couched in terms of "equal rights" for all citizens.

There is but a small step between assimilation and *ethnocide* or *cultural genocide*. Generally, these two terms refer to the same thing, but the latter has the additional sting of associating intentional destruction of a people's way of life with the more immediately destructive acts of mass killings. The term *ethnocide* came into common use in discussions of cultural destruction in Central and South America in the 1970s and 1980s, such as resulted from Brazil's policy of Indian "emancipation," which pressured educated Indians to sign papers eliminating their Indian status and, by extension, their protection as Indians under Brazilian law; and from Mexico's policies of *indigenismo*, which sought through economic development and education to divest the "unprivileged" members of the indigenous population of their "backward" ways and to include them in the mainstream society. In an example that blurs the boundary between cultural destruction and actual mass killing, the term *ethnocide* has also been used in the context of the strategic apathy of the Brazilian government during the 1980s gold rush in the Amazon rain forest, with its devastating consequences for the ten thousand Yanomami living in the region (Maybury-Lewis 1997, 22–25). More recently the term found its way into article seven of the UN's draft Declaration on the Rights of Indigenous Peoples, in which the "collective and individual right not to be subjected to ethnocide and cultural genocide" immediately follows the allocation of rights "to full guarantees against genocide or any other act of violence" (United Nations 1995).

The parameters of ethnocide cannot be fully understood without recognizing that the actual mass killing of native peoples in North America has achieved genocidal proportions. Russell Thornton, in his authoritative overview of Native American demographic history, finds that for the region of the United States alone, the Indian population "decreased from 5+ million in 1492 to about 250,000 in the decade from 1890 to 1900. . . . Such a population decline implies not only that some 5 million American Indians died during the 400 years but that, in fact, many times the approximate figure of 5 million died, as new but ever numerically smaller generations of American Indians were born, lived, and died" (1987, 43). Thornton reports a proportionately similar population decline in Canada, from roughly 2 million in 1492 to 125,000 at the close of the nineteenth century. Since then, native populations have steadily recovered, to about 1.3 million in Canada and 2 million in the United states, but still 3.7 million fewer than in Thornton's estimate of the population five centuries ago.[2] Only a small portion of this disaster is directly attributable to organized mass killing—epidemics, resulting from pathogens of European origin to which indigenous peoples of the New World had no natural immunity, were the main killer—but so-called Indian wars, more correctly described as wars of extermination, were waged by the Spanish expeditions of Francisco Vásquez de Coronado in the Southwest in 1540–41 and Hernando de Soto in the Southeast in 1540–42; by the British, most notably the "Pequot War" of 1637; and by the Americans in the era of the United States' westward expansion, in which hundreds of massacres accompanied directives for the "complete extermination" of Indians who resisted displacement from lands and subordination to federal authority (Stiffarm and Lane 1992, 34). These bloody episodes came to an end in 1890 with the massacre in Wounded Knee, South Dakota, in which over three hundred Lakotas were killed (an event discussed further in chapter 5). It was the implementation of alternative means of "pacification" through the more outwardly peaceful guises of spiritual conquest that hastened the end of the "Indian wars" of the nineteenth century, an approach that, as Lyman Legters writes, "brought outright massacre to an end, but otherwise signified only that less bloodthirsty means were at hand for destroying what was left of the basis for Indian existence" (1992, 107). The peaceful termination of indigenous peoples had long been a part, sometimes a pivotal part, of colonial enterprises in the New World, often taking the form of missionary efforts struggling for human souls in the midst of the chaotic destruction of human lives. But at the close of the nineteenth cen-

2. Such estimates of population decline are widely variable. Thornton's estimates are conservative in comparison with Stiffarm and Lane's (1992, 44) estimate of at least 7 million original inhabitants of today's continental United States in 1492, and exaggerated relative to Ubelaker's (1988, 291) very conservative estimate of decrease in all of North America from 1,894,350 at contact to 1,051,688 in 1800.

tury, bloodshed became largely superfluous. Philanthropic eradication of the last vestiges of "savagery" through Christianization and "civilization" became the strategy of choice for the construction of culturally uniform nations.

Such associations between ethnocide and organized campaigns of killing raise an important question: what are the consequences for people's lives (in both the dominant and dominated societies) of the intentional elimination of human cultures? The semantic connection with actual mass killing can be extended to imply that cultural genocide truly does have consequences for the well-being and survival of individuals, and that attachment to a stable identity is a human need that cannot be denied without causing suffering.

Simone Weil once observed, "All oppression creates a famine in regard to the need of honour, for the noble traditions possessed by those suffering oppression go unrecognized, through lack of social prestige" ([1949] 1996, 19). Under the circumstances in which indigenous peoples were colonized, traditions were not merely unrecognized; they were acknowledged only as targets of derision, as dangerous for the soul, or as fragile reminders of disappearing ways of life. What are the consequences of active repression of tradition for the human sense of honor? When oppression takes the form of actions intended to destroy traditions, does the crisis of honor become all the more acute?

At the same time it should be recognized that evangelical doctrines and new educational regimes were not always imposed upon aboriginal peoples by force. Native North Americans, in their relationships with dominant societies, cannot always be portrayed as victims of ethnocide; one must also take into account frequent examples of partnership and cultural exchange. Christianity and ideas of "progress" also came to native peoples at times of loss and hardship, with new isolation on reservations, and along with racism and dependency in relations with neighboring white communities. Under these conditions many sought a new understanding of the reasons for their suffering and had a new expectation of moral justice in prophetic movements that combined elements of Christianity with Indian visionary traditions. For others the answers lay in a more uncompromising acceptance of what was being offered by outsiders—formal religion, education, "civilization"—in the hope that even if it did not improve their lives, it might at least provide their children with a better chance in a world of hostile change.

Understanding native North American religions, therefore, includes much more than interpreting ritual symbolism or receiving the wisdom of elders. All local practices have complex, usually undocumented, histories of influence from (and upon) other native traditions; and most have been subject in one way or another to the pressures of Christian evangelism, political control, biomedical exclusivism, and mass popularization. This is not to say that connections with the ancestral past do not exist or that these are unimportant, but that even the essential aspects of indigenous spirituality are reflected upon, defined, and chosen. Maintaining a practice or belief in the face of opposition implies an arranging of priorities, a definition of what is vital to one's integrity, and sometimes a shift in perception that makes communion with spirits simultaneously an act of defiance.

CHAPTER 2

The Conquest of Souls

God's providence constantly uses war to correct and chasten
the corrupt morals of mankind, as it also uses such afflictions
to train men in a righteous and laudable way of life, removing to a better state those whose life is approved, or else
keeping them in this world for further service.

St. Augustine, *The City of God*

At the time of European colonization in the Americas during the sixteenth and seventeenth centuries, the religious and metaphysical beliefs
of the immigrant peoples were not always as remote from those of the
First Americans as might be assumed. When George Fox, founder of the
Quaker religion, experienced visions and acted upon them, he was behav-
ing little differently from the Iroquois, among whom the Quakers were
later to live. Fox's diary abounds in entries describing his active commitment to his visionary experiences, confident that his experiences, if
acted upon, would later reveal an important meaning. On the outskirts
of the town of Lichfield, England, for example, Fox received a command
from the Lord to remove his shoes. He then walked about a mile in the
winter cold until he arrived within the town, and

> the word of the Lord came to me again, saying: Cry, "Wo to the bloody city
> of Lichfield!" It being market day, I went into the market-place, and to and
> fro in the several parts of it, and made stands, crying as before, Wo to the
> bloody city of Lichfield! And no one laid hands on me. As I went thus crying
> through the streets, there seemed to me to be a channel of blood running down
> the streets, and the market-place appeared like a pool of blood. . . . Afterwards
> I came to understand, that in the Emperor Diocletian's time a thousand Chris-
> tians were martyr'd in Lichfield. So I was to go, without my shoes, through
> the channel of their blood, and into the pool of their blood in the market-place,
> that I might raise up the memorial of the blood of those martyrs, which had
> been shed above a thousand years before, and lay cold in their streets. (cited
> in James 1990, 16–17)

To the Iroquois, Fox's behavior would very likely have made perfect sense. As the Jesuit missionary Father Fremin wrote of the Seneca in 1668, "The Iroquois have, properly speaking, only a single Divinity—the dream. To it they render their submission and follow all its orders with the utmost exactness. . . . Whatever it be that they think they have done in their dreams, they believe themselves absolutely obliged to execute at the earliest moment" (cited in Wallace 1969, 59). The difference between waking visionary experiences and dreams in this example is insignificant. George Fox behaved in a way that was fully consistent with the Iroquois moral universe.

At the local level, Spanish Catholicism made use of the intercession of saints in order to control natural forces such as hail or locusts. In seventeenth-century Spain, locust trials, in which vermin were put on trial and excommunicated, were commonly performed by both lay professionals and, less commonly, local clergy. In one such trial, held in 1650 in a monastery near Segovia, witnesses for the prosecution were patron saints and souls in purgatory, while the judge who pronounced the excommunication on the grasshoppers was Our Lady Saint Mary (Christian 1981, 29–30). Doctors of the church, such as Saint Ambrose, Saint Thomas Aquinas, and Saint Augustine, were invoked in the ritual excommunication of grasshoppers and other insect pests because, as William Christian explains, "in an ecclesiastical trial what lawyer could present a more convincing case than a doctor of the church?" (ibid., 44). Theologians may have objected to this behavior, but it would not have seemed at all unusual to the Indians of the pueblos in New Mexico, for whom deities controlling the seasonal cycles of the land required attention and propitiation.

Both the Catholic Church and the Protestant Churches of the Reformation were pervaded by belief in the almost ubiquitous presence of evil. In the sixteenth and seventeenth centuries, misfortune and suffering were frequently explained as the work of those who harnessed spiritual power in order to harm or destroy others. Belief in witchcraft was rife in England during this period as evidenced by witchcraft prosecution in the secular courts. Witchcraft was treated as a branch of heresy, an ecclesiastical offense to be punished by the state. An "act agaynst conjuracions inchantments and witchecraftes" of 1563 called for imprisonment of one year with four appearances in the pillory for the first offense, and death for the second in cases where people or property were injured by witchcraft. A more severe act was passed in 1604, in which the list of actions to be punished was extended to include the invocation of spirits and removal of dead bodies from their graves to be used as spiritual weapons. Injury of a person or property was henceforth to be punished by death for the first offense (Macfarlane 1970, 14–15). That the fear of witches was extremely widespread can also be seen in the wealth of literary evidence indicating that people protected themselves from witches and other supernatural evils through a wide array of magical instruments and gestures (ibid., 103).

Witchcraft manifestations and their repression in England were far more orderly than in continental Europe. Although children were permitted to give evidence against their parents in English trials, contrary to procedures used for other offenses, confession was not commonly pursued through the use of torture. As Macfarlane (1970, 20) points out, indirect pressures, "sharp speeches," threats of imprisonment and death, mounting suspicions of neighbors, and promises of clemency by clergy and justices were more responsible for confession of witchcraft than the imaginative and sadistic tortures used in inquisitorial proceedings in continental Europe.

By the late seventeenth century, at a time when missions were being established in North America, witchcraft was disappearing in Europe. The last ecclesiastical court case in Essex appeared in 1638, while in other parts of England prosecutions continued until the beginning of the eighteenth century. The last execution for witchcraft in Holland was in 1610, France 1745, Germany 1775, Poland 1793; and in Italy the Inquisition condemned people to death until the late eighteenth century, while inquisitorial torture was not abolished in the Catholic Church until 1816 (Sagan 1996, 413). Yet these changes did not fully bring to an end the belief in witchcraft and satanism among North American missionaries. The repression of witchcraft, the idea that control over evil forces including the Devil could be used for private ends, was a significant part of the background to missionary activities among native North Americans. Those who were among the first to try to change the souls of the Indians were not principally theologians or doctors of the church working with a view merely to create new congregations of active Christians; they were above all concerned with the Indians' use of spiritual forces, including witchcraft, with which they were familiar from the European experience. Again, this was amply confirmed by the beliefs and practices of many native peoples of North America for whom witchcraft was a social malaise that could be combated (and engaged in) by spiritual experts, sometimes referred to by the Europeans as shamans, "witch doctors," medicine men, or "conjurers."

Each missionary enterprise seems to have had its own personality. Even within the Catholic Church, the goals and behavior of the Franciscans in the American Southwest, with their readiness to extract labor and tribute, contrast with the more studious and systematic strategies of the Jesuits in the Northeast. Added to the variety of native spiritual systems and church strategies for conversion were the missionary offshoots of the Reformation that came to the New World in a spiritual colonial scramble, with overlapping and competing jurisdictions, to establish a presence in a realm where new souls were available to add strength and legitimacy to religious enterprises. By 1872 the Sioux agencies of Dakota were divided among three groups—Roman Catholics, Episcopalians, and the Hicksite Friends—to which have been added in recent years "fundamentalist" Christian groups such as the Body of Christ Independent Church and the Church of Jesus Christ of Latter Day Saints (DeMallie and Parks 1987, 11–13). This may not be typical, but neither is it an unusual degree of interdenominational competition in a native community.

One of the most important sources of disparity and conflict between missionaries and native peoples was not belief or practice, but the use of the powers of the state for evangelical efforts that went beyond religious instruction to include denigration of native practices, characterizing them as unwholesome or satanic. Colonies in North America that undertook spiritual conquest used different strategies to impose a version of monotheistic Christianity upon peoples who, in their own distinctive systems of belief, understood the universe as populated by a vast array of spiritual beings and forces with powers to influence human prosperity. Each of the examples I discuss here is associated in one way or another with disaster. The Spanish occupation of New Mexico, intended to enable Franciscan proselytizing, can be seen as a catastrophe lasting throughout the eighty years of occupation before the Pueblo Revolt of 1680. The praying towns of New England were built upon the aftermath of epidemics, warfare, and the marginalization of those native peoples at the center of English immigration, and destruction of these native peoples came about as those who had retained much of their military strength and had resisted Christianity made a final effort to put a stop to colonial encroachment and domination. And the Jesuits of New France came to be seen by many Hurons among whom they preached as harbingers of intertribal warfare and pestilence who could be given a place in their lives only because of the great spiritual power they seemed to possess. The spirit wars of North America in the seventeenth century were as much actual as metaphorical, out of which emerged some of the patterns of evangelism, assimilation, and resistance that accompanied the later growth of nations.

THE PUEBLO REVOLT OF 1680

The monumental plunder of the Aztec state in the valley of Mexico from 1519 to 1521 by Hernán Cortés and his band of four hundred soldiers realized, far beyond any expectations, the Spanish goal of amassing gold and slaves and spreading salvation. This amazing success (from the conquistador's point of view) inspired reckless exploration of far-flung, uncharted regions of the New World, including the regions of today's Florida, the Mississippi valley, and the American Southwest, by soldiers, missionaries, and would-be settlers. They forced their way into the New World with whatever military power could be mustered, pushing themselves almost beyond the limits of human endurance into sometimes forbidding environments, where the absence of social rules and the frustration at continually receding hopes for great discovery were backgrounds for the pillage, enslavement, rape, and slaughter of indigenous populations. Some of these expeditions concluded with few or no survivors among their members as the explorers fell to illness, accidents, or the defensive strategies of the Indians.

One such ill-fated expedition to the Southwest, survived by the Franciscan friar Fray Marcos de Ninza, brought rumors of a kingdom greater than either Mexico or Peru. Claiming to have seen the fabled city of Cíbola, capital of the Seven Golden Cities of Antilla, Fray Marcos expounded on its beauty and size. Although the pueblo he had seen (Hawikuh) was probably impressive in its own right, Fray Marcos's overwrought imagination led him to describe the "city" as a source of untold splendor and wealth. His tale was convincing enough to result in the assembly of a sizable, well-armed expedition. In 1540 Francisco Vásquez de Coronado, the twenty-nine-year-old governor of Nueva Galicia, was dispatched to accompany Fray Marcos with 292 soldiers and 800 Mexican Indian allies to conquer Cíbola (Gutiérez 1991, 42).

The Pueblo villagers who encountered this expedition, who saw for the first time horsemen armed with muskets, whose village succumbed within hours of the first attack, probably saw them as unusual *katsina*, spiritual ancestors who controlled village prosperity. Gutiérez describes the way this initial conquest may have been perceived by the residents of Hawikuh: "The katsina approached amid a cloud of dust. The earth shook, the heavens showered fire (gunfire), large stones were hurled through the air like hail (stone mortars), and strange birds shrieked a deafening cry (trumpets). Riding atop ferocious monsters (horses), the katsina were bedecked in the sun's glittering radiance (gilded armor) and were crowned with feathers (plumed helmets)" (1991, 43). Although the soldiers were initially given cornmeal offerings and treated in almost every respect as powerful gods, their indiscriminate use of force and demands for blankets, corn, and sexual use of Indian women without socially prescribed gift-giving led the puebloans to a defensive reaction. The Indian declaration of war at Alcanfor Pueblo resulted in swift retaliation by the Spaniards, with one hundred warriors being burned at the stake and hundreds more massacred as they fled (ibid.). But cold and hunger through the fall and winter of 1541 had taken their toll on the conquistadors. The failure of wealth to materialize and the likelihood of repeated skirmishes with the Indians led to the retreat of the expedition from New Mexico in April 1542.

Although smaller expeditions were subsequently sent to reconnoiter the Pueblo region, it was not until 1598 that a more substantial group arrived with the goal of establishing a colony. This party was led by Juan de Oñate, son of a Spanish governor, who had a pedigree built up through marriage to the granddaughter of Hernán Cortés, the fabled conqueror of Mexico. This colonial enterprise was originally intended to be peaceful and apostolic, though it was soon to replicate the brutality of earlier Spanish expeditions.

Oñate's colonizing program in New Mexico had, however, a much grander scale than any previous venture into the region. He spent three years in Chihuahua prior to his departure in 1598 assembling a party consisting of some four hundred colonists, soldiers, servants, and missionaries, together with eighty carts and one thousand head of cattle. His ultimate objective was to establish Spanish government, with himself at its head, over a region that stretched north to south from Taos to El Paso and from Pecos in the east to the Hopi villages 250 miles westward, a region of some eighty-seven thousand square miles (Spicer 1962, 156–57). The colony of New Mexico was to be divided into seven missionary districts, bringing the people, the Franciscans hoped, from their mesa strongholds and idolatrous beliefs into a peaceful, organized, and unified Christian domain. This was to take place in a region populated with some forty thousand villagers speaking numerous dialects of at least four distinct languages, who were divided into autonomous village communities ranging in population from several hundred to two thousand.

These villages were surrounded by nomadic hunters, principally the Apaches, whose adoption of the horse gave them access to a vast domain extending from present-day Texas to Arizona (Lamar and Truett 1996, 57). Even after three years spent before embarkment in Chihuahua, Oñate's expedition was poorly prepared for its campaign to establish Spanish rule and Christianity among the eastern Pueblos. Once under way, the expedition was frequently divided, with Oñate and a party of soldiers in armor riding ahead of the main cavalcade to meet with the *caciques* of the villages,[1] telling them of the king of Spain, offering protection from enemies, and explaining the main principles of Christianity, especially the importance of baptism. The main objective of these meetings, from the Spanish point of view, was to obtain promises of allegiance to the king, but there is, as Edward Spicer points out, "no record of how the Indians interpreted the idea of obedience and submission, nor of their understanding of what Oñate proposed to carry out" (1962, 156). In spite of all obstacles, Oñate's colonizing program was initially successful, with all the Pueblos pledging allegiance by the end of 1598.

Nevertheless, factions existed in some villages, which were divided by the issue of submission to the Spanish government and its zealous missionaries. In 1598 the Keres village of Acoma, under the leadership of Zutucapan, displayed violent opposition to Spanish rule, killing Oñate's aide, Juan Zaldívar, and his party of soldiers after inviting them into the village. In 1599 a punitive expedition of seventy Spanish soldiers laid siege to the village and eventually conquered it, capturing five hundred Acomans, then sentencing them to the amputation of one foot and to twenty years at hard labor (ibid., 157). This punishment sent the message to other villages that defiance of the Spanish crown and the new Christian dispensation would be met with severe reprisal.

The contradiction between the Christian values of peaceable humility and the fury of the Spanish repression of the indigenous villages of New Mexico is in some ways not surprising given the earlier episodes of Spanish brutality and the frequent disdain of the Spaniards for the original inhabitants of their colonies. A common view of the Indians of the New World among the conquistadors sent to subdue them was that their humanity could not be established; and since they were less than human it would be fruitless to try to make them human by efforts to Christianize them. The historian and conquistador Gonzalo Fernandez de Oviedo

---

1. The term *cacique,* meaning "chief," is one the Spanish borrowed from the Caribbean Arawaks (Clendinnen 1987, 6).

held the view that Indians were closer to sturdy animals than humans, advising his fellow warriors that when it came to hand-to-hand fighting one must be careful not to break one's sword on their heads due to the thickness of their skulls. Oviedo was an advocate of the genocidal solution to the Indian problem, proclaiming that with the Spanish conquest of the island of Hispaniola and the demise of the Indian, Satan's influence had disappeared; he concluded, "Who can deny that the use of gunpowder against pagans is the burning of incense to Our Lord" (cited in Todorov 1984, 151).

The Franciscan friars' view of the Indians, while stressing the latter's perfidy and association with the Devil, was at least inclined to acknowledge their humanity, a view that actually lent credence to the Franciscans' urgent calls for support of the missions. The Indians of the pueblos were recognized as peaceful and resourceful, according to Fray Lope Izquierdo, writing in 1601 that they were "a humble people, and in virtue and morality the best behaved thus far discovered" (cited in Knaut 1995, 59).

At the same time, however, they were seen to readily give themselves over to satanism, and their crowded calendar of religious activities—punctuated with fasting, prayers, sacrifices, and public dances—was seen in terms of idolatry and Devil worship. Although, under the guiding principles of the new colony, Indians were not subject to the authority of the Inquisition—they were, after all, not apostates but merely ignorant of Christianity in a region where evil had long enjoyed free reign and the light had not yet penetrated—the evangelical zeal of the Counter-Reformation came to bear on the Franciscans' understanding of Pueblo religion. Fray Nicolás de Freitas provided an interpretation of Pueblo dances that stresses a hedonistic use of satanic powers: "If they are asked for what purpose they perform these dances, they say that it is to obtain the woman they desire, and that the devil will give her to them, or, that he will give them corn, or any other thing that they request. One or more of them seize small palm leaves, and cruelly beat until they bleed one or more of the dancers who desire to make that sort of blood sacrifice to the devil; they all become so frenzied that they seem to be beside themselves without having previously taken any liquor whatever which might intoxicate them" (cited ibid., 111).

The uneasy coexistence of religious and lay powers in the New Mexico colony was largely responsible for the undoing of the policy of benevolent apostolic conquest. Since, even in his initial voyage of settlement, Oñate did not prepare adequately, he was compelled to extract tributes of food and clothing from the Indians. As the Spanish presence became established, onerous levies of resources and labor, referred to as *repartimiento,* were imposed. The colony was to have an evangelical purpose, and neither gold nor silver was found in the region, yet the lay authorities established a pattern of extracting as much food, clothing, and labor from the Pueblos as could be humanly endured—and then more. Every year after the harvest, ox-drawn carts went through the villages to collect set amounts of wheat or shelled corn. In lieu of corn or wheat, labor around the household of the padre could be negotiated. Governors, though frequently replaced, were rumored to waste no time in amassing personal fortunes before being recalled by the viceroy (Sando 1979, 194). One Franciscan chronicler, Fray Alonzo de Benavides, expressed a complicitous optimism concerning a situation in which both church and lay powers demanded resources from the Indians: "The first of their fruits they offer to the church in all reverence and good will. . . . They are all very happy and recognize the blindness of idolatry from which they have emerged and the blessings they enjoy in being the children of the church" (Kessell and Hendricks 1991, 344). Other friars focused upon the suffering caused by the lay authority's collection of tribute. As early as 1601 Fray Juan de Escalona wrote to the viceroy with his concern that the exploitation had reached the point where it was compromising the preaching of the gospel and conversion of souls: "Soon after [Don Juan Oñate] entered the land," Escalona writes, "his people began to perpetuate many offenses against the natives and to plunder their pueblos of the corn they had gathered for their own sustenance; here corn is God, for they have nothing else with which to support themselves" (ibid., 126). The situation, moreover, had deteriorated to the point where Indians were starving, and the future of the colony itself was being jeopardized: "All the corn they had saved for years past has been consumed, and not a kernel is left over for them. The whole land has thus been reduced to such need that the Indians drop dead from starvation wherever they live; and they eat dirt and charcoal ground up with some seeds and a little corn in order to sustain life" (ibid., 127). In the same year, Fray Lope Izquierdo complained of the collection of clothing by Spanish soldiers, a tribute that normally consisted of the payment of one cotton blanket, and a tanned buckskin or buffalo hide per Pueblo household per year: "During the winter . . . our men, with little consideration, took blankets away from the Indian women, leaving them naked and shivering with cold. Finding themselves naked and miserable, they embraced their children tightly in their arms to warm and protect them, without making any resistance to the offenses done to them" (cited in Knaut 1995, 59).

Adding to the complexity of the situation, the lay government based in Santa Fe unceasingly struggled with the Franciscans over jurisdiction and control of the Indians. Disputes over the collection of tribute, labor, and human souls divided the Spanish into two camps whose differences only deepened as the region became more thoroughly settled.

In 1613 the tension between lay and religious authority reached a new benchmark when Father Ordóñez excommunicated Governor don Pedro, posting a notice to this effect on the doors of the church in Santa Fe. In a sermon following this event Father Ordóñez, having cast don Pedro's usual chair outside the church, made a statement that outlined his perception of his own powers: "Do not be deceived. Let no one persuade himself with vain words that I do not have the same power and authority that the pope in Rome has, or that if his holiness were here in New Mexico he could do more than I. Believe you that I can arrest, cast into irons and punish as seems fitting to me any person without exception who is not obedient to the commandments of the church and mine" (cited in Kessell 1987, 97). In four years of leadership in New Mexico, Father Ordóñez established a precedent of overbearing authority and abuse of power that had consequences for the ways other friars perceived their roles.

It is difficult to say with certainty how many villagers became Christian and, among those who did, how deep their commitment to the faith really went. The focus of evangelism in New Mexico was clearly on the sedentary Pueblo Indians, the Tewas, Tanos, Keres, Tiwas, Pecos, Picuris, and Taos villages, with the surrounding nomadic tribes, which displayed sometimes formidable skills in fighting and evasion, remaining virtually unreachable by the message of salvation. Fray Alonzo de Benavides, like most Franciscan chroniclers, had a tendency to wax eloquent about the successes of conversion efforts on tens of thousands of Indians: "Today they are so well instructed in everything, especially in what pertains to the Faith and Christianity, that it is wonderful to consider that ever since they began to be baptized less than twenty years ago, and particularly during the last eight years when the harvest of souls has been most abundant, they have given the impression of having been Christian for a hundred years" (cited in Espinosa 1988, 23). Certainly in the vicinity of the missions, established near well-populated pueblos, the Indians could be seen as models of piety, with instruction beginning with the "veneration of the cross and the Blessed Virgin, respect for the missionaries, the teaching of basic Catholic prayers stated as a profession of faith in the fundamental beliefs of the Catholic religion, instruction concerning the sacraments, and regular attendance at mass and other religious services conducted by the friars" (ibid., 21). But in pueblos that lay beyond the immediate reach of the Franciscans, those who were unwilling to give up their traditional influence and practices, the "medicine men," held sway, supported by the native political and military leadership, maintaining healing practices and observance of the ritual calendar, and at times striving to disrupt the efforts of the missionaries by inciting converts to resist mission discipline. The punishment of recalcitrant Indians by the Franciscans and lay authorities speaks more eloquently of resistance to conversion efforts than the chroniclers could have imagined.

In a political context in which the Pueblo Indians were militarily dominated and brought to the point of starvation by onerous demands for tribute, the friars could not be expected to pursue their goals of bringing enlightenment in a spirit of fraternity and benevolence to those who in their view had long lived in darkness. And indeed they did not. For most of the seventeenth century, serious punishments, some of which were taken from the experience of the Inquisition, awaited those whom zealous and watchful friars caught practicing traditional ceremonies (Knaut 1995, 55). In their first attempts to crush Indian discontent and the stirrings of messianism Spanish civil and religious authorities instituted witch trials, corporal punishment, and executions against those who expressed fear of and doubt about Spanish rule and the Franciscan missions that accompanied it (Reff 1995, 71). Among the formal complaints lodged by Indians against friars is an account of the excesses committed by friars Velasco and Guerra. In 1655 these friars reacted against a group of Indians who had complained to the governor concerning conditions in the missions by having the Indians "brought to him [Guerra], and he went to their homes to search them. He found some feathers or idols and consequently seized [the people] and ordered turpentine brought so as to set fire to them" (cited in Knaut 1995, 107). Guerra then set fire to one of the men accused of worshiping idols and ordered him sent home, but he was unable to move and soon died from his burns. Although Guerra and Velasco were arrested and sent to Santa Fe for an investigation, they both eventually returned to the missions (ibid.).

The Spanish were frustrated by the Indians' continued observance of their rituals, finding it nearly impossible to replace local expressions of "satanism" with Christianity, either by the number of missionaries brought in or by the severity of punishments inflicted for "idolatry" (Hackett and Shelby 1942, xxii). In 1661 the Franciscan custodian took formal action against Indian ceremonials, with a decree prohibiting all kachina dances, instructing missionaries to seek out all objects of "idol-atry." Kivas, the ceremonial rooms of the pueblos, were raided, result-ing in the appropriation or destruction of sixteen hundred kachina masks as well as prayer feathers and other items (Spicer 1962, 160–61). In 1675 Governor Treviño took matters into his own hands, directing his actions not toward the materials of worship as much as toward the worshipers themselves: "Having captured forty-seven medicine men, who were alleged to be guilty of sorcery and witchcraft, he hanged three of them, as a warning to future soothsayers, and inflicted severe punishments upon the others" (Hackett and Shelby 1942, xxii). Among those who survived was Popé of San Juan Pueblo, whom the Spaniards later credited with inciting and leading the Pueblo Revolt.

After over eighty years of Spanish exploitation, missionary assaults on native ceremony and belief, and frustration over fruitless efforts to seek redress, Popé began to meet with Tewa and Northern Tiwa war chiefs to find a solution. The initial intention of these meetings was to formulate an ultimatum to be presented to the Spanish authorities in order to mitigate the effects of colonial domination. As more Pueblos joined these secret meetings, and particularly as more leaders joined who were familiar with Spanish intentions and motivations, the idea of an ultimatum geared toward ultimate compromise gave way to a carefully worked out plan to evict the Spanish by force.

The timing of the revolt was arranged to precede the arrival of a car-avan that came every three years from Mexico to replenish Spanish sup-plies. The intention was to strike the Spanish at a time when they would be low on weapons, horses, and ammunition. The ingeniousness of this plan was made all the more apparent by the fact that it succeeded in spite of being revealed to the Spanish authorities by two messengers from the planning group who were arrested, taken to Santa Fe, and brought before Governor Antonio de Otermín for interrogation. News of this arrest quickly reached the Pueblos. The timing of the revolt was brought for-ward by a spontaneous release of hatred for the Spanish military and Franciscan missionaries, sparked by the capture of the two messengers.

The Pueblo Revolt of 1680 began with an uprising in the Tewa region of Rio Arriba, which soon spread to the rest of the Pueblos. When news of the beginning of the revolt reached the Pueblos, the Franciscans were first ordered to leave by the local Pueblo leaders. In most cases they refused to go, and were killed in the ensuing destruction of everything that represented the Spanish occupation and the religion they brought with them. By the end of the violence twenty-one of thirty-three Franciscan friars, together with some four hundred Spanish soldiers and colonists, were killed (Sando 1979, 196). The death toll among the colonists was, in fact much lower than it could have been had the Indians been intent on their destruction. The fact that nearly two thousand colonists were given the opportunity to flee suggests that the main objectives of the revolt were to destroy the mission system and drive the Spanish from the region (Spicer 1962, 163).

Testimony from Indian captives following the Pueblo Revolt of 1680 linked the violent expulsion of the Franciscans and settlers to Spanish exploitation and the repression of Indian culture. Two Indians who had been sent with a letter from the father custodian and mayor of Santa Fe requesting news from the neighboring villas returned fleeing from the countryside, reporting that five hundred Indians were on their way to "destroy the governor and all the Spaniards, so that the whole kingdom might be theirs. . . . They were saying that now God and Santa Maria were dead, that they were the ones whom the Spaniards worshiped, and that their own God whom they obeyed never died" (cited in Hackett and Shelby 1942, 13). A Christian Indian who was arrested among the "hostile rebel apostates," when asked the reason for the rebellion and treason, replied that "they were tired of the work they had to do for the Spaniards and the religious, because they did not allow them to plant or to do other things for their own needs; and that, being weary, they had rebelled" (cited ibid., 24–25). Governor Otermín, on a march to review the aftermath of the revolt, saw for himself signs that it had been inspired by hatred of the religion that was being forced upon the Indians. In the pueblo of Sandia, he found that in the church "the images had been taken. . . . And on the main altar there was a carved full-length figure of Saint Francis with the arms hacked off by an axe" (cited ibid., 26).

Yet, as Daniel Reff (1995) points out, the evidence that stressed Indian grievances was largely ignored. The Spanish instead chose to focus on the testimony of those who could be understood to have witnessed Popé, the leader of the revolt, talking or communicating with Satan, such as the statement by two young men caught at the outset of the rebellion who said that "there had come to them from very far away toward the north a letter from an Indian lieutenant of Po he yemu to the effect that all of them should rebel, and that any pueblo that would not agree to it they would destroy, killing all the people. It was reported that this Indian lieutenant of Po he yemu was very tall, black, and had very large yellow eyes, and that everyone feared him greatly" (Hackett and Shelby 1942, 4–5).

When an elderly Tiwa man captured on a road north of Socorro was interrogated by Governor Otermín, and was asked what had possessed him and his fellow villagers to forsake their God and king, the old man replied "that the resentment which all the Indians have in their hearts has been so strong, from the time this kingdom was discovered, because the religious and the Spaniards took away their idols and forbade their sorceries and idolatries; that they have inherited successively from their old men the things pertaining to their ancient customs; and that he has heard this resentment spoken of since he was of an age to understand" (cited in Kessell 1987, 237).

The Pueblo Revolt ushered in a period of twelve years in which the Pueblos were free from Spanish domination. Previously prohibited ceremonies once again flourished, and the only secrecy was that which was intended by Indian standards for initiation, transmission of knowledge, and ritual control. The Spanish returned in 1692 with military considerations and the goal of political control overriding missionary objectives. That is not to say that the friars were left out of the picture or unwilling to return to a region that had ultimately proven so inhospitable to their war against the forces of darkness. In a Statement of the Missionaries of the Custody of New Mexico, a group of eight friars pledged their willingness to take on the dangerous task of spiritual reconquest in the pueblos: "Jointly we all have agreed that it was indeed our obligation to carry out the . . . designated ministries as regards both the obligations or our consciences and the credit to our seraphic order, even though we should be in danger of losing a thousand lives, which we would gladly give as well employed for these two highly justifiable aims as well as in the hope of thus being able to redeem them with the Precious Blood of our Redeemer" (Espinosa 1988, 86). There is little evidence, moreover, that revolt and martyrdom had tempered the Franciscan view of Indian "idolatry" and "deviltry." "With regard to these of New Mexico," the friar Casañas writes during the reconquest of New Mexico, "one can only believe that they still are drawn more by their idolatry and infidelity than by the Christian doctrine, for we see in them that with their little loyalty, at every full moon they rise in rebellion, foaming at the mouth" (ibid., 228).

Yet in the new phase of missionary conquest the Pueblos were to resist the Christian teachings more effectively. Lacking the power they once had, no longer wielding the powers of the Inquisition over lay authorities, the Franciscans did not succeed in exterminating the Indian practices they so despised. The atrocities of the early phase of Spanish conquest only served to reinforce attachments among the Pueblos to beliefs and practices that had been under assault. The successful revolt of 1680 showed that their sacred powers had not entirely disappeared.

The Franciscan religious colony in New Mexico was largely corrupted by institutional conflict between state and church, each insecure in its jurisdiction, each jealous of its control over the Indians, the one resource from which they could expect to profit. Whatever struggles for power may have occurred within the Spanish colony, the foundation of evangelical success became domination by the powers of the state, whether wielded by lay or church authorities. In this context the perception of satanic opposition could be acted upon with a destructiveness that rivaled the atrocities committed by the Spanish elsewhere in the New World,[2] atrocities that the founders of New Mexico sincerely, but vainly, wished to avoid.

EPIDEMICS AND THE "BLACK ROBES" OF NEW FRANCE

Although indigenous healers throughout North America at the time of early contact with Europeans had developed effective strategies for intervention in a wide range of illnesses and accidents, by the time missionaries arrived there was in most regions a widespread state of health crisis. Pathogens of European origin swept through native populations, often before the Europeans themselves arrived on the scene. Some diseases carried by explorers and early settlers, such as measles, smallpox, several varieties of influenza, whooping cough, tuberculosis, and syphilis, had not previously existed in the New World, and the indigenous population did not have immunological defenses against them. The result was a succession of epidemics that struck different regions at different times, but with similar catastrophic results. Dense populations, such as those that inhabited the cities of the Mississippi valley in the fifteenth century, were decimated, while those who lived in scattered hunting camps experienced epidemics that moved more slowly, with insidiously fatal results.

2. Although comparisons with other Spanish colonies cannot be elaborated on here, a useful example of domination by lay and religious authorities can be found in the Jesuit mission program among the Tarahumaras of the San Pablo Valley. Here, opposition to "witches" and black magic, seen by the missionaries as having their source in the Devil, provoked the Tepehuan revolt, a bloody and ultimately unsuccessful attempt to eliminate the Spanish presence in New Spain (Spicer 1962, 25–45). The later period of Spanish domination in California is covered in Heizer and Almquist 1971. A useful account of Spanish conquest and Franciscan mission programs among the Maya peoples of the Yucatan Peninsula can be found in Clendinnen 1987.

Native healers were often faced with insurmountable crises just at a time when missionaries arrived to bring a new religious dispensation and to question, or if possible eradicate, practices seen by them to be inspired by the forces of evil. It is easy to assume that such timing of missionary intervention would have led to the wholesale abandonment of healing strategies that were ineffective against the new, inexplicable illnesses, but this was not always the case.

In the seventeenth century, the establishment of permanent Jesuit missions among the Huron of the Great Lakes region corresponded with the first historically recorded spread of epidemic disease in the New World. Although descriptions of the diseases that swept through Huron country in this period are not specific enough to enable definitive identification of them, the result was that neither Europeans nor Indians were able to stop the spread of illness or effect cures (Trigger 1985, 229). On the surface it seemed that this conjunction of suffering and Christian evangelism placed the missionaries at an advantage. James Axtell (1988, 106) finds that "in the midst of widespread epidemics, Catholic priests baptized hundreds of natives who lay at death's door, after only a modicum of instruction and the most circumscribed assent of the stricken. Perhaps a third of the 16,000 natives anointed by the Jesuits between 1632 and 1672 soon expired, often from imported European diseases."

One pattern of these epidemics, however, fostered more suspicion than acceptance of the missionaries: the "black robes" and their French allies did not suffer from them nearly as much as the Indians. With European childhood diseases this was particularly noticeable. In 1637, for example, an outbreak of illness, probably scarlet fever, occurred in Huron country in which thousands of Indians who became sick died within two days, but none of the French traders or missionaries in the region became ill (Trigger 1985, 231). Bruce Trigger convincingly demonstrates that such tremendous disparity in the effects of epidemics did not lead to an invalidation of Huron spirituality or methods of healing. A more complex understanding of their own weakness and the apparent Jesuit infallibility to disease seems to have developed: "It was widely accepted that the Jesuits were the agents by which the epidemics were being spread. No other reason could account more plausibly for why the French had insisted that these priests be allowed to live in the Huron Country. Their celibacy also suggested that they were nurturing great supernatural power, and their generally sound health and the speed with which they and their workmen recovered from influenza were additional proofs that they could control these diseases" (ibid., 246). Such suspicions were not allayed by the Jesuits' attempts to heal. "Their baptismal water and the sugar, food, and drugs that they gave to the sick were thought to be the charms that they were injecting into the bodies of their victims" (ibid., 247).

The Huron's fear of the Jesuits which followed from these observations was offset by their dependency upon European goods and maintaining trade relations with the French. After a century of trade relations, European items had become permanent fixtures in the indigenous technologies and prestige systems of the Northeast. More significant, economic reliance and perceptions of Jesuit sorcery did not lead the Huron automatically to abandon their own spiritual system. "The florescence of ritualism that accompanied the epidemics bears witness to the dynamism and resilience of traditional Huron religious beliefs. The failure of particular rituals to cure the sick did not discredit the Huron religion. Instead, it spurred shamans to communicate more intensively with the spirit world in an effort to discover rituals that would be effective" (ibid., 248–49).[3] The great loss of life that followed epidemics and warfare resulted in, if anything, a questioning of Christianity more than of Huron practices. The Huron leader Aenons, in a meeting with the Jesuits, said, "What profit can there come to us from lending ear to the Gospel, since death and the faith nearly always march in company?" (Ronda 1977, 82).

Epidemics destroyed Huron religion more through demography than delegitimation. Diseases of European origin were particularly lethal among the very old and the very young, and with the sudden loss of entire populations of elders came the disappearance of their knowledge of spiritual matters that had not yet been passed on to the next generation. "Traditional religious lore," Trigger (1985, 250) speculates, "tended to be a prerogative of the elderly, and many must have died before they could transmit what they knew to their heirs. The loss of such a broad spectrum of knowledge must have made the Hurons economically still more reliant on the French and less able at a theological level to resist the attacks of the Jesuits."[4]

---

3. Further evidence of the vitality of Huron beliefs comes from Alexander von Gernet's 1994 discussion of the sophisticated philosophical discourse between Hurons and Jesuits concerning the nature of the human soul, with the Hurons defending the apportionment of the human persona into a plurality of souls, in contrast to the Christian conception of the unitary soul.

4. Similarly, Walker and Hudson (1993, 116) find that among the Chumash of California the loss of elders through epidemic diseases lead to a decline of esoteric healing techniques: "The loss of medical knowledge was accelerated by the secretiveness of

French missionaries were also the first Europeans in the New World to use institutions of healing and education to further the compatible goals of charity and Christian conversion. In 1639 a small hospital, founded by the Duchess d'Aiguillon and operated by Ursuline nuns, was opened to serve the Hurons in Québec. The nuns were immediately challenged with a catastrophic epidemic of smallpox. "Scarcely had they disembarked," writes Father Le Jeune, "before they found themselves overwhelmed with patients. The Hall of the hospital being too small, it was necessary to erect some cabins, fashioned like those of the Savages, in their garden. . . . In a word, instead of taking a little rest, and refreshing themselves after the great discomforts they had suffered upon the sea, they found themselves so burdened and occupied that we had fear of losing them and their hospital at its very birth" (Thwaites 1896–1901, 19:9). Between August 1639 and May 1640 more than one hundred patients were admitted to the hospital for long-term care, while more than two hundred received temporary treatment or lodging. Of these, twenty-four died, a modest figure given the lethal nature of smallpox epidemics in native populations; but it seems that not all the patients at the hospital were mortally ill. The permanent residents included, for example, two blind women, one of whom had a two-year-old daughter who "led her mother, and warned her in her childish jargon of the rough places where she might stumble" (ibid., 13).

European medicine in a time of catastrophic illness was definitely one of the appeals of the French mission in Québec. The Mother in charge of the hospital reported to Father Le Jeune, "The remedies that we brought from Europe are very good for the Savages, who have no difficulty in taking our medicines, nor in having themselves bled" (ibid., 21). Two years later the Mother was able to make a similar comment on the popularity of the hospital among its Huron patients: "This year we dispensed over four hundred and fifty medicines. Our supply of drugs is exhausted; but our hearts are still quite whole, so that we can rejoice at the Baptism of these good souls" (ibid., 22:173).

As the Mother's statement indicates, the hospital at Québec was a religious institution as much as a place of healing. "All our sick are very careful to pray to God," she reports. "It is a great consolation to us to see them attentive to prayers evening and morning. They waken one

---

Chumash herbalists, who were paid for their services and had an economic incentive not to divulge remedies."

another as soon as the time for prayers draws near" (ibid., 15). The Ursulines' hospital was ultimately as concerned with salvation as biomedical intervention.

For children orphaned in a time of disease and warfare, the French missionaries had another small-scale institutional solution, one based on the observation by Father Le Jeune that "only education, and not intelligence[,] is lacking in these people" (ibid., 39). In 1640 Madame de la Pelletrie and the Ursuline nuns began a seminary to provide religious instruction to Indian orphans, with eighteen girls taking up residence in de la Pelletrie's house. In the Seminaire des Sauvages, as it was called, the children were given lessons in literacy and religious instruction intended to prepare them for Communion. They were also required to dress and behave "à la Française," and de la Pelletrie herself reported with pride that her "principal occupation is to make their clothes, comb their hair, and dress them" (ibid., 57). Yet the change in their outward appearance did not take away many of their emotional attachments to their lives in the Huron villages. As Mother Marie de Saint Joseph commented, "Their favorite recreation is to dance, after the fashion of their country; they do not do this, however, without permission" (ibid., 43). The ultimate goal of the seminary was to raise the Huron girls to the point at which they "have left their savage nature at the door . . . [and] have brought no part of it with them" (ibid., 53). The Mother Superior praised those who "are not moved at seeing Savage girls or women come and go—they show no desire to follow them, they salute them in the French way, and leave them smilingly" (ibid., 53–55). The seminary was one of the first tightly controlled institutions to use education as a tool of exclusively religious instruction, in which the manners and appearance of the French were requisite, and Indian "superstitions" forbidden.

The French mission, despite its accomplishments in converting, educating, and healing the Hurons, was destabilized and ultimately overwhelmed by raids from the Iroquois, which were supported and armed by the Dutch. Father Jerome Lalemant, writing in 1642, complained of the "petty wars" of the Iroquois, using this term "because they come by bands and by surprise; but this is so harassing, that there is no battle we would not wage rather than see ourselves always in danger of being taken unexpectedly" (ibid., 22:247–49). It was immensely frustrating for the French missionaries to be prevented by "a mere handful of one or two thousand Iroquois" from converting all the regions of Canada "into a great Christian Empire" (ibid., 49:213–15).

Missionaries often undertook their work among the Indians at times when the loss of elders to disease compromised indigenous spiritual and healing traditions. At the same time, it was unusual for missionaries to live in communities that were not faced with continuing, almost over-whelming challenges to their health. Epidemics, loss of subsistence, war, and forced relocation were common backgrounds against which mis-sionaries plied new religious ideas—and new strategies of healing.

PURITANS AND "PRAYING INDIANS" IN NEW ENGLAND

By 1600 the European colonization of the eastern seaboard had been destructive, though not catastrophic, for the indigenous North Ameri-cans. Until then, the British, French, and Dutch colonists were outsiders to native communities. The depredations of settlers had started the process of removal, the impact of disease had destroyed some villages, the introduction of European goods had brought with it change to mate-rial culture, subsistence strategies, exchange, political organization, and patterns of alliance and rivalry (Salisbury 1996, 399). But societies' elas-tic capacity for change had not yet been surpassed; the core values of each society remained intact.

This situation was to change as European rivalries deepened and turned to violence, bringing Indian allies into their conflicts, as settlers began changing the landscape and pressing for Indian removal, and as missionaries in the wake of upheaval began their efforts to provide those whose existence had been irrevocably transformed with what some saw as the spiritual secrets of European dominance.

The New England Puritans who fled the religious repression of Stuart England brought with them the experience of worldly struggle for eternal values. And in the New World the agents of resistance to the divinely ordained Truth were the "savages," seen by some as descendants of the lost tribes of Israel who had for many years lived in ignorance, guided only by the dark counsel of Satan. Repeated characterization of Indians as some-how dominated by satanic influence and therefore devoid of normal human virtues such as generosity, compassion, and cleanliness confirmed the Puri-tans' sense of moral superiority and provided a rationale for occupation of, dispossession of, and violence toward indigenous populations that char-acterized the founding of the new colony (Cave 1996, 17).

Captain John Smith, who participated in the founding of a permanent English colony in Virginia in 1607, provided reports, later to be studied by New England's Puritans, on the behavior and dispositions of the natives. The Indians were, in Smith's view, shrewd, yet basically cruel, irrational, vengeful, treacherous, and barbaric, even among themselves. He mistakenly understood Indian puberty rituals to involve the sacrifice of children to the Devil (ibid., 14), providing an assessment of Indians in which they embodied all that was antithetical to humanity and Christianity. Even sympathetic writers were inclined to consider native spiritual practices as satanism. Roger Williams, a clergyman from Salem who was exiled from the Massachusetts Bay Colony in 1636 for expressing such views as the need for separation of church and state and respect for Indian land rights—views unacceptable to the Puritan ruling elite—and who, in exile, made perceptive, sympathetic observations of Indian life, nevertheless understood Indian "priests" to be "no other than our English witches" (cited ibid., 24). So deep were the prejudices of Puritan settlers toward native spirituality that they could not look upon the curing ceremonies of the powwows (an Algonquin word referring to their healers and spiritual intermediaries) without recoiling in horror. The shaman's control over a variety of animate, inanimate, visible, and invisible entities was narrowly understood as satanic. The invocations and manipulations of spirits were not understood by Europeans as control of powers whose benevolence was necessary to ward off evil for the sake of health and prosperity, but as "Devil worship." Witches in seventeenth-century Europe, let us not forget, were not only prosecuted for using diabolical powers to redress grievances by injuring or killing their victims, but also punished for manipulation of sacred power with benevolent intentions, such as finding treasure or lost articles or attempting "to provoke any p[er]son to unlawful love" (cited in Macfarlane 1970, 15). And while Algonquin and other native peoples often attributed sickness and misfortune to the malicious use of sacred power, they were not inclined to attack or discredit all shamans, especially not those who controlled the forces capable of relieving them of their afflictions; yet powwows were not seen by Europeans as leaders and healers who had an important place in the Algonquin community, but were equated with the marginalized and presumably usually malicious witches of Europe, even though specific observations did not support the comparison (Cave 1996, 24–25).

So far this sounds a great deal like the Spanish perceptions of Indians in New Mexico; but the English were not to begin the process of spiritual colonization in earnest until their domination was seemingly secure. Settlement and mercantile interests, pursued in ways that promoted competition with the Indians as well as rival colonies, were the first preoccupations of New England's Puritans. Only when the Indians were all but decimated by epidemics and, in the case of the Pequots, by a punitive military offensive, did the English immigrants begin to attend to their salvation, calling for help from the God-fearing in establishing missions (see figure 1).

There is a connection between English misunderstandings of native ritual and their similarly unenlightened views of the Indians' ties to the land. The English, almost from their arrival on the shores of the New World, interpreted much of what they saw in terms of mercantile possibilities; and the lack of such understanding and initiative by the Indians led many Europeans to see them as "shiftless" and "lazy," as squandering the resources available to them (Cronon 1983, 56). In a tract defending "the Lawfulness of Removing Out of England into the Parts of America," Robert Cushman sets the minds of would-be immigrants at ease by telling them of the wastefulness of the Indians, who are "not industrious, neither have art, science, skill, or faculty to use either the land or the commodities of it; but all spoils, rots, and is marred for want of manuring, gathering, ordering, etc.," while the Indians "do but run over the grass as do also the foxes and wild beasts" (cited ibid.). The legal principle of *vacuum domicilium,* which provided a basis for the occupation of land not being "used" by its original inhabitants, was challenged by Roger Williams, who observed that, while only a small portion of Indian land was cultivated, virtually all of it was used for hunting, and that if the English wanted to lay claim to these hunting lands the Indians were equally entitled to the hunting parks of the English royalty and nobility (Salisbury 1982, 197–98). Williams's tract outlining this view was burned (surviving secondhand only in the writings of his opponents), and the occupation of Indian land following the principle of *vacuum domicilium* was upheld by the New England magistrates.

By focusing on the "Devil-worshiping" powwows as the source of Indian spiritual ideas and by stressing commercial uses of land, the New England Puritans also failed to see the interconnectedness of spiritual and subsistence practices among native peoples. The observation made by the anthropologist Frank Speck in the 1930s that "hunting is a holy occupation" (1977, 72) in which strict, tacit codes of behavior are underpinned by belief in animal reincarnation and human spiritual development through participation in killing and ritual respect toward hunted animals, does not find expression in colonial chronicles and is certainly

Figure 1. Seal of the Governor and Company of Massachusetts Bay from 1681 by John Foster, depicting an Indian with
a scroll reading "Come over and help us." (Courtesy of
American Antiquarian Society)

not acknowledged by those who had interests in removing Indians from
the land. The Pilgrim apologists' depictions of Indians as morally and
spiritually depraved, and as "running over the land" like animals without industry or ambition, is a significant part of the background to
removal, warfare, and, ultimately, missionary enterprises.

English hegemony was secured in the Pequot War of 1636–37, in
which the British, in their terms, taught the recalcitrant Pequots a "salutary lesson" by waging an all-out military offensive intended to inflict
the maximum number of casualties, and which included a massacre at
Fort Mystic, a fortified Indian village, in which noncombatants were
deliberately killed, male prisoners of war summarily executed, and surviving women and children given into slavery, among either England's
Mohegan and Narragansett allies or Caribbean slave-traders. When the
fighting was over, the victorious English abolished Pequot sovereignty
and prohibited use of the tribal name (Cave 1996, 2). The Pequot slaughter encouraged evangelical ambitions. Puritan commentators saw the
defeat of the Pequots as God's intervention in punishing those who
expressed "pride" and "defiance of authority." William Bradford's awe
of what he saw as divine intervention was not atypical: "It was a fear-

ful sight to see them thus frying in the fire and the streams of blood quenching the same, and horrible was the stink and scent thereof; but the victory seemed a sweet sacrifice, and they gave the praise thereof to God who had wrought so wonderfully for them" (cited in Salisbury 1982, 224). And if divine will could be seen in the "righteous smiting" of England's enemies, God's favor could also be understood as an incentive to bring Christianity to the unenlightened.

It was in the aftermath of the Pequot massacre that John Eliot, a pastor at Roxbury, set out to convert the Indians, "to persuade them to pray unto God, to turn from their lewd and lazy life to the living God, and to come forth from the dark dungeon of their lost and ruined condition, into the light of the Lord Jesus" (Eliot [1671] 1980, 63). After their defeat it was easier to see the Indians as living in a "lost and ruined condition," even if Eliot was using a metaphor for their spiritual state of being. With their communities depleted and scattered, many Indians, especially the Pequots and Massachusetts, who were hardest hit by the epidemics and warfare of the 1630s, sought new spiritual insight and new possibilities for hope. After such calamitous events, few aspects of their lives could have remained unexamined; and those who gave polite hearings to the first English missionaries and who asked sincere, probing questions of them seem to have been looking for ways to understand the spiritual sources of English domination.

Missionary enterprises had their greatest success among those furthest removed from the centers of the fur and wampum trade, where choices were limited and viable negotiation of English political domination and expansionist pressures was difficult—the geographically isolated islands, including Martha's Vineyard, and eastern Massachusetts, where English settlement was concentrated (Salisbury 1990, 84–85). It was also in these locations that missionaries found it possible to isolate their Indian congregations from outside influences, to prevent backsliding through contact with powwows and other nefarious "idolaters."

In 1641 Thomas Mayhew purchased a group of sixteen islands, including Martha's Vineyard and Nantucket, honoring land claims, purchasing title, then reselling the lands to English settlers. His son Thomas Jr., who already knew the Massachusett language, was given direction of the first settlement at Edgartown on Martha's Vineyard, and soon began evangelizing the Indians. In 1652 a covenant for a Christian community was drawn up, and by 1670 there were some three thousand native Christians in the islands. At the same time, the first Indian church, with Indian officers, was established (Beaver 1988, 431).

In 1646 the General Court of Massachusetts passed an act encouraging the propagation of the gospel among the Indians, accompanied by a recommendation to the elders of New England's churches to consider how this goal might be accomplished. John Eliot responded by first learning the Massachusett language and, with the help of a bilingual assistant, translating the commandments, the Lord's Prayer, some of his favorite passages from the Bible, and a few of his own exhortations and prayers. Having prepared himself in this way, Eliot then visited a camp five miles from his home in Roxbury, where he delivered a one-hour discourse in the Massachusett language to the assembled Indians. The thoughtfulness of Eliot's listeners is apparent in the record that has been left of their questions to the missionary. One Massachusett pointed out that "God made hell in one of the six days" and reasoned from this the pointed question, "Why . . . did God make hell before Adam sinned?" Another asked, "If [sinners] repent in hell, why will not God let them out again?" (Ronda 1977, 71).

Enough of his listeners, however, were persuaded by his message that Eliot could develop more ambitious plans for his Indian ministry. Between 1651 and 1674, Eliot created fourteen praying towns in the Massachusetts colony based on his vision of a "Christian Commonwealth" and his understanding of scriptures "for every Law, Rule, Direction, Form or what ever we do" (cited in Salisbury 1974, 32). Native practices seen to diverge from biblical or English norms, whether in spiritual practice, marriage, economic pursuits, or hygiene, were forbidden, with censure and fines imposed for violations. Tribal mechanisms of leadership and social control were considered defunct. The Natick code, a set of rules established for Eliot's praying town in Natick, Massachusetts, calls for a fine of five shillings for idleness. Women were forbidden to wear their hair short, or men their hair long; both sexes were required to "weare their haire comely, as the English do" (cited ibid., 33). The use of body grease was prohibited, as was the custom of killing lice between the teeth (ibid.). Eliot's goal in propagating the gospel among the Indians was therefore to civilize as much as to Christianize them. "I find it absolutely necessary," he wrote, "to carry on civility with religion" (cited in Moore 1842, 69–70). Above all, the praying towns were to be isolated from the influence of nonpraying Indians. They were to be bulwarks against the pernicious sachems and powwows who threatened to lead his congregation astray. As Eliot metaphorically explained, "The fox came to the lamb's door, and would fain come in, but the lambs refused" ([1671] 1980, 123).

In his Indian dialogues, used for instructional purposes in his missionary work, Eliot created the character of Piumbukhou, who instructs his kinsmen in the "filth and folly" of their previously unenlightened way of life. With the light of Christianity, he tells his wayward kinsmen, "we plainly see the sinfulness of our own former, and of your still continued[,] ways, and I desire that God will help me to open among you some of the divine light which God hath showed us, that it may shame you from such filthy practices and shine them away forever, as the rising sun doth dissipate and drive away all the darkness of the night and maketh wolves, bears, and all other wild beasts hide themselves in thickets, and not dare to be seen in the day light" (ibid., 64). Eliot's use of animal metaphors suggests that the natural world, the realm of wild beasts concealed in darkness and thickets, was as much to be controlled and tamed as the souls of the Indians.

As events were to prove, there was also more than a grain of truth to Eliot's concern that the world outside the praying towns was potentially a predatory danger to his ministry. Those who struggled to maintain an existence on the land, now circumscribed by a competitive fur trade and immigrants' land hunger, looked upon the praying Indians, who fully adopted the settled life and religion of the English, with more than a trace of suspicion. King Philip, who was later to lead an ill-fated war against the English, was said to have once taken hold of John Eliot's coat and told him that he "cared as little for his gospel as he did for the button on his coat" (Moore 1842, 45–46). Mission historians were later to comment on the active hostility of the "heathen" Indians: "Nothing, indeed, but the dread of the English, prevented them from murdering all the converts" (Religious Tract Society [183?], 20).

Not all non-Christian Indians, however, shared this hatred; and there were tangible benefits for those who joined the Christian communities. Their conversion, following the "Eliot Plan," was not only to Christianity but also to "civility," to a settled way of life involving household production of food and handicrafts, together with an explicit renunciation of native practices and beliefs. In exchange for giving up portions of their land and providing unskilled and semiskilled labor to English merchants and employers, the "praying Indians" obtained a sense of security in a time of overwhelming change. The missionaries served as protectors against further loss of land and the abuses of neighboring English settlers. The praying Indians were sheltered from the tribute demands of rival Indian groups and from resistance to Christianity from within their own bands. At the same time, they resisted complete isolation in the pray-

ing towns, trading many of the items given to them to encourage their
"civilization"—such as clothing, tools, and sewing materials—with non-
Christian natives outside the communities in exchange for items of Indian
manufacture (Salisbury 1990, 84–85).

King Philip's War of 1675–76 destroyed all but four of the praying
towns and seriously disrupted those that survived; all were to disappear
by the end of the seventeenth century. The Christian Indians had no allies
in this conflict other than the missionaries themselves and were victim-
ized by both non-native settlers and non-Christian Indians in the struggle for supremacy in New England (Beaver 1988, 431). The aftermath
of the war was similarly disastrous. The so-called allies of the English—
the Pokanoket of Plymouth, the Mohegan in Connecticut, and the Narragansett and Eastern Niantic in Rhode Island—had most of their lands
seized during and immediately following the hostilities, and thereafter,
as Salisbury relates, "continued their descent to the position of a sub-
proletariat, often intermarrying with blacks who, like themselves, were
confined to the economic and social margins of pre-industrial New
England" (1982, 238). From this point until recently, the surviving native
communities were to exist as enclave cultures with minimal resources,
still attracting the interest and sympathy of missionaries intent on propagating Christianity and the virtues of "civility."

PRELUDE TO NATION BUILDING

Perceiving the beliefs, customs, and practitioners of other spiritual traditions as alien, maleficent influences that must be destroyed in order to
improve the human condition through the power of Truth is not an
inevitable consequence of a deep commitment to a scriptural faith by a
dominant people. Not every devout Christian making personal sacrifices
to live among the Indians as an example of piety and industriousness was
drawn into the destruction or appropriation of sacred objects and the
marginalization of those who used them. The Quakers living among
the Seneca in the eighteenth and nineteenth centuries were tolerant of
the Indians' beliefs and practices, basing their approach to religious differences on a passive evangelism by example, inspired by the belief, as
Wallace portrays it, "that every human being, not merely the Christian,
entertains an inner light that evinces itself as the voice of natural conscience. Since this inner light is the mystic presence of divinity in every
man, the Seneca were in no danger of damnation if they but heeded the
voice" (1968, 176). The Society of Friends was scriptural, universalis-

tic, sober, and orderly, and it stressed the values of hard work, honesty, cleanliness, and marital fidelity—all the virtues that in some other missionary programs came to be associated with ethnocidal evangelism— yet the Quakers' direct interventions in Seneca practices were minimal. When Henry Simmons, a Quaker working to educate the Seneca, became exasperated with the "dancing frolicks," the social dances frequently taking place in the village, he burst into the house of Chief Cornplanter, a prominent Seneca leader, and, as Wallace narrates, announced to a room filled with the chief's family and friends that "these frolics were 'the Devil's works,' and that before he would suffer such doings in *his* house, he would 'burn it to Ashes & live in a cave'"(1969, 231). Such occasional outbursts were tolerated and, in fact, resulted in social reform largely because of the Quakers' general tolerance of the significant events of Seneca ritual observance.

This leads us to a pivotal question: why were the Quakers an exception? What led most missionaries in the North American colonies to act upon their convictions so destructively? Part of the answer can be found in the "civilizing" goals of many missions, which were largely absent from the Quaker approach, and of which some tribes, such as the Pequots discussed by Kim Burgess below, successfully divested themselves. One of the features shared by Spanish, French, and English missions was, as Robert Berkhofer points out, a fusion of religious and colonial ambitions: "The work of the English missionaries, like that of the *religieux* engaged in the *Francization* program and of the Spanish friars proselytizing on the frontiers of New Spain, can be viewed not only as bringing the Indians more fully under White law and jurisdiction but also making them more amenable to White economic exploitation" (1978, 133). This combination of goals was a common outgrowth of the colonial situation, in which conversion efforts and occupation complemented European views of Indians, which portrayed them as lacking both religious edification and the motivations necessary for hard work and improvement of land.

The apostolic ideal of bringing enlightenment to those who had long lived in ignorance and darkness certainly had a place in inspiring the missionary zeal that led to both an acceptance of martyrdom and a tactical readiness to destroy the material and ideological foundations of error. For some, not only was there a positive impulse to truly universalize a universal Truth, but also a more sinister perception of evil, particularly in the context of indigenous control of spiritual forces, at times fitting perfectly with European understandings of satanic power.

It is also important to note the wider context in which the missions were developed. Christianity in Europe at the time of early missions in North America was undergoing profound changes, not only through the upheavals of the Reformation and the rise of Protestant churches but also through, and during approximately the same period as, a shift in the use and understanding of magic and witchcraft. Witchcraft accusations and the use of magic for protection against spiritual harm declined radically in the seventeenth century for reasons that are not fully understood by historians. Keith Thomas, in his magisterial survey of the use of magic in sixteenth- and seventeenth-century England, posits as the background to this decline the intellectual changes that constituted the scientific and philosophical revolution of the seventeenth century, which underscored the flaws of witchcraft prosecutions, discredited astrology, and inculcated skepticism toward enthusiasts who claimed inspiration from God (1971, 771); new technology and uses of bureaucracy led to such changes as the development of insurance, fire fighting, improved sanitation, and improvements to living standards in which the environment was amenable to control. More important, as Thomas points out, was the rise of new aspirations, positive efforts to improve human lives that had a greater effect in challenging the worldview of magic than almost anything else. The development of hospitals may initially have done more to spread disease than improve medical conditions, but "they helped to displace the amateur, the empiric and the wise woman. They also reflected a new practical, optimistic attitude" (ibid., 789). We can also surmise, beyond Thomas's findings, that the "discovery" of the original inhabitants of the New World in itself contributed to a decline in the vitality of the Inquisition, drawing attention and energy away from European heresy toward the unsaved souls across the ocean, like a new affliction easing old wounds.

These changes in Europe that occurred as the Reformation overturned the powers of the Catholic Church—at the same time that people began to reach for a scientific explanation of the universe—are reflected in the missionary enterprises of the New World. The Puritans of New England were the clearest exemplars of this change in the foundations and functions of knowledge. Those who inspired the industrial revolution in Europe—the hardworking, frugal Protestant reformers—became influential missionary ambassadors to the Indians, striving to teach them not only how to worship but how to live.

This was the model that later came to be underwritten by governments in efforts to instill in "savages" the virtues of "civilization."

Through this process, the enemy of the true faith became perceived less as Satan or his minions on earth and more often as "superstition," the very antithesis of the rationalism and frugality that would make the Indians true citizens. In order to achieve this new and ideal measure of equality, Indians were expected to leave behind their "fanciful" beliefs and "superstitious" practices. Christian missions themselves paradoxically took on the task of instructing native children not only in religion and the values of thrift and industry but also in the discoveries and benefits of science. They were to disappear as Indians by thoroughly following the example of their "civilized" neighbors.

The Pequots' Conversion to Christianity

Kim Burgess

After the Pequot War of 1637, the English ensured that the remaining Pequots, those neither killed nor given into slavery, were politically, socially, and economically incapacitated. Although it may have been politically strategic for the Pequots to convert to Christianity after the massacre, they demonstrated considerable resistance to the efforts of religious practitioners for more than a hundred years. They withstood numerous restrictions placed upon them as they struggled to regroup and retain their separate identities and lifeways.

For example, by the end of the 1650s, two groups of Pequots exhibited considerable initiative and moved back to their own territory in Connecticut, set up encampments, and were granted colonial representatives with whom to negotiate their political affairs. These two groups are today known as the Eastern Pequots (historically known as the Stonington group) and the Mashantucket-Pequots (known as the Groton group).

The English restricted the remaining Pequots in numerous ways. They were prohibited from engaging in their own subsistence activities, speaking their own language, purchasing or receiving guns from non-Indians, and shooting weapons without penalty or corporal punishment (Salisbury 1987, 91). Colonists and foreigners were prohibited from trading with the Pequots, and non-Indians were barred from settling with them. The limitations placed on their economic strategies fostered a dependency on colonists for subsistence (ibid., 95). Although the Pequots experienced severe economic deprivation and social isolation, for more than a hundred years they demonstrated considerable resistance to the attempts of missionaries to convert them to Christianity and eventually, against all odds, accepted Christianity on their own terms, in such a way that it complemented rather than destroyed indigenous spiritualism.

The English found several ways to pressure the Pequots to give up their indigenous spiritualism and convert to Christianity. Church elders were ordered to preach to the Pequots twice yearly, in accordance with the 1650 Code of Laws. In 1657 the Reverend William Thompson was hired to preach to the Pequots in Stonington, but gained no converts. In the 1660s the Society for the Propagation of the Gospel applied greater pressure on the Pequot leaders to convince tribal members to convert to Christianity. Six coats were given to the tribal leaders from the Society "to reward them for their services in governing the Pequots, and to persuade them to attend [church] on such means as should be used for bringing them to a knowledge of God" (DeForest 1852,

273). As an added incentive, "Indians who would put out their children to 'godly English' were also offered a coat every year, besides food and clothing for their children" (ibid.). In addition, Connecticut passed a law in 1675 forbidding practices of Native American spiritualism.

Since the Pequots were initially stalwart in their resistance to Christianity, why did they eventually become receptive to missionary efforts? The earliest Pequot conversions may have been strategic: The people were handicapped when dealing with colonial authorities because of illiteracy in English. Reading and writing were taught only in Christian church schools; and without access to secular educational facilities, those who wanted to develop literacy skills could be taught only by evangelical Christians.

Archaeological evidence reveals that the Pequots retained indigenous lifeways until they began to convert to Christianity in the 1740s during New England's "Great Awakening" (a term given by missionaries to their first years of success) and the New Light Movement. Kevin McBride (1990) notes that implements associated with animal husbandry and frame dwellings are not found in the archaeological record until the eighteenth century.

The New Light Movement, led by an Englishman named George Whitefield, swept through New England and appealed to Native American groups as it called for a rejection of the traditional, restrictive churches and advocated acceptance of a new order premised upon the salvation of the individual. It also contested many of the elitist attitudes of the upper classes, including the idea that the uneducated were largely ignorant (Simmons 1983, xxiii). George Whitefield preached to large crowds in Groton and Stonington and introduced itinerant teaching (Comrie and Kimball 1987, 17). The New Light approach was more acceptable to the southern New England tribes because its teachings included revelations, visions, and trances, which were prevalent in Indian ceremonies and rituals. The New Light reformers also challenged the doctrine of the standing clergy, claiming that the latter's knowledge of Christianity was purely intellectual and did not have any revealed religion at its foundation. The Puritan clergy was criticized for being opportunistic and interested only in the lucrative aspect of their positions, rather than love of God (ibid.).

Surprisingly, the adoption of Christianity served to strengthen intertribal communication and alliance formation, rather than weaken tribal ties. During the Great Awakening in the 1740s, there emerged Native Americans who became political activists as well as religious leaders (Samuel Niles of the Narragansetts, Samson Occum of the Mohegans, and William Apess of the Pequots). Samuel Niles, who was ordained by his fellow tribal members, separated from the New Light Movement in 1745 and, with a "Separate" faction, established a Separatist Narragansett church on the Rhode Island reservation.

Members of many tribes attended meetings at the Narragansett church to hear Samuel Niles preach, including the Mohegan, Groton and Stonington Pequot, Western Niantic, and Montauk tribes. One ritual that began in the

1740s at the Narragansett church continues to this day: it is called the August Meeting, and people from many tribal origins, including both Pequot tribes, come for several days of feasting, socializing, dancing, and spiritual services (Simmons 1983, 263).

Samuel Niles also traveled to the Groton Pequot and the Mohegan reservations to administer communion (ibid., 8). This created some tension, as the standing clergyman, a man of English descent named Joseph Fish, head of the Stonington Congregationalist Church, objected to Niles's preaching, which he saw as working against his own success with the Eastern Pequots. Fish had baptized a number of Eastern Pequots in the years spanning 1740–43 and looked after a school for them while he was representing the Company for Propagation of the Gospel in New England. Although Christianity gave the Eastern Pequot children access to education, Fish found the Pequots largely resistant to his preachings, and he complained that they preferred the Separatist teachings of the Narragansett ministers (ibid., xxviii).

Native Americans, as well as other poor and isolated groups, found the New Light preachings appealing because New Light preachers could be Indian or white and did not have to be literate. There was also a basic continuity between New Light Christianity and indigenous practices. Simmons notes, "Eighteenth-century accounts of New Light itinerant preachers are remarkably reminiscent of seventeenth-century descriptions of powwows, particularly with reference to their bodily movements, singing, visions, and trance behavior. Both powwows and Separate preachers were recruited . . . by dreams, visions, and other forms of direct supernatural insight" (ibid., 266). Indian tribes could thus remain "Indian" even though they adopted Christianity.

However appealing the Separate preachers were to some, there were others who could not tolerate the demoralizing aspects of living as a native person in New England. In the 1770s many of the Pequots, Mohegans, and Narragansetts who were Christian converts followed the Mohegan minister Samson Occum to the Oneida Iroquois reservation near Brothertown, New York, where land was deeded to them. There they lived until 1833, when, with the Oneida, they moved on to Brothertown, Wisconsin (Speck 1928).

The tendency of the Eastern Pequots to worship outside the established church was again evident in the early 1900s when Calvin Williams, an Eastern Pequot, served as preacher to his tribe and led religious meetings in members' homes or out of doors if the weather permitted. When Williams became too ill to continue his role as preacher, Simeon F. Dickson, a Narragansett, traveled to the reservation and served as preacher.

The legacy of the Eastern Pequot maintenance of their own brand of worship while fostering tribal cohesion continued thereafter. By 1930 there was no formal preacher on the reservation, but prayer meetings were still held among tribal members on a regular basis. When the weather was fair, meetings were held on the reservation on the first Sunday of the month. The group that gathered was predominantly composed of Eastern Pequots: joining them were worshipers from nearby tribes, blacks, and a few whites who were friends of the tribal members and who were, according to Eastern Pequot elders, "interested in Indians." The meetings were considered nondenominational, although Separatist Baptists were the majority of the attendees, and were spiritual, social, and political in function, with prayers followed by picnicking and discussions of family issues.

In the 1970s, the Eastern Pequots resurrected their tribal powwows, which continue to this day. These powwows, unlike most intertribal dances of the "pan-Indian" movement, are private affairs, attended by family members, friends from other tribes, and a few non-natives. Drumming and dancing occur throughout the two-day event, with breaks taken for prayers, naming ceremonies, speeches by tribal members, and the sharing of food. Although many of the Eastern Pequots are baptized Christians, they still embrace their Native American traditions. To date, the Eastern Pequots have been able to negotiate Christianity in such a way that it does not hamper their Indian identity or sense of indigenous spiritualism.

CHAPTER 3

Learning to Forget

A great general [Sheridan] has said that the only good Indian is a dead one, and that high sanction of his destruction has been an enormous factor in promoting Indian massacres. In a sense, I agree with the sentiment, but only in this: that all the Indian there is in the race should be dead. Kill the Indian in him, and save the man.

> Richard H. Pratt, *Official Report of the Nineteenth Annual Conference of Charities and Correction*, 1892

Evangelism by itself could not be counted upon to effect the desired transformation of "savages" into "civilized" human beings. Missionaries whose efforts failed utterly or, perhaps even worse, remained stagnant after initial success, vented their frustrations on the recalcitrant Indians by attributing their refusal to accept the truths of Christianity to stupidity, indolence, or the satanic influence of "witch doctors" whose insidious control over their spirits and intellect could not be uprooted. Something more than mere persuasion was needed to overcome these basic defects.

That "something" was developed during the earliest evangelical efforts in North America but was not fully implemented until after the pacification of the nineteenth century: the marriage between evangelism and formal education. In the mid- to late nineteenth century, when most Indians were settled on reservations, effectively displaced by the western expansion, the squalor and desperation of their new situation pricked the consciences of some members of the eastern elite. The humanitarians who sought a new solution to the "Indian problem" worked within a heavily Christian framework to bring the Indians into civilization. Although the precise means for accomplishing assimilation was never fully agreed upon, there was a general consensus in influential philanthropic groups, like the Friends of the Indian (a coalition of academics, clergy, policymakers, and society women), that civilization and Christianity must go together and that the best work of this kind could be done by dedicated men and women who volunteered to promote the complementary goals of Indian welfare and Christian evangelism. At the beginning of the new, vigorous drive for Indian education, the work of churches and their representatives was seen as praiseworthy and indispensable, even to the point of garnering government support (Prucha 1973, 281). This view was expressed explicitly by Edward H. Magill, president of Swarthmore College, in an address to the Lake Mohonk Conference of 1887: "The religious organizations of the country must continue the noble work which they have so well begun, and upon them the chief burden must rest. It will be worse than vain for the government to attempt it, without their constant cooperation and their most efficient aid. A merely secular education, a training of the intellect alone, will not accomplish it. . . . No truth is more trite than that a purely intellectual education can only make the recipient a more efficient agent for evil" (Prucha 1973, 283).

It was soon to be confirmed that, by isolating young Indians from the influences of their families, they could be made to forget their barbarous practices and acquire the knowledge and benefits of civilization. An age-old practical truth, that those in the formative period of youth can more easily be broken down and rebuilt to live in a new way, was applied with enthusiasm after the settlement of Indians on reservations. Young people, whose personal sovereignty was still fragile and whose beliefs were still malleable, were the focus of a new phase of cultural annexation.

ENLIGHTENMENT AND EVOLUTIONISM

Programs of Indian education in the United States and Canada cannot be understood without first considering the intellectual currents that, directly or indirectly, influenced Indian education policy. Eighteenth-century Enlightenment ideas provided lasting notions of universal human perfectibility, while "vulgar" evolutionism in the nineteenth century was built upon notions of the innate backwardness of some races of humankind and the superiority of others (almost without exception that of the particular theorist). The combination of these intellectual currents, harnessed to the more immediate ideals of frontier domination, pride of civilization, and the simple expediency of what to do with those newly confined to reservations, was integral to efforts to "uplift," "improve," and "civilize" the Indian.

Until late in the eighteenth century, the dominant intellectual models of human history stressed processes of degeneration and decay, usually expressed in the biblical conception of the Fall, in classical ideas of a primitive golden age, or in cyclical patterns attributed to social life (Stocking 1987, 16). A prominent expression of degenerationism can be found in Joseph-François Lafitau's *Moeurs des sauvages américains,* based upon his observations of Iroquois life while serving as a missionary at Caughnawaga from 1717 to 1721, which presents a detailed argument that customs seemingly shared by native peoples and ancient Greeks, Romans, and Hebrews had survived from a divinely ordered era of religious virtue, and that differences between Indians and ancients can be attributed to the abandonment of ancient values and the loss of understanding of God's commands (Trigger 1985, 22–23). The frequent concern of missionaries in North America with the pervasive influence of Satan was thus more than religious bigotry: it was based upon a version of degeneration theory, explaining differences between Indians and Europeans as stemming from a savage fall from primitive religious grace. The Indians, according to most early missionaries, whether Spanish Franciscans, English Protestants, or French Jesuits, had at some point in human history been led away from God's favor into a realm of moral darkness. The principal goal of evangelism, therefore, was religious conquest, to erode the influence of Satan by disseminating knowledge of the true faith.

The Enlightenment introduced a competing, progressive conception of history that was to have important implications for later Euro-American goals and strategies in reforming Indian lives. European thinkers in the seventeenth and eighteenth centuries, buoyed by the discoveries of science, the development of a global commercial network, and the conquests of nascent colonial empires, shifted increasingly toward a view of history in which human progress was partially removed from formal Christianity and connected more directly to human reason and opportunities for individual improvement. The Enlightenment period cannot be portrayed as unified by a single, dominant theme or approach to history or human development. Joseph de Maistre, for example, represented a reactionary support of the trinity of classicism, monarchy, and the church at the same time that others were inspired by a new and restless spirit and sought to challenge old, constraining forms of intellectual and religious orthodoxy (Berlin 1990, 92–93). More innovative notions of human progress, however, came to prominence. Montesquieu, in *The Spirit of the Laws,* and Vico, in *The New Science,* for example, looked to ancient society, in the manner of Lafitau but with different premises, to find sources of pluralism, arguing that human differences do not stem from inferiority or degradation but from productive adaptations to varying political and environmental circumstances. Radical views that challenged the practices of formal Christianity and European ethnocentrism supported the equally radical corollary that human life could be self-consciously improved. In different ways, human perfectibility was understood by Locke, in *Of the Conduct of the Understanding,* and Rousseau, in *Emile,* to be accomplished more by practical educational strategies than mere religious instruction, discipline, and devotion.

Enlightenment ideas were also evident in missionary accounts of native people and their potential for Christianization. The Jesuit historian Pierre-François-Xavier de Carlevoix (1682–1761) developed, like Lafitau, a view of native peoples based on both wide reading and first-hand experience. He shared the popular conviction, articulated most clearly by Montesquieu, that nations, including Indian nations, have unique characteristics very much like individual personality that cannot easily be laid aside; the differences between the French and Indians could be explained by the latter's lack of education, which resulted in superstition and violence; and even the most savage people could be improved by association with more rational beings (Trigger 1985, 24–25). The Enlightenment vision of human progress and moral improvement was also a central intellectual force in the Great Awakening, the flurry of Protestant missionary activity in New England from the 1730s to 1760s. In the thoughts expressed by such renowned missionaries as Cotton Mather, Experience Mayhew, Eleazar Wheelock, Samson Occom, and John Sergeant, an anthropocentric appeal to the mind and reason was combined with a theocentric appeal to the heart and human spirit to create a forceful impetus behind missions in the New England and Middle Colonies,[1] with Christian schools opening in Pennsylvania, New Jersey, Rhode Island, Connecticut, New York, and Massachusetts, and on Martha's Vineyard (Szasz 1988, 191). In the Moravian settlements, which began construction in the 1740s with the Mahican community at Shekomeko in New York and soon sprang up across the Alleghenies, the fundamental importance of Christian education was reflected in their

---

1. Margaret Szasz (1988, 191) considers these two modes of thought to be in a state of "friction," but evidence of the energy with which they were applied suggests rather that they were fully complementary.

order of priorities: "in each case the church was built first, next the school, and the houses last" (Kohnova cited in Szasz 1988, 204).

The influence of Enlightenment ideas on policies applied to native North Americans was indirect and did not always have the effect of inspiring visions of social tolerance. Conceptions of human progress eventually came to the fore, resulting in a shift away from degenerationism and almost relativist pluralism in favor of ideas of human progress in which European civilization was seen to have steadily advanced, leaving "savages" in an undeveloped state. By the late eighteenth century a view had gained currency that presaged nineteenth-century socioevolutionism, situating native North Americans as representative of an earlier form of life from which Europeans had emerged as the pinnacle of human achievement. Adam Ferguson, a luminary of the Scottish Enlightenment, wrote in 1767, "It is in their [the Indians'] present condition that we are to behold, as in a mirror, the features of our own progenitors" (cited in Berkhofer 1978, 47). And in France and Scotland, the term *civilization* took on a modern meaning resonant with moral implications: a conception of superiority in material progress and social organization (Stocking 1987, 20).

In the mid-nineteenth century, evolutionism and nationalism developed this starting point of the Enlightenment into powerful and complementary intellectual currents with great influence on popular philanthropy and formal policy. Charles Darwin's *On the Origin of Species by Means of Natural Selection, or the Preservation of Favoured Races in the Struggle for Life,* published in 1859, was only the focal point of an intellectual movement that demolished the temporally shallow biblical chronology of human life and presented civilization as developing from savagery according to basic natural laws.[2]

Far from being incompatible with scriptural religion, however, nineteenth-century science took on some of the flavor of Christianity, especially in its pursuit of orthodoxy with respect to ideas of human progress and the virtues of civilization. Once evolutionism in its various forms had become acceptable to most thinkers, the division of humanity into races entered the mainstream of scientific classification. "Scientific" racism, in which the principal tenet was that light-skinned people ruled the world by virtue of superior physical and mental endowment, stimulated the investigation of a wide range of human differences, most noto-

---

2. This original, and revealing, title of Darwin's treatise is presented by Berkhofer (1978, 50).

riously the supposed measure of human intelligence through a simple measure of cranial capacity, sometimes with a length-breadth ratio referred to as the "cephalic index" (Berkhofer 1978, 55–61; Stocking 1988). Evolutionism, racism, and exclusivist Christianity were compatible ideas that situated Indians in an inferior position in the scale of human progress, simultaneously justifying their dispossession and calling for their improvement.

In terms of public policy applied to native North Americans, few works of the nineteenth century were as influential as Lewis Henry Morgan's *Ancient Society or Researches in the Lines of Human Progress from Savagery through Barbarism to Civilization,* which argued for the great antiquity of human life and situated "civilization" as the outcome of humanity's "natural as well as necessary sequence of progress" ([1877] 1974, 3). Morgan's paradigm presented this sequence as occurring through the earlier stages of Lower, Middle, and Upper Savagery followed by Lower, Middle, and Upper Barbarism, ultimately progressing to Civilization. Native North Americans were usually situated in Upper Savagery or Lower Barbarism, depending upon Morgan's assessment of their material and political development. This approach to human progress called out for something to be done, some forceful strategy to bring the Indians out of their supposedly inferior and lethargic state to enjoy the benefits of civilization.

One of the earliest and clearest expressions of a connection between the progress of civilization and the requirements of Indian policy was made by Morgan in his pioneering ethnological study, *League of the Ho-de-no-sau-nee, or Iroquois,* which appeared in 1851. Through a chance encounter in a bookstore in Albany with Ely S. Parker, an educated Iroquois leader, Morgan gained an unusually productive entry into Iroquois society; and with Parker as his translator and principal source of information, Morgan succeeded in assembling a detailed and, for the time, accurate picture of Iroquois society. His concluding chapter, which begins with the subheading "Future Destiny of the Indian," however, is concerned with the more practical implications of a complex Indian society overwhelmed by the demands of civilization: "Our primitive inhabitants are environed with civilized life, the baleful and disastrous influence of which, when brought in contact with Indian life, is wholly irresistible. Civilization is aggressive, as well as progressive—a positive state of society, attacking every obstacle, overwhelming every lesser agency, and searching out and filling up every crevice, both in the moral and physical world; while Indian life is an unarmed condition, a negative state, without inherent vitality, and without powers of resistance" ([1851] 1962, 444).

This understanding of the Indians' situation raised for Morgan an important issue, what he calls "the question of his reclamation" (ibid., 445), in which the government is seen as the proper guardian of the Indians' welfare, and education is a central tool of Indian improvement. The way the question is posed by Morgan squarely situates the best possibility for the Indians' "emancipation" in their assimilation into the nation that is displacing them: "Should the system of tutelage and supervision, adopted by the national government," Morgan asks, "find its highest aim and ultimate object in the adjustment of their present difficulties from day to day; or should it look beyond and above these temporary considerations, toward their final elevation to the rights and privileges of American citizens?" (ibid.). Morgan believed that the particular strategies best suited for this transformation of Indian life were education and Christianity, while one of the key obstacles to Indian "reclamation" was Indian "mythology" or "thraldom": "There are but two means of rescuing the Indian from his impending destiny; and these are education and Christianity. If he will receive into his mind the light of knowledge, and the spirit of civilization, he will possess, not only the means of self-defense, but the power with which to emancipate himself from the thraldom in which he is held" (ibid., 447–48).[3] Although Morgan praises missionaries for what they have accomplished, principally in demonstrating the potential for Indians to achieve a state of "improvement," it is clear that for Morgan (as it was for policymakers later in the century), Indian education was too important to be left exclusively in the hands of religious societies. The state was to have a central place in the important project of reclaiming Indian lives.

Although a variety of sometimes fuzzy notions stemming from evolutionism and an unshakable belief in the dominating powers of civilization had gained almost universal currency in Euro-American society by the late nineteenth century, the application of these ideas to Indians was by no means uniform. In frontier settings in particular, attitudes toward Indians and their potential for improvement were usually pes-

3. There were important influences upon Morgan's thinking that may explain, at least in part, the apparent discrepancy between his sincere appreciation of Iroquois life and the values of assimilation that he presents so forcefully in these lines. His wife, Mary Elizabeth Steele Morgan, was a devout, strict Presbyterian, and Morgan's close friend the Reverend Joshua Hall McIlvaine was a source of both evolutionist and possibly Christian ideas in Morgan's writing. These and other influences on Morgan's thought are presented by Trautmann (1987).

simistic and often virulently racist. William McKewen, Clerk in Charge of the Ouray Agency in Utah Territory, writes in 1886 that the Utes under his charge, whom he reports as having no religious beliefs or understanding of the truths of Christianity, refused to listen to the Reverend Mr. Bond, a Unitarian minister who had come to preach among them: "He soon concluded that they were so intolerably stupid and sullen, and so little inclined to give him even a respectful hearing, that he took his departure after a stay of three weeks, without accomplishing anything" (Government of the United States 1886, 448). Other missionaries found that the Indians' progress was confined to the settled communities, that as soon as they returned to the wilderness, old habits returned. Frank Pedley, Deputy Minister of Indian Affairs in Canada, commented on the difficulty experienced by Ottawa and the churches in changing Indian behavior: "It must not be forgotten that we are working in a material that is stubborn in itself; that the Indian constitutionally dislikes work and does not feel the need of laying up stores or amassing wealth. The idea which is ingrained in our civilization appears to be that a race must be thrifty and surround itself with all manner of wealth and comforts before it is entitled to be considered civilized. The Indian has not yet reached that stage, and it is doubtful if he will" (cited in Miller 1996, 185).

Other attitudes, especially among the eastern elite, tended to be more humanitarian and reformist in orientation, while usually acknowledging the Indians' temporarily inferior state. Richard Pratt, the most outspoken Indian educator of the nineteenth century, was clear in his view that the defects of Indian life were social rather than stemming from innate racial inferiority: "It is a great mistake to think that the Indian is born an inevitable savage. He is born a blank, like all the rest of us. Left in the surroundings of savagery, he grows to possess a savage language, superstition, and life. We, left in the surroundings of civilization, grow to possess a civilized language, life, and purpose" (Prucha 1973, 268). An author in a Canadian Anglican journal presented the widespread view that Indians were more capable of permanent improvement than other races: "There is a certain innate dignity about the Indian that marks him off from the negro, who in adaptability his superior, is inferior in those qualities which, when cultivated and developed place him on a level of acknowledged equality with civilized peoples" (cited in Miller 1996, 187). Views that combined racism and social Darwinism were still often optimistic toward the possibility of "satisfactory results" in the pursuit of Indian education. The call for government involvement in Indian improvement, expressed with such clarity by Lewis Henry Morgan earlier in the nineteenth century, gained momentum, and Indian education came increasingly to be a public concern.

THE ORIGINS OF THE INDIAN RESIDENTIAL SCHOOL

Uncharacteristically, education was one aspect of their relationship with the dominant society in which Native Americans were to receive preferential treatment. Rayna Green, in an overview of Indian education in the United States, concludes that "the idea of schools for Indians was irresistible, even as blacks and poor whites were being excluded from similar consideration" (1989, 11). Why did native North Americans merit an unusually determined effort to improve their lives through schooling when in other aspects of their existence, such as protection of the land on which they lived and even the preservation of their lives, they often received no such consideration? The answer becomes apparent when we look past the philanthropic self-congratulations of educators and politicians to consider what they actually accomplished. It was in the forced, institutionalized transformation of the children entrusted to their care that the masters of Indian schools blundered, like sculptors ignoring the inherent qualities of their material, inadvertently reducing their creation to rubble.

From the beginning of North American missionary enterprises, schools were the preferred means of "civilizing" Indians. A comfortable fit was perceived between the goals of education and the evangelical efforts of missionaries. The earliest schooling projects, however, did not always result in a meaningful transmission of knowledge to native communities. The Franciscans in the American Southwest developed programs that stressed vocational skills over literacy and academic development; and whatever attempts they made to instill moral improvement could not have had much of an impact prior to the revolt of 1680. The British made some early efforts to develop programs for Indian higher education, intending to build upon the foundation laid by missions. The endowments of such academic institutions as William and Mary, Harvard, and Dartmouth were partially contingent upon the establishment of programs for Indian education, but these philanthropic impulses became institutionally sidetracked, with fewer than fifty Native American graduates of Dartmouth, for example, before 1970.

A determined, widespread effort to "civilize" Indians resulted from the crisis following the defeat of the nomadic Plains peoples and their settlement on reservations in the 1870s and 1880s. A dual system of civil and military jurisdiction over Indians was rife with confusion and conflict; the Indian Bureau often failed to keep its treaty obligations, while the army was faced with the task of forcing unwilling, bitter nomadic peoples onto reservations. With the buffalo herds on which they depended for subsistence all but extinct, and without the mobility to roam the land for even the most meager resources, the Plains tribes were forced to rely upon rations supplied by the American military. This food allowance began as inadequate and was reduced further by the Indian Bureau. At the same time, like all nomadic peoples being forced by an expanding state to settle, they resisted taking up agriculture; in any case, the land they were allocated was often the least arable. For those who did plant crops, several seasons of drought in 1889 and 1890 resulted in starvation. Conditions on the new reservations were widely recognized as deplorable. Bishop W. H. Hare, an Episcopal missionary among the Sioux, was a sympathetic witness to the injustices and suffering of those among whom he worked to spread the gospel. With government promises of payment for lands unfulfilled, crops failing, and disease rampant, Bishop Hare saw a solution in the transformation of the Indians: "No doubt the people could have saved themselves from suffering if industry, economy, and thrift had abounded; but these are just the virtues which a people emerging from barbarism lack" (cited in Mooney 1991, 841). This juxtaposition of a clear, honest report of the dire consequences of the government failing to keep its promises with an advocacy of the virtues of thrift and industry shows an unwillingness to consider the actions of government as being improper or immoral. The solution to a situation resulting from a failure of government, according to Bishop Hare, was not to be found in lobbying those in power. The actions of legislature may be slow, haphazard, even dishonest, but in his view nothing was to be gained by challenging the inevitable course chosen by duly elected lawmakers. This aspect of the catastrophe on the new reservations had, for Bishop Hare, the same inevitability as the weather conditions causing the drought: it was a challenge to be overcome by the virtues of hard work and economy. The only way to save the Indian race from extermination would be to provide them with the habits of "thrift and industry," acquired through knowledge of civilization and the moral underpinnings of Christianity.

Following this logic, westward expansion in the late nineteenth century brought schools in its wake, which appeared almost as soon as, if not before, reservation communities could be established. This was an

initiative largely brought about by missions following the simple principle articulated by J. G. Wright, the Indian agent for Rosebud Agency,
Dakota, in 1886: "Christianity and civilization go hand in hand,
and . . . education is an assistant thereto" (Government of the United
States 1886, 300). The government Indian-school system, as Francis Paul
Prucha points out, was from its inception closely tied to missionary
efforts in which the values of faith and citizenship were tightly inter-
woven: "It was a principle agreed to by both Protestants and Catholics
that instruction in Christianity was fundamental in the education of
Indian youth. To fit Indians for citizenship in a Christian nation (which
all considered the United States to be), it was imperative that religious
training precede or parallel the industrial and literary learning that was
intended to prepare the pupils of the tribes for full participation in white
American society" (1979, 161).

The example that proved the feasibility of Indian education, that
demonstrated tangibly the potential for their transformation from "blanket Indians" into human beings capable of learning and yielding grace-
fully to discipline, was undertaken by Lieutenant Richard Pratt in 1875
with a group of seventy-two prisoners of war under his charge. These
were Kiowa, Comanche, Cheyenne, and Arapahoe warriors branded as
"notorious offenders" and banished to a remote eastern location, Fort
Marion, near St. Augustine, Florida, where they would no longer be able
to incite raids in the American frontier. They arrived in the beginning of
hot, humid weather. Several died, as Pratt explained, from the fatigue of
the long train journey and "the depressing effect of their being in irons"
(1964, 118) (see figure 2). He used the prison setting, with its tight security and strict routines, to effect a moral transformation of his charges.
He began, immediately after removal of their shackles, by having their
hair cut and giving them a change of clothes, an initial step that immediately provoked deep-seated resistance from the prisoners: "Soon after
the clothing was issued, a number [of prisoners] cut off the legs of the
trousers at the hip, laying aside the upper part and using the trouser legs
as leggings in the Indian way" (ibid.). "Correction," combining a mandatory model of dress and hygiene with a willingness to enforce it with punishment, eventually resulted in the external appearance that was to
become a starting point for inner transformation.

Once he was confident in the obedience of his prisoners, Pratt began
to further liberalize the conditions of their confinement, encouraging
them to produce works of art for sale, allowing them to visit the nearby
beaches and even to consort with the curious residents of St. Augustine.

Figure 2. A ledger drawing made by Howling Wolf, circa 1876–77, depicting a stop on the train journey to Fort Marion, Florida. One soldier is giving the Cheyenne prisoners water while others stand guard with fixed bayonets. (Field Museum of Natural History, Chicago. Photograph by Diane Alexander White; negative A111807)

English lessons were started with the help of some "excellent ladies" of the town who had previous teaching experience. For recreation, expeditions were arranged for oyster gathering and, on occasion, shark fishing, an adventurous and dangerous undertaking that reminded the inmates of the buffalo hunts that must have seemed a world away. Their word for the sharks was "water buffalo."

At the apogee of this liberalization, several Indian dances were staged for visitors, including several "persons of importance" from St. Augustine. Pratt himself could not contain his effusiveness in describing one such event: "Night was selected as the best time. Wood was brought for a bonfire in the court and the terreplein was crowded by the audience. Necessary paint was procured and the best dancers selected. They carried out their home methods of dress and adornment, stripping to the skin, wearing only the gee string and the breech clout which it supported, and painting their bodies most impressively. They made tom-toms, provided a chorus of singers, and gave a varied exhibition of different tribal dances.

This was perhaps as picturesque and thrilling a performance as any of its kind ever produced on the continent" (Pratt 1964, 121). After granting permission for another performance of this kind, following "urgent requests" from the townsfolk, the events were discontinued, ostensibly because they did not produce "interracial respect" (ibid.). We can assume, moreover, that from Pratt's point of view, they did little to promote the kind of inner transformation he was seeking from his inmates.

By sharply restricting the inmate's symbolic attachments to their earlier way of life on the western plains, and molding them as much as possible into the image of the "civilized" American, Pratt managed to perform what must have seemed to his selected audience to be an astonishing conjuring trick: to turn the "ruthless barbarians" most had only read about in newspapers and dime novels into people closely approximating "human beings." Mrs. J. Dorman Steele, in the August 1877 edition of the *National Teacher's Monthly*, was unable to conceal her surprise at the change she had witnessed in the prisoners at Fort Marion. Those who a mere two years previously had come to Florida convicted of "the grossest outrages and murders" had been transformed into "a military company neatly dressed in United States uniform, with hair cut and brushed, nails cleaned, manners respectful and faces more or less intelligent" (cited ibid., 181).

The miracle of Fort Marion showed that the most recalcitrant and dangerous of "savages" could be purposefully shaped into civilized humans. Breaking down the walls of outward appearance and language enabled the personalities of the inmates to become visible to their captors, the residents of St. Augustine, and eventually the country at large. "We have," in Pratt's expression of the ideal public response to his work, "accepted as brothers our natives whom this recent experiment has proved to be susceptible of transformation and responsive to Christian teaching" (ibid., 182).

But the experiment ended without being fully complete. In 1878 the War Department released the prisoners to the jurisdiction of the Indian Bureau. After three years at Fort Marion they could return to their families. The disappointment Pratt felt at seeing many of his charges "return to the blanket" was allayed only by the willingness of some others to continue their work elsewhere. Seventeen of the younger Fort Marion "students" elected to continue their training through sponsorships that allowed them to attend the Hampton Agricultural School for Negroes in Virginia.

The Hampton school was founded in 1868 with the backing of the American Missionary Association and was directed by General Samuel Armstrong, former commander of a regiment of African American troops in the Civil War. At the Hampton Institute, the Indian students found much that was familiar from their days at Fort Marion: order, discipline, dormitories, classrooms, work, prayer. As the renowned African American educator Booker T. Washington observed from his days as a student and teacher at the Hampton Institute, "No white American ever thinks that any other race is wholly civilized until he wears the white man's clothes, eats the white man's food, speaks the white man's language, and professes the white man's religion" (1965, 62).

An education at the Hampton Institute in the 1870s involved total immersion in the English language and a hands-on curriculum that emphasized vocational training, particularly in farmwork and domestic maintenance. An "outing" system gave students contact with New England families for whom they performed services and from whom they learned, in return, the habits of "industrious and thrifty people" (cited in Hultgren and Molin 1989, 31). Hampton also emphasized the imparting of Christian values, or what General Armstrong referred to as the "education of the heart." Although the Hampton Institute was officially nonsectarian, Christian practices and teachings permeated daily life. General Armstrong was clear in his advocacy of Christian education, stating, "Of all our work, that upon the heart is the most important; there can be no question as to the paramount necessity of teaching the vital precepts of the Christian faith" (ibid.). In practical terms, the imparting of faith involved not only Sunday morning services but also mandatory afternoon and vesper services in the school's nondenominational chapel; and from the arrival of the first Indian students in 1878 until the end of the nineteenth century there were 48 baptisms, 3 marriages, 141 confirmations, and a congregation of 190 communicants (ibid., 32–33). Clearly, General Armstrong's commitment to "education of the heart" was one of Hampton's highest priorities and, for those who wanted to witness a spiritual transformation of its Indian students, one of its proudest accomplishments.

Satisfaction with the Hampton Institute's accomplishments, however, was not universal among Indian educators. Richard Pratt in particular was not satisfied with the racial integration of its students, preferring to see the Indians take their lessons in civilization from the source, from the Anglo-American families who took in students in the "outing" program:

"I told the General [Armstrong] my dissatisfaction with systems to educate the Negro and Indian in exclusively race schools and especially with
educating the two races together. Participation in the best things of our
civilization through being environed by them was the essential factor for
transforming the Indian" (Pratt 1964, 213). Pratt's view was that, however civilized the former slaves or their descendants at Hampton might
be, their influence over the Indian students was not as salutary as exclusive contact with "national families" working from the purest motives
of Christian charity to overcome the Indians' "tenacity to savage life."

Pratt's solution was to establish an exclusively Indian school, situated
as far as possible from the "blanket Indians" of the western frontier. He
found a site for his school in a former Civil War barracks in Carlisle,
Pennsylvania. The Carlisle barracks, which had formerly housed the
Army School of Instruction for Cavalry Recruits, had been abandoned
in 1871 because of a petition by the religious people of the town to have
Sunday dress parades stopped. "These [parades] were," Pratt explains,
as though the reason was self-evident, "in the afternoon and crowds
came to witness" (ibid., 218). Rather than allow these buildings to fall
into decline, they could be used to house Indian students in a school that,
in a departure from the Fort Marion experiment, would start with the
very young. After successfully lobbying in Washington to secure use of
the barracks and the start-up money he needed, the next, most challenging task was to find the students who, with parental permission,
would attend the school.

The recruiting effort began with an address to about forty delegates
from Rosebud Agency, including the chiefs Spotted Tail, White Thunder,
Milk, and Two Strike. In his presentation, Pratt made the following
appeal: "The Government now realized that by keeping [Indian students]
separate from us and on reservations remote from any material chances
to learn our ways, the acquirement of our qualities was a very slow operation. . . . The purpose in establishing a school so far east was to bring
them near Washington[,] where all the people could see the improvement
and where members of Congress and the administrative officials of the
Government could visit and witness their progress and ability to learn"
(ibid., 221). Spotted Tail's initial reply summarized the injustice of
treaties, especially that which several years previously had led to the
annexation of the Black Hills,[4] soon followed by a flood of settlers in a

---

4. This complex case is considered more fully in Lazarus (1991) and Prucha (1994,
388–90).

gold rush. He described how Indian people had settled on the edge of the reservation boundaries, but surveyors had been sent and the lines of the reservation were established a long way inside of where Indian negotiators had agreed with the government they should be. "We are not going to give any children to learn such ways," he concluded (ibid., 222).

In his rejoinder, Pratt astutely turned Spotted Tail's objections to his advantage by pointing out the wisdom of having some Indian youths educated in the white man's knowledge to protect the tribes against further exploitation, deception, and encroachment: "Because you were not educated, these mountains, valleys, and streams have passed from you. Your ignorance against the white man's education will more and more hinder and restrain you and take from you, in spite of everything that can be done by yourselves, as long as you are so ignorant and unable to attend to your own affairs. . . . If you, yourself, had had education you might be owning the Black Hills and be able to hold them. . . . Spotted Tail, do you intend to let your children remain in the same condition of ignorance in which you have lived, which will compel them always to meet the white man at a great disadvantage . . . ?" (ibid., 223). Spotted Tail acceded to this line of reasoning. Fifty-six students for the new school at Carlisle were accepted from Rosebud Agency, including five of Spotted Tail's children. The school began its first year in 1879 with 136 students from the Sioux, Cheyenne, Kiowa, and Pawnee agencies, 16 more than authorized for the establishment of the school.

Pratt's real objectives were never presented to the chiefs who eventually agreed to send their children to the Carlisle Indian Industrial School. The children were not merely to be taught English and writing. The principal goal of their residency in the school and of its "outing" system was transformation: "Americanization," Christianization, the full participation of the Indian in the life of the nation. And the model for this difficult process was the "experiment" previously conducted with the adult prisoners of Fort Marion.

The routine developed at Carlisle that proved most effective in uprooting what were seen to be barbarous practices and superstitions involved institutional isolation of native children from family and community; removal and prohibition of all symbols of their Indian identity, including names, hairstyle, clothing, food, and, most important, language; and a regimented school routine based explicitly upon a military model found to reinforce discipline and conformity. This was supplemented by a regular barrage of ideas intended to demonstrate the iniquity of their elders and ancestors, the path to their redemption, and the benefits that

Figure 3. Richard Henry Pratt
(1840–1924), founder of the Carlisle
Indian Industrial School, 1879. (Courtesy of Hampton University Archives)

would await them if they would only give up their barbarous practices
and try to be good Christians.

As in Fort Marion, the first step was physical transformation: removal
of all reminders of "savage" life and their replacement with things seen
to be more conducive to the orderly life of the classroom and the virtues
of productive labor. Barbers were hired to cut the hair of the boys who
had arrived at the new Carlisle school. Luther Standing Bear, a member
of the entering class of 1878, remembers that when it was announced
though an interpreter that their braids were to be shorn, one of the boys,
Robert American Horse, made a speech to the others in which he concluded, "If I am to learn the ways of the white people, I can do it just as
well with my hair on" (1928, 140). Despite the anxiousness of most boys
to conform, several resisted the haircut. One in particular refused firmly
to have his long hair removed, resulting in a scene reported by Pratt in
his memoirs: "Late that night [Mrs. Pratt] was aroused by a very discordant wailing, which grew in volume. . . . When the interpreter came
he gave the explanation that the young man who had refused to have his

Figure 4. Spotted Tail, in a portrait made in Washington, D.C., 1872. (National Anthropological Archives, Smithsonian Institution)

hair cut afterwards relented and did the job himself with a knife. He then said his people always wailed after cutting their hair, as it was an evidence of mourning, and he had come out on the parade ground to show his grief" (1964, 232). Luther Standing Bear remembers the emotional confusion that followed having his braids cut off, a sense that he had misunderstood what was expected of him in coming to the white man's school: "After having had my hair cut, a new thought came into my head. I felt that I was no more Indian, but would be an imitation of a white man" (Standing Bear 1928, 141).

New names were another part of the intended transformation. These were allocated by writing a list of Christian names on the blackboard and copying them onto pieces of tape. The boys were called up one by one and asked to point to the name they wanted, before even being taught the rudiments of the alphabet. The name they pointed to was taped, then sewn, onto the back of the boys' shirts. Luther Standing Bear recalls, "When my turn came, I took the pointer and acted as if I were about to touch an enemy" (ibid., 137). Even among students who were later to accommodate themselves to the school routines, the assignment of names was understood as an act of hostility. For those just arriving at Carlisle, new names and outward appearance added to the already bewildering experience of displacement (see figure 5).

Not every aspect of their new lives was as painful as some of the early experiences. The new school uniforms, when they arrived, were a source of pride and excitement, with deep pockets, shiny buttons, and boots that squeaked on the floors. The start of a music program was another break from the routine. Standing Bear was among a group of boys who were given music lessons and who were both thrilled and consternated by the instruments distributed to them. He says, "Although we tried our best, we could not produce a sound from them. [The music teacher] then tried to talk to us, but we did not understand her. Then she showed us how to wet the end of the mouthpiece. We thought she wanted us to spit into the horns, so we did. She finally got so discouraged with us that she started crying" (ibid., 148).

Even with the occasional appreciation of new experiences, however, life at the school was oppressive for most students. Food rations were meager, even by the standards of children who had lived in the deprived conditions of the new reservations. The dormitories were cold, and before their new beds arrived the children of the entering class slept on a cement floor. Loneliness was a debilitating aspect of their lives at school. Some children simply did not adjust to their new surroundings. The death rate among the students at Carlisle was to become a stumbling block to future recruitment efforts, as notorious as the failure of the school and local Indian agents to properly inform parents of their children's condition when they were ill.

Some of these conditions were already apparent when thirty-one Sioux chiefs, on a trip to Washington in 1880, took time during their journey to visit the school at Carlisle. After a lengthy tour, Spotted Tail asked to have the Sioux children assembled with the visiting chiefs to talk about the school. The chiefs then discussed the situation among themselves, and Spotted Tail was their principal spokesman. Pratt reports in his memoirs their view of the school: "[Spotted Tail] found fault with the school because we were using soldier uniforms for the boys. He said he did not like to have their boys drilled, because they did not want them to become soldiers. He also found fault with the sleeping accommodations and the food" (Pratt 1964, 237). Pratt explained to the visitors that he was constrained by limited funding and had to buy the best-wearing clothes for the money, which just happened to be army uniforms. As for the drilling, he saw this as being beneficial for the boys' health.

Figure 5. Pueblo youth as they arrived at the Carlisle School, 31 July 1880.
(National Archives and Records Administration, Washington, D.C.)

Something in Pratt's reasoning must have sounded hollow. Spotted
Tail removed his children from the school, paying for their travel himself. He attempted, without success, to have all the Sioux children
removed and returned home. We can only imagine the impact on Spotted Tail, who was among those who led the bloody struggle against the
American invaders to secure his community's claims to land, of seeing
his children dressed in the uniforms of his erstwhile enemy, parading for
the sake of their "health." The argument that the school had to econo-
mize must have sounded strange to him since the children were already
wearing durable clothes when they arrived, and could if necessary have
been sent more from home. And what greater benefit to health could
there have been, if activity outside the classroom was needed, than the
games the children already knew? But Pratt, for his part, could not understand why Spotted Tail was being so unreasonable, and interpreted the
behavior of a man sick at heart as the moodiness of one who was alone
in the exercise of authority.

Despite Spotted Tail's objections, there was still wide support among
administrators for the idea of residential education away from reservations. A letter dated 12 February 1880, to Captain Pratt from John Miles,
an Indian agent among the Cheyenne, concurred with Pratt's advocacy

of removing children from camps to attend boarding schools away from home. Remaining with their families, Miles wrote, the children "will still be the same dirty, ignorant, camp Indians" (ibid., 242), while keeping the children in industrial schools or "training schools" (like Carlisle) would secure important benefits, not the least of which was the greater compliance and peacefulness of those whose children were being lodged in government residential schools: "The child being in school the parents are much easier managed; are loyal to the Government, to the Agent, and take an interest in the affairs of the Agency, and never dare, or desire, to commit a serious wrong. I am yet to know of the first individual Indian on this reservation who has joined in a raid, that has had his child in school" (ibid.). Sedentarization also seemed to follow, for similar reasons. Having their children in school "induces [in an Indian parent] a desire to locate in the vicinity of the agency, and his habits are consequently localized" (ibid., 243).

Those who expected noticeable results from these education efforts were not to be disappointed. Captain Pratt sent photographs of the students at Carlisle (as in figure 6) to government officials, including Secretary of the Interior Carl Schurtz and even President Rutherford Hayes, to advertise the success of the Carlisle school in efforts to secure increased funding. A letter to Representative T. C. Pound illustrates one of Pratt's proudest accomplishments, held out as a promise in the development of Indian education elsewhere in the country: "I send you today a few photographs of the Indian youth here. You will note that they came mostly as blanket Indians. . . . Isolated as these Indian youth are from the savage surroundings at their homes, they lose their tenacity to savage life, which is so much of an obstacle to Agency efforts" (ibid., 248).

Boarding schools were, by the 1880s, commonly seen as the answer to the civilizing initiative begun a decade earlier; and it was usually clearly understood that parents would not be willing to give up their children to school superintendents, that schools must impose such a form of education by force, if necessary. This, at any rate, was recognized by W. M. McKewen, Clerk in Charge of the Ouray Agency of Utah Territory, who observed in 1886 that the solution to the "Indian problem" lay in education and that his district urgently required boarding school facilities. This "solution" was not a response to a request by the Indians of the agency. McKewen recognized that the initiative necessary for the Indians' redemption would inevitably be met with resistance: "That the Indians will decline to allow their children to attend school, and will bitterly

Figure 6. A group of Omaha boys attending the Carlisle School, circa 1880.
(National Archives and Records Administration, Washington, D.C.)

oppose such a scheme in every shape, way, and form is certain; but their wishes in this respect should not be consulted. The power should be here to force them to give up their barbarous practices, superstitions, and narrow prejudices, and walk in the paths laid out for them" (Government of the United States 1886, 447). Mandatory education, with boarding schools as the vehicle of assimilation, was called for as a way to resolve the "Indian problem," the problem faced by expansion of the state into territories occupied and used by people with no conception of "improvement" of the land.

Not every Indian agent saw a need for schools that would isolate children from their families and communities as a means to maximize the civilizing effect of education. W. W. Anderson, reporting from the Crow Creek and Lower Brulé Consolidated Agency in 1886, expressed a strong preference for the "wholesome and refining influence" of reservation day schools, mainly because "the children . . . do not outgrow their surroundings and become ashamed of their parents . . . but rather keep their parents abreast with themselves" (ibid., 285). This kind of opinion, however, was not enough to prevent off-reservation boarding schools from becoming the foundation of a nationwide effort to "Americanize" the American Indian.

The realization of the goal of full Americanization involved building upon the example set by the school at Carlisle. A rapid expansion in Indian education occurred simultaneously with a shift in strategy. In 1842 the federal government had sponsored 37 Indian schools, most of them day schools on reservations run by missionaries; by 1885, 106 were in operation, with many schools occupying abandoned military installations far from reservation communities. In 1889 General Thomas J. Morgan, as Commissioner of Indian Affairs, spearheaded a Republican effort to stop government funding of all missionary schools and to establish a government-controlled plan for Indian education, a plan that called for compulsory school attendance and a standardized curriculum. As part of this new design, Congress passed laws permitting Morgan to enforce the school attendance of Indian children by withholding rations and annuities from Indian families whose children were "truants" (Reyhner 1990, 47).

But while forced education increased, it did not provide the kind of skills that Spotted Tail was promised when he placed his children in the care of Captain Pratt. Indian education for nearly a half century was strongly geared toward compelling children to forget, toward teaching students that their ancestors were barbarians and that they must forever let go of their language, style of dress, ceremonial practices, and spiritual attachments. At the same time, the vast majority of Indian students were taught only the rudiments of the English language, literacy, and mathematics. More emphasis was placed on "the education of the heart," on learning Christian rituals and values, usually accompanied by a vocational trade intended to instill an appreciation of hard work, earning, and saving for the future.

By the late 1920s it came to be recognized that the national experiment of educational "containment" was seriously flawed. The 1928 Meriam Report, commissioned by the U.S. Senate to provide information on the state of Native America, condemned this system of education, with its strong emphasis on forced removal of children to boarding schools. It found that Indians were not being improved by education in terms of economic autonomy or health and that the forcible removal of children from their homes was an inappropriate foundation for their educational development.

In the 1930s the findings of the Meriam Report were acted upon. John Collier, Commissioner of Indian Affairs, led a sweeping effort to abandon an entrenched legacy of assimilation, "civilization," and "Americanization." The bureaucratic reorganization of tribes in an effort to provide a form of structured sovereignty, though not endorsed by every recognized tribe, did eventually reduce the incidence of vigorous recruit-ment for off-reservation schools, at least in those facilities directly con-trolled by the Bureau of Indian Affairs (BIA). At the same time, Chris-tianization efforts in federal schools were largely discontinued. There still remained, and continue to remain, religious schools with aggressive and questionable campaigns to bring Native American students into the classroom (Green 1989, 13), but the goals of federal education were no longer infused with Christian evangelism.

At the time of the 1928 Meriam Report, 27 percent of Indian children in the United States were enrolled in reservation and off-reservation boarding schools; 14 percent were in federal day schools and mission schools; 45 percent were in public schools; and the remaining 14 per-cent were not in any school. The report concentrated its criticism on the boarding school system. It was for the sake of those children in board-ing schools who did not have contact with their families, even in sum-mer, and who were similarly isolated from the cultures of their home communities, that education reformers challenged the policies of the BIA (Szasz 1977, 18). The reason for this focus of criticism was not so much the boarding schools' assimilationist approach to education as the fact that their budgets were maintained at a level that kept conditions of health and nutrition below minimum standards. The government's penury meant that Indian children "subsisted on a diet that was the equivalent of slow starvation[, a problem] . . . compounded by lack of medical care, dangerous overcrowding, and the excessive labor required of the children because of the lack of funds" (ibid., 19). Nevertheless W. Carson Ryan, after being appointed Director of Education for the Indian Bureau in 1930, did not press for closure of the boarding schools, arguing that this would result in children from remote areas not receiv-ing any education at all. Instead his approach to reform focused on the boarding school curriculum.

The removal of most Christian missionary curriculums from Indian education did eliminate the most overt efforts to assimilate Indian chil-dren through education, but this did little to improve the school experi-ence for many native children. After World War II, assimilationist voices again prevailed in Congress, this time pressing for Indian "freedom" through termination of tribal status. Education policy was drawn into this wider rejection of Indian sovereignty. A 1944 report of the House Select Committee to Investigate Indian Affairs and Conditions, for exam-ple, recommended a return to greater use of off-reservation boarding schools. It deplored the movement toward community day schools that had taken place in earlier decades, suggesting that children attending these schools were disadvantaged by "having to spend their out of school hours in tepees, in shacks with dirt floors and no windows, in tents, in wickiups, in hogans where English is never spoken . . . and where there is sometimes an active antagonism or an abysmal indifference to the virtues of education" (cited in Szasz 1977, 109). A study conducted at the Pine Ridge Sioux reservation in the early 1960s found that unequal power relations discouraged parents of Indian children from participating in school activities, and that while the curriculum, did not overtly stress assimilation and discarding of native culture, it still stressed "sharing in the material benefits associated with the culture of the teacher" (Wax et al. 1989, 6). The elders of the Pine Ridge community had distanced themselves from their customary place as educators of local knowledge: "the Sioux elders, faced with the power of the educational establishment, simply withdrew" (ibid., 129).

The Civil Rights movement of the 1960s swung the pendulum of federal Indian policy back toward limited acceptance of tribal autonomy. The Kennedy Report of 1969 (chaired by Senator Robert Kennedy), a national survey of Indian education in the United States, described the education of Indian children by the BIA and public schools as a "national tragedy" and found fault with virtually every aspect of the Native American educational experience, including teaching practices, curriculums, funding, Indian control of Indian education, limited sponsorship of bilingual education, and the continued use of boarding schools. In response to such criticism, from 1972 to 1975, Congress signed into law three major bills influencing Indian education: the Indian Education Act of 1972, a law creating the American Indian Policy Review Commission in 1975, and the Indian Self-Determination and Education Assistance Act of 1975. These bills were, Margaret Szasz writes, "milestones for the Indian people. They meant that the web of government control had been loosened. Henceforth, direction and leadership in Indian education should come increasingly from Indians themselves" (1977, 201).

Whether or not this new approach has uniformly taken hold, the political climate generated by the Civil Rights movement of the 1960s favored a reversal of termination policy and a new degree of Native American participation in education. A trend became established in which public schools or BIA schools were "contracted out" to tribal governments. In 1966, the Navaho's Rough Rock School, the first locally administered school in a Native American community, was established; eventually, more tribally controlled institutions followed, such as the Navaho's Rock Point School (Reyhner 1990, 67–69) and the Mesa Valley School (McLaughlin 1992). As other tribes take up the challenge of local organization and leadership, and as more schools open with locally developed curriculums, the legacy of schools attempting to teach children to forget will be an even more dimly remembered thing of the past.

RESIDENTIAL EDUCATION IN CANADA

In Canada this legacy is still a vivid nightmare. At the time of the founding of the Carlisle school, the American model of boarding schools was taken up with alacrity by the Canadian government as a way of integrating Indians into mainstream society. The main point of departure from the American system was that Canada had much more confidence in missionaries as educators of the Indians. In 1879, word of the American "experiments" in Indian education had already traveled widely, prompting the Canadian government to commission a report evaluating their effectiveness and potential applicability to Canada's Indians. Nicholas Flood Davin, sent to investigate the boarding school system in the United States, was convinced it would be necessary, in civilizing the native population, "to take away their simple Indian mythology" (cited in Titley 1986, 77), and he built this goal into his proposals to the Canadian government. The outcome of his inquiry, the Davin Report, approved of the American model, with the cost-saving proviso that missionaries be given the task of directly operating Indian schools. The Department of Indian Affairs accepted these recommendations and provided funds for missions to upgrade existing schools and construct new ones. Thus began a period of Canadian policy sometimes referred to as "the Bible and the plough," in which education featured prominently in a wide-ranging government initiative aimed at controlling and reshaping aboriginal political behavior, coercing native hunters to become sedentary farmers, and eliminating what were seen as unsavory and unhygienic ceremonies, such as the Potlatch of the Pacific Coast and the Sun Dance of the Plains Indians (Miller 1996, 186). Preference was given to large, industrial, vocationally oriented boarding schools located away from reservations and, several years later, to boarding schools for younger children located closer to reservation communities (Barman et al. 1986, 6). As a supplement to the new system of residential schools, the government funded a network of day schools (as in figure 7). Those

Figure 7. A mission day-school at Fort Resolution, Northwest Territories, circa 1910. (Hudson's Bay Company Archives, Provincial Archives of Manitoba)

who lived in urban settings or in areas remote from residential schools could by this means still be included in the civilizing effort.

Aggressive recruiting was undertaken by missionaries to persuade parents to send their children to school. In some cases children were detained against their will and the wishes of their parents. Some efforts to hold children in schools were met with resistance. The 1884 *Annual Report of the Department of Indian Affairs,* for example, mentions an uprising at the school in Kyutka on the west coast of Vancouver Island, in which the superintendent "was held by some of the Indians until others of the band, sixty of whom had forcibly entered the house for the purpose, had released two Indian boys who had been detained by the teacher in school over the usual hour as a punishment for irregular attendance" (Government of Canada 1884, lviii). Yet, by 1900 this joint federal-missionary initiative had already borne fruit, with 3,285 students enrolled in 61 industrial and boarding schools and 6,349 students in 226 day schools, out of a total population of approximately 20,000 native children aged six to fifteen (Barman et al. 1986, 7).

At a time when the Bureau of Indian Affairs in America was beginning to reconsider its education policy, Canada was stepping up its efforts to educate and assimilate its Indian population. In 1920, an amended Indian Act dispensed with any pretense of voluntary enrollment and made it mandatory for Indians to attend school. Further amendments to the Indian Act were made in 1930 to enforce school attendance. Legal penalties, including denial of food rations, were levied if parents refused to send their children to school, and truant officers were assigned the task of ensuring compliance. Many parents, despite the most determined efforts of the federal government, were successful in keeping their children out of school. But by the 1940s, approximately 8,000 Indian children were enrolled in 76 residential schools across Canada (York 1989, 24).

A challenge that many educators set themselves was to transform their "savage" pupils as much as possible into productive, civilized citizens who could function in the social and occupational margins—but without encouraging them to acquire the literate skills that might eventually make some of them difficult to manage. In many of the on-reservation day schools this was not an issue. Students were often given only a rudimentary education or, as one student from a day school in the 1890s recalls, no formal education at all: "I do not remember any book learning acquired there. A bell was rung each morning to announce that school was opened. . . . To insure his attendance the next day, each child was given a biscuit of hardtack before leaving" (cited in Barman et al. 1986, 7). Few schools, however, were so narrow in their goal to Christianize that they did not teach some reading, writing, and English. In some cases, Indian students excelled and wanted to pursue their studies further. The best efforts of missionaries, moreover, were not successful in obliterating all vestiges of attachment to ancestors, land, and a reflected native way of life. The combination of these influences could result in the sort of person that educators most abhorred: the educated, "retrograde" Indian.

The two means used to prevent this outcome were restricted education and thorough exposure to Christian teachings and practices. The experience of one student attending the Kamloops Indian Residential School in Kamloops, British Columbia, in the 1930s was typical of those subjected to the Christian exhortations that accompanied Indian education: "We spent over a hour in the chapel every morning, every blessed morning. And there they interrogated us on what it was all about being an Indian. . . . [The minister] would just get so carried away; he was punching away on that old altar rail . . . to hammer it into our heads that we were not to think or act or speak like an Indian. And that we would go to hell and burn for eternity if we did not listen to their way of teaching" (Haig-Brown 1988, 59). An elder I spoke with in Chisasibi, Québec, remembered a similar emphasis at the St. Phillip's Indian and Eskimo Anglican Residential School on forgetting the iniquities of the past and becoming an obedient Christian: "Growing up in school, you learn to behave yourself and leave your tradition behind. That's the way I was taught to become a Christian." With missionaries given control of Indian education in Canada, "becoming a Christian" without opportunity for question or discussion was an experience shared by thousands of native students across the country (see figures 8 and 9).

At the same time, the academic accomplishments of native students were kept at a very basic level. Students in Indian schools progressed slowly, with academic subjects usually given a fraction of the time devoted to vocational skills and religion. Interest in students' progress normally ended once they reached the age of fifteen or sixteen, an age at which they would be fortunate to have completed grade seven. Even if a school superintendent wished his or her students to continue on to high school, they were usually discouraged. Basil Johnston remembers a situation in the 1940s in which Father Oliver, a Jesuit priest in charge of St. Peter Claver's Indian Residential School in Ontario, encountered resistance from the Department of Indian Affairs against his effort to develop a high school program for his most promising students. Not only were there problems of funding and a lack of precedent for such a program, there was government resistance to Father Oliver's initiative, summarized by Johnston as follows: "What possible benefit would Latin, algebra and chemistry be to the boys if they did not have a corresponding familiarity with the basic etiquette and social graces of the civilized world?" (1988, 169). The high school program was eventually funded, but only through the persistent effort of a relatively farsighted priest. Far more commonly, education in mission-operated schools was associated with minimal academic aspirations.

Change in Canada's residential school program did not occur until the decades after World War II, when the federal government stepped up its direct involvement in all aspects of Indian affairs. In the 1950s and 1960s a new policy was implemented that required native children to attend provincial schools. By the 1970s nearly all mission-operated residential schools were closed or transferred to state control. This decline of church control of education was not entirely inspired by the goal of

Figure 8. A classroom at St. Joseph's Residential School, Cross Lake, Manitoba, circa 1955. (Archdiocese of Keewatin-LePas)

Figure 9. St. Joseph's Residential School, Cross Lake, Manitoba, circa 1955. (Archdiocese of Keewatin-LePas)

curtailing assimilative efforts in schools; in fact, it gave assimilation a new direction, a shift toward secular inclusion in the state system. As Geoffrey York points out in an overview of social conditions in native Canada, "Although the provincial schools were better funded than the federal schools, the threat of assimilation was much stronger there, where Indian students were overwhelmed by white teachers and white students and native culture was ignored or denigrated" (1989, 25). Randy Fred, for example, remembers what it was like being bussed to a provincial school when he had finished his schooling at the Alberni Indian Residential School near Port Alberni, British Columbia: "Immediately we were labeled as Indians, but we had a second label because we were being bussed in from the residential school: a lower class of Indian. The shock was too much for me; my grades dropped, my sense of self-worth disappeared, learning became a chore" (1988, 20). While native students no longer have to deal with discipline and conformity within a religion-oriented school setting, many now face the challenge, in some ways more overwhelming, of adjusting to the racism and the foreign way of life of their peers.

THE HIDDEN CATASTROPHE

Absolute, unchecked institutional control over the powerless is a recipe for social disaster. Native children in the United States and Canada who were sent far from their homes to residential schools in which nearly every detail of their lives was regimented and supervised, in which their adult superiors held everything but the power of life and death in their hands, were in serious danger of severe physical and emotional abuse. Added to the almost unrestricted power of supervisors were the ideological underpinnings to Indian education, which categorized students in these schools as something less than civilized, as fundamentally flawed beings in need of correction. There was only a small step from this to the idea that the "Indian" needed to be punished, that domination of the body would lead to a transformation of the spirit. We have already seen this in the shaping of outward appearance that was a common initiatory experience in residential schools.

Memories of abuse and loneliness are by no means universal among former students of residential schools. A woman from Cross Lake, Manitoba, for example, recently spoke favorably about her experience in St. Joseph's Residential School: "I never used to get spanked by the sisters.

We were treated well. That's why I learned a lot from the sisters, especially my religion. . . . Now I'm sticking to my own faith. I'm a Roman Catholic, and that's what I'm hanging on to."[5]

In the institutional vacuum that gave almost unlimited power to school authorities, however, the implementation of punishment and control in many schools crossed the line into the pathological. As the 1996 *Report of the Royal Commission on Aboriginal Peoples* points out, "In the vision of residential education, discipline was curriculum and punishment an essential pedagogical technique" (Government of Canada 1996, 366). It often happened, as one elder in Chisasibi, Québec, understood it, that anger and violence came together in the behavior of school officials: "Today I still have that mark . . . from the white man's anger. When somebody has anger in his heart, it has no room for anything else."

The Alberni Indian Residential School was one of many institutions of its kind that seem to have fostered sadism. In the 1920s Randy Fred's father was punished for speaking Tseshalt by having sewing needles pushed through his tongue. From then on, he rejected his native language and refused to teach it to his children. Fred remembers from his own childhood that the selection of school employees made this kind of treatment almost inevitable: "Most of the boys' supervisors were sadists, consisting mainly of men kicked out of the RCMP [Royal Canadian Mounted Police] or retired from the armed forces. . . . One supervisor used to stand us in line for hours at a time and amuse himself with sadistic acts" (1988, 21). The risk of excessive punishment, torture, or sexual abuse for Indian students in residential schools almost anywhere was extremely high and had devastating and lasting consequences for the victims. A former pupil of the residential school in Gordon Reserve, Saskatchewan, remembers the suffering endured at the hands of supervisors, older students, and teachers: "[The] guy that sexually abused me, I remember leaving his room at three and four o'clock in the morning, just hitting my head on the pillow, just falling asleep and all of a sudden they are there with the lights on. Get up. Time to clean up. Wash up. Go do your chores. Then set off for school. But I never went to school to go learn anything. I wanted to, but I was so tired . . . that I fell asleep in [the] classroom. . . . Then when we got to the school, we were abused

5. Statement recorded by Multi-Channel Television (Cross Lake's television broadcasting station) at a meeting honoring survivors of the 1930 residential-school fire at Cross Lake, 15 May 1998.

there again by the teachers who didn't understand that we were up half the night being sexually abused."[6]

The frequency with which serious incidents of abuse occurred in church-run schools is impossible to estimate with any accuracy because of the trauma associated with disclosure. Victims are often unable to revive painful memories of the suffering they endured as children. Geoffrey York's harrowing survey of social conditions among Canada's First Nations peoples, *The Dispossessed,* includes a finding that as many as 80 percent of Indian children in Canada's mission-operated residential schools were sexually abused. Although this figure may seem high and be impossible to substantiate, the mere fact that social service professionals could arrive at such an estimate does shed light on the magnitude of the problem.

How could men of the cloth, who presumably devoted their lives to religious observance and ethical self-examination, be guilty of committing such atrocities? How could the goal of teaching Indian children the basic principles of Christianity and civilization become so commonly misdirected under the authority of missions? These are questions that many victims themselves have difficulty answering. A former student of St. Phillip's school in Fort George, Québec, was confused by the experience of abusive punishment by a clergyman: "I must have sinned, really was a sinner, I guess, to be strapped by this minister. . . . A minister cannot make a mistake. He's a man of God." The *Report of the Royal Commission* points out that school officials, teachers, and employees were often underpaid, undervalued, and unprepared for their positions of authority over native children, resulting in an "atmosphere of considerable stress, fatigue and anxiety that may well have dulled the staff's sensitivity to the children's hunger, their ill-kempt look or their ill-health and often, perhaps inevitably, pushed the application of discipline over the line and transformed what was to be a circle of care into a violent embrace" (Government of Canada 1996, 367).

For many students in residential schools this "violent embrace" was made all the more painful by separation from the comfort and commiseration of family. The powerful loneliness felt by those suffering abuse in isolation was expressed by a former student of the residential school in Gordon, Saskatchewan: "I lived about a hundred yards across the lake from the school. And I would stand at the window and would be cry-

---

6. Statement presented in a public meeting, Cross Lake, Manitoba, 8 October 1998, recorded and transcribed by the author.

ing, thinking Mum and Dad didn't love me. Angry with them. Blaming them because I was in the school. I could see my home across the lake, not even a hundred yards. Used to hate my Mum and Dad. How come they don't love me no more? How come they don't want me home? Many times I seen my sisters standing at the window, crying to go home. You were hit. You were slapped and shoved. I wanted to go home."[7]

One of the lessons of the Indian residential school experience is that religious personnel are not immune from the dangerous combination of institutionalized racism and power over a marginalized population. The particular combination of ideas about Indians and control over their children (the very young almost everywhere being the epitome of power-lessness) was the common denominator in a very wide distribution of institutional abuses that were not prevented by Christian commitments or positions of responsibility.

It is instructive to consider the Holocaust as a more intensely lethal version of a similar phenomenon. For centuries, anti-Semitism in Europe was associated with an almost visceral hatred of those seen to embody the antithesis of Christian norms. "The conception of Jews in medieval Christendom," writes Daniel Goldhagen, "with its uncompromising, non-pluralistic and intolerant view of the moral basis of society, was one which held the Jews to violate the moral order of the world" (1996, 37). Similarly, Indians were perceived by many devout Christians in North America to violate the moral order through satanic practices, the drumming, singing, dancing, and visionary experiences common to their spiritual observance. In the attitudes of dominant societies toward both European Jews and Native Americans, there were religious and racial justifications for state policies oriented toward solving the "problem" posed by the mere existence of a population defined as moral violators. The central difference was that Indians were perceived to be morally redeemable. Their state of savagery was the result of the sins of ancestors being visited upon their sons. Genocidal killing in North America was not the only, nor the most commonly preferred, option in resolving what was seen as the moral corruption or backwardness of the Indian. It was discovered that Indians could be transformed, perhaps not entirely but at least in essence, into docile, obedient, "civilized" beings through a school experience that taught them the iniquity of their ancestors and the true path to righteousness.

7. See note 6.

Or at least so it seemed. There were always "success stories" that could be produced by educators to justify perseverance in pursuit of a situation in which, as Captain Pratt stated, "all tribal relations are broken up . . . [and] the Indian loses all his Indian ways" (1964, 266); but this sweeping goal of social and cultural elimination could not always be realized, even through a bewildering and often effective combination of brutal discipline and patient instruction. There were persistent problems in every residential school, problems with disobedience, attempts at escape, petty crimes, even arson, committed by students who failed to adjust, whose entire educational experience was based upon defiance, resistance, and stoicism in the face of punishment.

But the most serious failure of the residential system of education for Indians occurred beyond the school ground. Success was almost always measured while children were still in the hands of their supervisors, where their appearance and behavior were strictly controlled. Much less attention was paid to what happened when they returned to their families. Even here the most common examples presented were of those who had learned a trade and built successful lives in the white man's world, or who could be held up as model citizens on the reservation, like one individual praised by Pratt as "an efficient helper in the agency and in the business affairs of his tribe[,] . . . a sturdy, highly respected, and useful man among his people" (ibid., 244). This was a fatal oversimplification of the social consequences of the educators' work. While there may have been dismay at those who "returned to the blanket"—the "retrograde" Indians on whom the efforts of their teachers were presumably wasted—Indian educators seem to have been almost completely unaware of the serious problems encountered by those attempting to find a place in family and community after several years at school.

The native communities of Canada's North illustrate the social impacts of state- and mission-sponsored programs of assimilation most clearly because of the relatively late arrival of all aspects of colonial and state domination. Harsh winters and the nuisance of biting insects during the short summers made the North unattractive to settlers. The fur trade was ushered in with a 1670 British Royal Charter to the Hudson's Bay Company for a vast portion of the North American subarctic, but even though settlement around trading posts changed Cree patterns of movement, the overall impact of the fur trade on native uses and spiritual attachments to the land was minimal—certainly in comparison with the social devastation in the plains region of the United States in the nineteenth century. Christian evangelism began in earnest in northern Canada only in the mid-nineteenth century. In Fort George, Québec, the St. Phillip's Indian and Eskimo Anglican Residential School operated into the late 1970s, when it was demolished during relocation of the community to the mainland following hydroelectric construction (Niezen 1998). In this community, as in more than a dozen others that I visited in Québec, Ontario, and Manitoba, many of those in the middle generation experienced residential education, and living elders experienced painful transitions in their own lives by having their children taken from them to be raised by mission educators.

The most immediate indication that the first generation of those who had been to school was different from others in their communities was in their use and knowledge of language. As one Cree elder remembers from his childhood in Fort George, Québec, the first impression he had upon returning home from residential school was that his parents were ignorant: "When I came out [after] all those years in school . . . I thought I was a different person. I thought my parents didn't know any English. That is what my impression was. This is what the school did to me." For another young man returning to his Shuswap community after attending the Kamloops Indian Residential School, the problem was one of inhibition more than loss of knowledge: "When I first came out of school, I was embarrassed to speak my language in front of white people. . . . It took about three or four years . . . to get away from that embarrassment of speaking it on the street. . . . They just about brainwashed us out of it" (Haig-Brown 1988, 120). And, as Randy Fred of Port Alberni remembers, the punishment endured by his father in residential school for speaking Tseshalt made him unwilling to pass his language on to his children: "My Dad's attitude became 'Why teach my children Indian if they are going to be punished for speaking it?' so he would not allow my mother to speak Indian to us in his presence. I never learned how to speak my own language" (1988, 16). Use and knowledge of native languages often declined among successive generations of those who experienced compulsory residential education.

Children who attended school outside their community also often failed to learn the subsistence skills they normally would have acquired over years of participation in the domestic economy.[8] A Nishnawbe elder in Wunnumin Lake, Ontario, indicated to me the cause of a wide gulf between himself and his children: "When the school came in I had to

8. Such an observation was made as early as 1744 in the English colony of Virginia during the course of a treaty negotiation, when a group of northern Indians declined the

bring up my children here [in the village]. That's when I started to notice
that there was a big difference for the kids. . . . There are some who come
back from down south. When they come home, they don't know how
to use their language. And when the parents ask their daughter or son
to do something, they don't know how to do it . . . because they were
never taught. . . . There are no people who are teaching them about hunting, or any of those traditional things."

While parents may express dismay at the lack of knowledge and experience among those who return from school, for the students themselves
the experience of reintegrating with the community while lacking the
skills necessary for full membership could be devastating. A knowledge
base that is out of alignment with the needs and expectations of the older
generation has had consequences that go further than the individuals'
productive contribution. With language and economic pursuits usually
integral to the community's spirituality, those who attended residential
school were often unable to connect with elders on another level: they
lacked the qualifications for spiritual participation in the community.
Spiritual alienation could take a number of forms, including dissonance
between those whose school-acquired Christianity could not be made
consistent with the visionary practices of others in the community and,
in an opposite scenario, a lack of support for youth who reacted against
their institutional experience, who wanted to rediscover their traditions
in communities that had been almost uniformly Christianized.

Recognition of such problems of reintegration makes it possible to
understand how those who had suffered abuse during their school experience would be led to even deeper anguish upon return home. Mental
illness, often resulting in self-destructive behavior such as alcoholism and

---

offer of the Virginia government to educate their children. An account of the Indian position was made by none other than Benjamin Franklin:

> You who are wise must know that different Nations have different conceptions of
> things, and you will, therefore, not take it amiss if our ideas of this kind of educa-
> tion happen not to be the same with yours.
>   We have had some experience of it. Several of our young people were formerly
> brought up at the College of Northern Provinces. They were instructed in all your
> sciences. But when they came back to us, they were bad runners, ignorant of every
> means of living in the woods and unable to bear either Cold or Hunger, knew nei-
> ther how to build a cabin, take a Deer, kill an Enemy, spoke our language imper-
> fectly. Neither fit for Hunters nor Councillors, they were totally good for nothing.
> We are, however, not the less obliged by your kind offer, tho' we decline accepting
> it: and to show our grateful sense of it, the Gentlemen of Virginia will send us a
> dozen of their Sons, and we will take great Care of their Education, instruct them
> in all we know, and make Men of them. (cited in Green 1989, 11)

suicide, is so common among those who attended Indian residential schools that a new term, "residential school syndrome," has been coined by social service professionals to describe the pattern they often see in native communities. Although there are numerous causes of "social pathology" in native communities, including dramatic social change following large-scale resource extraction, the residential school experience is a common theme that emerges from many investigations of native villages in decline. By the mid-1980s it was widely recognized that the residential school experience throughout much of Canada was directly responsible for the devastation of native communities, and a finding of the 1996 *Report of the Royal Commission on Aboriginal People*s was blunt in its appraisal of the consequences of the residential education system: "In their direct attack on language, beliefs and spirituality, the schools had been a particularly virulent strain of that epidemic of empire, sapping the children's bodies and beings" (Government of Canada 1996, 376–77).

In 1995 the Nishnawbe-Aski Nation, a federation of forty-eight First Nation communities in northern Ontario, conducted public and private hearings on the causes, consequences, and possible solutions to the suicide epidemics that had devastated several villages during the previous decade. One of the themes commonly mentioned in these hearings was the residential school experience. Testimony from several respondents made explicit the connection between abuse in school and the deep personal crises that followed:

> Boarding school in those days, in the forties and early fifties, held very sad memories. I had lots of physical abuse in there. There I missed my family, my grandmothers and my parents. . . . I cried and cried in school, and when I cried in school I used to get straps. When I talked my Native language I was strapped. . . . Even before I was thirteen I used to want to be dead. A lot of times I used to think about that. I never actually formulated a plan, but I knew I just wanted to be dead because maybe it's better, maybe I wouldn't be lonely anymore, or shy of my colour. I would be okay with the way I looked and the way I acted. (Nishnawbe-Aski Nation 1996, 120)

Another contributor also remembered the teenage years following residential school as the most traumatic: "All of those times, I was at residential school and I held a lot of the anger, pain and hurt. It was too much to handle at times when I was a teenager. . . . I was confused. I didn't know how to cope with or handle those memories" (ibid., 162). For this individual, as for many others, sexual abuse in school and in the community were the cause of powerful emotions that led to suicidal impulses: "I went in the shack and picked out a shotgun and sawed it off. Then I wrote a suicide note. I went down to the bank and stood on the rock and I stuck the shotgun in my mouth and I held it there for about an hour deciding whether to pull the trigger. I was playing with the trigger, hoping it would go off. Somehow, deep inside I didn't want to do it" (ibid.).

The "Nishnawbe-Aski Youth Forum on Suicide" also reveals the disturbing fact that such profound emotional disturbance does not end with those who are the immediate victims of abuse but is, as one contributor put it, "a negative seed passed on from generation to generation" (ibid., 34). Children learn parenting skills from their parents. The institutional setting of residential schools, however, disrupted this learning process, accustoming students to an atmosphere of unquestioning obedience and emotional distance. One response to this experience among former students was to later imitate the emphasis on obedience with their own children or even to repeat patterns of violence and abuse in their homes. "I found I was always yelling at my kids," a social worker in Port Alberni, British Columbia, once told me, attributing this behavior to years of being ordered and disciplined in the Alberni Indian Residential School.

Reacting in an opposite direction against the harshness of their school experience, many former students of residential schools set very few limits upon their children's behavior. Such a family background is widely recognized as contributing to high rates of drug and alcohol abuse and unwanted pregnancy among teenagers, a pattern that prompted one elder from Port Alberni to say to me, "Children are not like grass. You can't just plant the seeds and watch them grow."

There are two features of the residential school legacy that provide some measure of hope. Like almost any centralized form of institutional control, residential schools fostered resistance as much as, or more than, compliance. The policies of educational assimilation in the United States and Canada were not at all successful in "killing the Indian" or breaking asunder all tribal relations. Those few students who eventually made it to high school often had the inspirational experience of turning their reading and writing skills toward meaningful subjects that informed their own native heritage. Billy Diamond, later to become the first Grand Chief of the Grand Council of the Crees, is reported in a biography by Roy MacGregor to have found just such a use for his English-language education: "Thanks in large part to the stories his Uncle Philip and Mark Blackned has [sic] passed around the campfire that summer, Billy began researching Indian legends. From the legends he moved quickly into the history, and the history soon brought him up to date with the Indian situation in Canada" (MacGregor 1989, 28–29). The false promise that Captain Pratt had once dangled before Spotted Tail in order to fill the enrollment list of the new Carlisle school was eventually, perhaps unintentionally, fulfilled.

Such experiences of discovery equipped a new native leadership with the knowledge and skills necessary for effective political advocacy. Agreements negotiated between native governments and the state in the 1970s, such as the James Bay and Northern Quebec Agreement and the Alaska Native Claims Settlement Act, are nothing like the treaties imposed on native peoples during the frontier expansions of the seventeenth to early twentieth centuries. The modern agreements may still be premised upon the inevitability of land transfer to the state and abridgment of native control over natural resources, but they are informed by a greater awareness on the part of native negotiators of the legal and political resources at their disposal. The result of these agreements in Alaska and Québec has been both greater financial cost to the state and a greater measure of regional political autonomy for native peoples.

One of the most significant consequences of higher education among native North Americans is reform of education systems themselves. Having made it through the residential school experience and, against all odds, found their way through high school and college, some native leaders have turned their attention to the educational system that had such an impact on their own lives. In 1974 the people of Sabaskong Bay staged a boycott of the Father Moss School at Sioux Narrows, Ontario. This integrated provincial school was controlled by a Roman Catholic school board that effectively excluded the Ojibwa parents from key decisions and did not address the issue of racism, had an extremely high dropout rate among native students, and followed a curriculum that failed to take into account the significant presence of native children. In defiance of the Department of Indian Affairs, the leaders of Sabaskong Bay hired their own teachers, set up their own classrooms on the reserve, and established their own curriculum, one that included the study of native culture and history and the Ojibwa language. In 1975, the school was funded by the federal government, making it one of the first native-controlled schools in Canada (York 1989, 25–26).

In the same year, the Cree School Board was established through section 16 of the James Bay and Northern Quebec Agreement. Its special powers include the hiring of native teachers (even those without formal teaching qualifications), and the development of "courses, textbooks and

materials designed to preserve and transmit the language and culture of
the Native people" (Government of Québec 1976, 269). Since the sign-
ing of this agreement in 1975 the Cree School Board has made full use
of its control over curriculum, making Cree the exclusive language of
instruction for the first three years of primary education, before introduction of French and/or English (depending on parental choice) in the
fourth grade. To meet its teaching needs, the Cree School Board has produced a sixty-thousand-word Cree-English dictionary, the first of its kind
in the eastern Cree dialect; and the James Bay Cree Cultural Education
Centre has published a series of primary textbooks depicting hunting,
fishing, and daily activities in forest camps and a series of books illus-
trating legends narrated by local storytellers, including the story of
Aayaasaau, a shaman who was able to perform "seemingly magical feats
by calling on the spirits of the land for help" (James Bay Cree Cultural
Education Centre 1990, 1). The Cree School Board is among a growing
number of native educational organizations trying to rebuild realms of
knowledge that earlier education efforts had attempted to dismantle, as
well as trying to bridge lines of communication between elders and youth
that Indian schools had once been designed to disrupt.

The government of Canada has recently acknowledged the connection between its programs of Indian residential education and an
immense toll of suffering still being felt in the native population resulting from cultural loss, separation from families, and victimization
through physical and sexual abuse (Government of Canada 1998). A
Statement of Reconciliation presented by Jane Stewart, Minister of
Indian Affairs and Northern Development, on 7 January 1998 admits
that Canada is "burdened by past actions that resulted in weakening the
identity of Aboriginal peoples, suppressing their languages and cultures,
and outlawing spiritual practices" (ibid.). The statement places special
emphasis on the damaging legacy of the residential school system, and
promises a "healing strategy" to deal with its remaining consequences.

Residential schools were only one part of a wider effort to radically
change Indian knowledge and behavior, to make Indians understandable
to "civilized" people and compliant with their plans for "improvement,"
and to do away with their awkward claims to sovereignty—to make them
"citizens." In the nineteenth and early twentieth centuries, assimilation
of Indians was both politically expedient and a philanthropic goal acted
upon with sincere moral conviction. Euro-Americans and -Canadians
commonly saw Indians as living in a state of savagery that was a danger
to their health, prosperity, and salvation. At the same time that schools

were being established as a widely applicable solution to the "Indian problem," some native practices were seen as being so degrading, so insidious in their influence on the Indian soul, that special efforts were required to stamp them out. Schools were not enough to put a quick end to the Sun Dance, the Potlatch, or the use of hallucinogenic drugs. More urgent measures were required that would bring the powers of the state to bear upon those who continued to engage in what was seen as social and spiritual self-destruction.

The Way of the Diné
Still Sustains Us

Manley Begay Jr.

On 8 January 1998, it was reported throughout the world in major newspapers that the day before the Canadian government had for the first time formally apologized to its 1.3 million indigenous people for 150 years of paternalistic assistance programs and racist residential schools that had devastated Indian communities as thoroughly as any war or disease (DePalma 1998). The apology was received with mixed feelings among native peoples. Some felt it was a historic stride toward healing unresolved issues between the federal government and indigenous peoples. Others thought the apology was insincere and did not address specific issues like land loss and forced relocation.[1] In addition to the apology a promise was made to establish a "healing fund" of $245 million for the thousands of Indians who were taken from their homes and forced to attend the schools where they were sometimes physically and sexually abused (ibid.). Some felt that this sum was not sufficient for their pain and suffering. I am sure that this apology and action forced many unrevealed and unresolved feelings to the surface and brought out stories from the generations of indigenous families that experienced such invasive government policies in Canada—as well as in the United States and other countries, such as Australia and New Zealand.

I immediately began receiving phone calls at my office in Harvard's Kennedy School of Government from various news agencies requesting my opinion of the Canadian government's action and asking whether such an apology had ever been given by the United States government, which had also painstakingly established residential schools (called boarding schools in the United States) for native children. Sadly, I had to report that thus far no formal apology has ever been rendered by the U.S. government and no "healing fund" has ever been established.

As these calls continued to come in, I had to stop and think about what was going on and why. How could anyone have let this concerted effort at cultural genocide occur? As I contemplated, I thought of my mother, someone who had experienced the U.S. government's experiment at bringing "civiliza-

---

1. What this expression of regret also failed to report was the statistical extent of the damage inflicted on the native population by its assistance programs and residential schools. The demographic measure of the North American genocide is mentioned above in the introduction to this volume and is covered in detail by Thornton (1987).

tion" and "Christianization" to native peoples. I telephoned my mother in the Navaho Nation and asked her to describe her boarding school experience. First, she mentioned those in our family who had been to boarding schools: "We had many family members that were sent off to boarding schools in Arizona, California, and New Mexico. Three maternal grandfathers, me, your father, four uncles, and three aunts were sent to boarding schools. Two of my brothers spent most of their lives in federal institutions. They both died young. One died in a federal TB [tuberculosis] institution and the other died at home."[2] It is noteworthy that she does not fully distinguish between family members sent to boarding schools and federal tuberculosis sanatoriums. The experience, for those who were separated, was essentially the same. What is not commonly recognized, and what follows from my mother's connection between boarding schools and sanatoriums, is that both were total institutions oriented toward the imposition of cultural change. The sanatoriums were, in effect, boarding schools that combined the goals of health care and formal education.

She continued, saying, "Even though my brother Robert did not go to boarding school, he spent most of his life in another federally operated institution—a TB institution. When he was about twenty-five years old, in 1948, he came home to die. Grandma took care of him for as long as she could. He died in Grandma's arms. Grandma still gets very emotional when we talk about Robert. It's still hard for her."

She went on to recall the recent past and vividly described her ordeal: "I ran away from Fort Wingate Boarding School with several other girls [because I was homesick]. I made it home and felt safe, but it wasn't for long because the BIA [Bureau of Indian Affairs] school officials eventually came for me. I was sent off to another place. It was much farther away, a place I had never been, the Sherman Institute in Riverside, California. As they took me away, I cried and fought to stay, but no one helped me and I couldn't understand why." Then, she shifted further back to the stories she had been told by my grandmother about the imprisonment of our people, the Diné, from 1864 to 1868 at a makeshift concentration camp located at Fort Sumner, New Mexico. This harrowing experience culminated in a treaty being signed between the Navaho Nation and U.S. government. Article VI of the treaty of 1868 states:

> In order to insure the civilization of the Indians entering into this treaty, the necessity of education is admitted, especially of such of them as may be settled on agricultural parts of the Reservation, and they therefore pledge themselves to compel their children, male and female, between the ages of six and sixteen, to attend school; and it is hereby made the duty of the agent for said Indians to see that this stipulation is strictly complied with; and the United States agrees that, for every thirty children

2. From a telephone interview, 11 January 1998, translated from Navaho by Manley Begay Jr.

between said ages who can be induced or compelled to attend school, a house shall be provided, and a teacher competent to teach the elementary branches of an English education shall be furnished who will reside among said Indians, and fully discharge his or her duties as a teacher. (Government of the United States, 1868)

With this educational provision, which was part of the national policy of "civilization" and "Christianization" of all natives, our people were mandated to attend schools, with the proviso that the U.S. government would provide appropriate physical facilities and competent teachers for formal education. Yet, as my mother testifies, "It was hard being at boarding school. The conditions were not always good. It was very cold in the wintertime. I remember that we only had woodstoves for heating. We also at times had to bring our own [sheepskin] bedding because there were not enough mattresses or beds for all of us."

Various religious groups, like the Presbyterian Board of Missions, were given the responsibility of establishing the first schools for the Diné. After several failures to permanently establish these schools as directed in the treaty, the federal government reverted to the boarding school approach: forced removal of children from their homes and communities was determined to be the only successful method to "civilize" and "Christianize" Indians. With this change in the original program, the first permanent boarding school in the Navaho Nation was established at Fort Defiance (Thompson 1975). In the eyes of Euro-Americans, this effort was the beginning of much-needed change toward "civilization," "Christianization," and the eradication of the traditional lifestyle of my people, the Diné. But it was not what we were promised: it was not local, it was not safe, and at times it was not education.

In a concerted effort to extinguish the traditional lifeways of the Diné, the federal government had, by 1930, forced nearly 50 percent of school-age Navaho children into schools. By the mid-1940s, since boarding school facilities on the reservation were not being expanded or improved, the Navaho school population dropped to approximately one-fourth (ibid.). In response to this reduction, plans were made to forcibly remove Navaho children from the reservation to schools like Intermountain School in Utah, Chemawa School in Oregon, Anadarko School in Oklahoma, and the Sherman Institute in California. By 1954, with this mandatory federal relocation initiative, the percentage of Navaho children enrolled in schools had increased to 82 percent.

The 1960s saw a native political renaissance, which became the impetus for much-needed change in federal Indian policy, tribal sovereignty, and education (Cornell 1988). An important part of this resurgence was the introduction of public and tribal schools for Navaho children. Consequently, more and more Navaho children began enrolling in public schools, both off and on reservations, and by 1968, 90 percent of the Navaho children were enrolled in schools operated by either federal or state governments or by the tribes (Thompson 1975).

But the problem of dislocation, and even the era of boarding schools, is not yet over. In the 1970s the Association of American Indian Affairs conducted a multiyear study that found, astonishingly, that one-fourth to one-third of all American Indian children were being separated from their families and placed in foster care, adoptive homes, or educational institutions (Graham 1997). Navaho children were part of this statistic, and although by the early 1970s over half of Navaho children attended public or tribal schools, 20,000 Navaho children in kindergarten through twelfth grade were still living in boarding schools on the reservation (ibid.). About a decade later (1979), the total number of native students living in boarding schools was 20,255, of which a majority were Navaho children (Geboe 1997). By 1992 there were 21,281 native students still living in BIA boarding schools, with a majority being Navaho children (Government of the United States 1992). Most recently, in 1997, there were 10,445 native students living in boarding schools, again with a majority of them Navaho children (Geboe 1997). For all intents and purposes, the federal boarding school system is still in effect.

It is within this historical context that four generations of my family have survived and overcome not only U.S. federal Indian policies but also Spanish and Mexican Indian policies aimed at dissolution, disintegration, and assimilation of our way of life. Each generation in my family has experienced these policies differently. I am the first member of my generation, in my family, to graduate from public school and college. My mother and father's generation was subjected to the federal government's boarding school experiment and did not graduate. My grandmother did not personally experience formal education. My children, however, have had the privilege of attending both public and private schools.

Although Indian education policies of the federal government have been overtly and subtly imposed on my family, and each of my family members from the various generations has changed culturally and socially, each has in his or her own way remained a strong defender of native rights and ways. Why have the odds against this remained so great? I believe that one of the reasons for my family's strength is the spiritual knowledge and practices of each family member. My mother also identifies this as what has sustained us through the generations:

> Even though being at boarding school was sad and hard, I made the best out of a situation I had no control over. I decided to learn as much as I could. I learned how to cook, sew, and take care of a family. I learned how to take care of myself, to be independent. I learned the white ways, but didn't forget my family. I learned the English language, but did not forget the Navaho language. I learned many things, but wished I had been learning more of the Navaho Way: family practices, traditional prayers, songs, and stories, and weaving rugs. In spite of having been sent away to boarding schools, I have relearned much of the Navaho Way through the years. The Navaho Way is what has sustained me and continues to sustain me and my family.

CHAPTER 4

Medical Evangelism

Drawing from a deep Western cultural source, philosophy in
ancient Greece developed a central distinction between reality
and appearance. Behind the changing surface of events rests
an immutable structure: an immortal soul, an imperishable
form of beauty, a universal and objective justice. . . . The
imperative [that there must be an intrinsic moral order] leads
to the castigation of anyone who does not accept or fit within
this monolithic moral order as an alien Other. The imperative's legacy is easily visible in the justification for stigmatiz-
ing and suppressing religious heresies, in the brutal oppression found in colonial movements of conquest, and more
prosaically, but equally fraught with dangerous consequences, in the antagonistic absence of respect accorded theories that fall outside the Western canons of philosophy and
science.

> Arthur Kleinman, *Writing at the Margin:*
> *Discourse Between Anthropology and Medicine*

When Spanish colonists first arrived in the New World, one of their discoveries was the comparatively sophisticated systems of healing among
the indigenous peoples. Medical knowledge was one of the first areas of
cultural exchange on the new continent, in a process that altered the healing practices of both Indian and immigrant cultures. Clara Sue Kidwell
points to herbal remedies in particular (1991, 21) as constituting "a case
of reverse acculturation, the adoption of native practices by the con-
quering civilization." The early colonists of North America were
impressed with the Indians' state of health, which, before diseases of
European origin found their way across the continent, seemed to be superior to that of the immigrant peoples and was attributed to their special
knowledge of indigenous medicinal herbs. Cotton Mather, an early his-

torian of North Carolina, reported that Indians effected "cures many times which are truly stupendous" (cited in Starr 1982, 48) and even advocated intermarriage with Indians, partially to obtain their remarkable medical knowledge.

Native North Americans drew upon an immense variety of plants for use as medicines. A census of medicinal plants in North America by Daniel Moerman (1991, 147) enumerates 17,634 uses of 2,397 species. His census does not include a wide variety of products from animals, such as the fat of bears, seals, and geese, and the wide use of beaver castoreum, which was especially common among northern Athabaskan and Inuit peoples, whose access to medicinal plants was more seasonal and limited to fewer species.[1] Plant sources throughout North America provided aboriginal peoples with cough and cold remedies, emetics, cathartics, diaphoretics, vermifuges, astringents, alteratives, stimulants, narcotics, and antiseptics (Russel 1980, 35).

The Indians' knowledge of the medicinal properties of plants and animal products was occasionally to prove crucial for the survival of explorers and settlers. When the three ships of Jacques Cartier were icebound in the St. Lawrence River in the winter of 1535–36, almost all of the 110 men of the expedition began to fall seriously ill. According to Virgil Vogel, "As the crisis deepened, Cartier had the good fortune to encounter once again the local Indian Chief, Domagaia, who had cured himself of the same disease with 'the juice and sappe of a certain Tree.' The Indian women gathered branches of the magical tree, 'boiling the bark and leaves for a decoction, and placing the dregs upon the legs.' All those so treated rapidly recovered their health, and the Frenchmen marveled at the curative skill of the natives" (1970, 4). There is, according to Vogel (ibid., 5), a "vast untold story" of Native American accomplishment in pharmacology which, despite a trial-and-error method of invention, has had a significant connection to many "scientific" accomplishments, including the discoveries of insulin and local anesthetics. Also credited to native North Americans is the use, independent of biomedical breakthroughs, of molds and fungi as antibiotics.

Aside from herbology, however, most indigenous healing practices were rejected by European colonizers from the earliest period of contact. Shamanic performance, ritual use of hallucinogens, and visionary expe-

---

1. This aspect of indigenous medicine would more accurately be called "vertebral" than herbal, even though use of animal and plant products were part of the same healing system.

rience were among many forms of native spirituality, central to healing systems, seen to be inherently, even if unintentionally, satanic. Joseph-François Lafitau, who served as a missionary in New France from 1712 to 1717 among the Hurons and Iroquois, found that the Jesuit missionaries in general did not apply themselves to research on Indian medicine, out of concern about seeming to approve of the "superstitions" and "foolish imaginings" of the "savages" toward their most simple remedies (Lafitau [1724] 1983, 117). Daniel Gookin, a missionary in seventeenth-century New England, observed that the powwows "are partly wizards and witches holding familiarity with Satan, that evil one; and partly are physicians and make use at least in show of herbs and roots for curing the sick and diseased" (cited in Russel 1980, 40). Sweat bathing was another indigenous healing method with very wide distribution in North America rejected by European immigrants. This seems at first to be an odd prohibition, considering the almost spiritual devotion of northern Europeans to the sauna; but in the North American colonies it was the association of the sweat lodge with non-Christian ceremony—singing, drumming, and visionary experiences—that led to its being labeled an instrument of the Devil (Bruchac 1993, 25).

We are by now familiar with missionary rejection of native healing practices, but beginning in the late nineteenth century, biomedicine came into its own as a source of insight and human improvement and brought with it a similar intolerance of native techniques seen to be at odds with "proper" diagnosis and treatment.[2] It developed a form of evangelism that acted in ways usually complementary to missionary efforts. The synergy of missions and medicine derives in part from their foundations in belief, in the acceptance of basic convictions that serve as strong influences on perception, judgment, and motivation for reform and improvement. As Byron Good observes, "There is—quite ironically—a close relationship between science, including medicine, and religious fundamentalism, a relationship that turns, in part, on our concept of 'belief.' For fundamentalist Christians, salvation is often seen to follow from belief, and mission work is conceived as an effort to convince the natives to give up false beliefs and take on a set of beliefs that will produce a new life and ultimate salvation. Ironically quite

2. The argument that follows, and other portions of this chapter, are revised versions of material that first appeared in "Healing and Conversion: Medical Evangelism in James Bay Cree Society," *Ethnohistory* 44(3): 463–91 (cited elsewhere as Niezen 1997). I would like to thank the editors for permission to reprint selections from this work.

a-religious scientists and policy makers see a similar benefit from correct belief" (1994, 7). Historical associations between religion and bio-medicine can also be drawn. Bryan Turner finds a direct confluence of medicine and religion in the Protestant imposition of discipline and subordination of the passions through "religio-magical management of the body . . . handed down from medieval monastic practice" (1995, 20). The increasing rationalism and bureaucratization of scientific procedures and belief, however, occurred, according to Turner, at the expense of religious influence: "The doctor has replaced the priest as the custodian of social values" (ibid., 35).

Turner's overview of medical puritanism does not make explicit the evangelical techniques by which doctor takes the place of priest. This aspect of biomedicine can be illustrated by considering its introduction to native North Americans and the ways it has negotiated (or failed to negotiate) cultural differences. Among the indigenous peoples of North America, the dissemination of Western biomedicine has paralleled the development of missionary religion, first being introduced through missionary enterprises themselves and then through independent medical administrations that used prohibition, coercion, and persuasion to attempt to transform native behavior into a more consistent reflection of biomedical belief. As health care has come increasingly under the control of autonomous native administrations, biomedical practice has had to respond, as have many missionary movements, to local priorities and values by accommodating local healing traditions.

The conduct of missions and medical institutions and their impact on native peoples are therefore not historically or socially uniform. Nor have aboriginal peoples themselves responded uniformly to their policies and actions. The dissemination of biomedicine in native communities can be seen, for purposes of simplification, to have unfolded in three phases. The missionary phase usually began with the earliest introduction of evangelism, varying, according to local history, from the sixteenth to mid-nineteenth century and lasting until the appropriation of medical services by government from the late nineteenth century to the mid-twentieth. During this period, Christianity and medicine acted as complementary realms of cosmology and practice that worked together toward changing "irrational" native beliefs and healing practices. With the establishment of permanent missions, the drive toward improvement in medical practice as an adjunct to conversion became formally articulated. Missions, medicine, and education acted together through complementary institutions of conversion.

By the mid-twentieth century, the missionary phase of biomedicine had in most places given way to government-initiated efforts to promote and enforce the assimilation of native peoples to the lifeways of the dominant society. Government involvement in health care eventually divested missions of their educational and medical portfolios and was associated with a secular drive toward cultural and administrative assimilation. Indigenous healing practices had no place in the central tasks of government involvement in native health care: to combat epidemics and change the health-related behavior of native peoples.

Finally, in recent decades biomedicine has in some communities entered a distinct phase in which medical administrations have demonstrated an increasing openness to indigenous healing practices. This has been occurring despite obstacles inherent in the structural attachment of semiautonomous native agencies to government laws, regulations, and funding. Missions and medicine have been subject to similar processes of cultural critique and pressure to accommodate a renewed commitment to tradition. A growing number of native leaders have insisted upon the value of local practices while questioning long-standing prohibitions enforced by missions and biomedicine. During this phase the opportunities for encouraging traditional healing inherent in regional administrative autonomy have been perceived, and are being acted upon within the limitations of government systems of health care and social services.

CONTRASTING STYLES OF HEALING

Medicine in nineteenth-century Europe and America developed a solid grounding in science and professionalism that was both a product of and response to the health-related problems of rapid industrialization. Rudolf Virchow, a German physician widely known as the founder of cellular pathology, was among the European medical reformers of the 1840s committed to the radical ideas that the poor and oppressed should not have to wait until they got to heaven for their rewards, that a healthful existence should be a right of citizenship in this life, and that the physician should be the "natural attorney of the poor" (Fee and Porter 1992, 251). Public health in America evolved as a separate professional specialty that employed not only medical doctors but also biologists, statisticians, engineers, and others with specialized training. But with professionalization in both Europe and America, as Fee and Porter indicate, there was a distancing from the social reform impulses that originally inspired the development of public health: "Scientific methods tempered, when they did not replace, the initial commitment to improving the lives and living standards of the poor" (1992, 249). It was this scientific, public health–oriented medicine that expanded its objectives to include Indians settled in reservations, who became subject to medical reform through the mediation of Indian agents and missionaries.

Although Indians and Europeans had exchanged medical knowledge in some parts of North America for several centuries, the biomedicine that developed out of the scientific and social upheavals of the nineteenth century was very different from the unprofessionalized medical knowledge of early explorers and settlers. Above all, it contrasted in fundamental ways with the indigenous systems of healing that, in the course of more than a century of medical reform and expansion in the reservation communities of the United States and Canada, it was frequently to displace. Biomedicine is plural and has by no means remained static in its goals, forms of administration, or especially its technology, but there remain several points of continuity from the late nineteenth century to the mid-twentieth century (many features of which continue to the present) that allow us to find basic points of contrast between biomedicine and indigenous systems of healing.[3]

1. SPIRITUALITY VERSUS BIOCENTRISM IN ETIOLOGY (THE EXPLANATION OF ILLNESS)

Many indigenous healing systems are grounded in two fundamental notions that can be combined to explain illness and events that, from a biomedical point of view, would be called "accidents" or misfortune: (1) Every living thing possesses life force, soul, or power capable of disrupting, and being disrupted by, other forces in the universe; and (2) the disruptions that cause illness can often be traced to a moral event, decision, or desire that has compromised an individual's relationship(s) with other powers. In a study of Iroquois medicine, for example, James Herrick (1995, 25) finds that the common explanations of illness point to an upset by "the exertion of life force or power by any person, place, thing, or event upon any other person, place, thing, or event," with similar

---

3. I will be drawing mainly upon my research on the traditional healing systems of the James Bay Cree of Québec and the Cree and Ojibwa of the Nishnawbe-Aski Nation of Ontario for illustrations of the points that follow. Although the basic features of these conceptions of health and medicine are common, not only in native North America but in the indigenous societies of many parts of the world, the specific examples that I use are not intended to illustrate, or argue for the existence of, a generic "native" system of healing.

explanations being offered for successful healing or "restoration of balance." Such imbalance can be caused by witchcraft, offensive acts (e.g., gathering medicine without a show of respect by offering tobacco [described below] may cause the joints to swell and stiffen), unfulfilled desires (birthmarks may be caused when a pregnant woman wants blackberries or raspberries but does not get them), or things, events, people, or places that exude evil (ibid.). It is also clear, as underlined by a description an elder in Mistassini, Québec, gave me of a woman suffering from a formally undiagnosed psychosis, that whatever the ultimate determinants of illness, there is a close connection between its physiological and behavioral manifestations: "I saw a lady one time whose illness was very strong. She never hit us but we often saw her hit her kids. . . . She had blackouts. There were times she would recover. . . . She would start doing her work just like any other normal person [and then her illness would come back]. . . . The most frightening thing we saw was when she took a gun and started shooting all over the place. . . . How it started was when she was giving birth to one of her children, some of the blood stayed inside her stomach. That's when [the elders] realized she was having mental problems." Such etiological holism is not used consistently to arrive at the same explanations for the same illness. The forces that can lead to sickness and misfortune are unique to each person and cannot always be called upon to explain a similar event. There are, however, cases of collective misfortune, as in epidemics, that call for a wider explanation, a perception of combined spiritual forces that can throw an entire village or region into violent disarray.

In most indigenous healing traditions of North America, the spiritual powers of plants and ritual action are seen as having a real potential to harm as well as heal; and a common way of explaining illness is to attribute it to the ill-feeling or sorcery of a jealous rival. A list of Iroquois explanations of illness compiled by Herrick reveals sorcery to be a common concern: "Soreness all over with the skin or muscle twitching is an indication of being witched. A poultice . . . is placed on the twitching area . . . and it will draw out an object in the shape of a bug of some kind" (1995, 52).

In contrast, the biomedical system remains true to its name in the explanation of illness. As Byron Good observes, "Over and over again I have been struck by the enormous power of the idea within medicine that disease is fundamentally, even exclusively, biological. Not that experiential or behavioral matters are ignored, certainly not by good clinicians, but these are matters separate from the real object of medical practice. The fundamental reality is human biology, real medicine, and the relevant knowledge is staggering in its scope and complexity" (1994, 70). Biomedicine may frequently have been introduced to native communities through missions, even with missionaries as medical practitioners, but this did not take away from a biological understanding of the origins of illness. The relationship between moral weakness and sickness could be perceived only in failure to perform the routines of hygiene and other acts or avoidances necessary to preserve good health. At base, the causes of illness are looked for in biological rather than spiritual processes.

2. SPIRITUALITY VERSUS SPIRITUAL NEUTRALITY IN THE TREATMENT OF ILLNESS

A pervasive spirituality in indigenous healing is the general source of differences between it and biomedicine. In some instances of crisis, such as those in which the patient is seen to suffer from sorcery, spiritual intervention in the human world can be considered both the cause and cure of serious illness. The spirit world's potential for alleviating uncertainty and human frailty, however, entered into even those aspects of curing that some might be tempted to call "experimental"—the selection and use of "natural" medicines. Every healing technique, even such seemingly instrumental practices as herbology or bone setting, was seen to have a connection with sacred power. The use of herbal remedies was, despite a high degree of effectiveness that so impressed early European immigrants, guided more by spiritual than practical concerns. Moerman to some degree overlooks this when he finds that Native American botanical medicine was more than "placebo medicine" or the result of random activity, but had true "efficacy" in treating illness, and goes on to explain how Native Americans may have learned the medicinal uses of plants: he points out that several categories of biologically active plants, such as those in the honeysuckle and poison apple families, produce substances that protect themselves from browsing, and they alert animals (including humans) to the presence of poison with distinctive odors or tastes (1991). Such signals would have alerted native healers to the presence of powerful biological effects in the plant's compounds, which would have led them to medicinal "discoveries." There is also, however, a strong symbolic element to the selection of medicinal plants. Roots of a wide variety of plant species were the most common source of botanical medicine, a fact that suggests Moerman's "poison apple" hypothesis explains, at best, only part of a complex process of practical experiment and discovery in the development of native North American pharmacologies. The Ojibwa Mide (members of the Midewiwin medicine society, a secret society of healers) let dreams guide them to useful plants; and, as Frances Densmore found, the symbolic appearance of a root can point a healer, whether in dreams or a conscious state of alertness, to its medicinal properties: "[I] showed a certain root to a medicine woman and asked her if she knew what it was. She replied that its use was familiar to her but she would have known it was a medicinal root if she had never seen it before. On being questioned further she said it was evidently an old root which had sent up a new stalk each year and had long roots extending downward. The stalk and the small roots were gone, but the life remained in the root itself, and this would be the part used for medicine" (1928, 325). This suggests that what was often looked for in medicinal plants was not initially or even most importantly their effects upon the body of the patient, but indications of life force or "power," of qualities that could provide a corrective to spiritual imbalance. The effects of medicine upon patients was only one of many possible ways such power could be discovered. From this starting point, detailed knowledge of the medicinal properties of plants could be developed into the healing systems whose biological efficacy impressed European observers.

The gathering of medicinal plants also commonly involved acknowledgment and propitiation of their sacred power. As an elder in a 1994 broadcast on community radio in Chisasibi, Québec, pointed out, "After the herbs are gathered, you in return have to put something back. The way this was done was an offering of tobacco to the Creator, to show your thanks." Densmore's study of the use of herbs by the Ojibwa Mide reveals the same practice: "An unfailing custom of the Mide in gathering plants for medicinal use is to dig a little hole in the ground beside the plant and put tobacco in the hole, speaking meanwhile to the plant." An example of what might be said to the plant was provided to her by a member of the Midewiwin medicine society: "You were allowed to grow here for the benefit of mankind, and I give you this tobacco to remind you of this, so that you will do the best you can for me" (1928, 325).

This recognition and propitiation of higher powers stands in stark contrast to the biological focus and instrumentality of formal healing. In biomedicine, healing is grounded in a naturalism that removes both illness and healing from supernatural or spiritual processes. Both the prevalent use of a systematic, biologically oriented diagnosis to discover the specific cause of illness in a patient, and the use of technology to intervene in biological processes to effect a cure, place physicians in situations of emotional distance from their patients. Arthur Kleinman, in highlighting the distinctive features of biomedicine that transcend its historical and social particularities, points to its links with Western monotheism, philosophical essentialism, and demands for orthodoxy. The single-minded objectivism and positivism of biomedicine, reinforced by essentialism and intolerance of competing paradigms, has the advantage of peeling back "layers of reality and [establishing] with precision what is certain and fundamental, and establishing criteria against which orthodoxy and orthopraxy can be certified" (1995, 29). Yet biological reductionism is dehumanizing in therapeutic practice, placing physicians in a difficult position when they care for patients with chronic illness. Having to balance personal care with the requirements of identifying and treating biological pathology, practitioners tend to discount patients' experiences of suffering. There is also, as Max Weber observed long before the recent controversy surrounding euthanasia, a tendency for biomedicine to overlook the emotional and spiritual significance of death and dying:

> The general "presupposition" of the medical enterprise is stated trivially in the assertion that medical science has the task of maintaining life as such and of diminishing suffering as such to the greatest possible degree. Yet this is problematical. By his means the medical man preserves the life of the mortally ill man, even if the patient implores us to relieve him of life, even if his relatives, to whom his life is worthless and to whom the costs of maintaining his worthless life grow unbearable, grant his redemption from suffering. . . . Yet the presuppositions of medicine, and the penal code, prevent the physician from relinquishing his therapeutic efforts. Whether life is worth living and when—this question is not asked by medicine. (1948, 144)

Biological reductionism in therapeutic practice frequently provides physicians with a narrow and sometimes self-contradictory goal—to preserve life and prevent suffering—which at the same time absolves them from the moral and emotional aspects of the transition toward death. The doctor, as Bryan Turner (1995, 35) says, may have replaced the priest as the custodian of social values, but the nature of medical practice often leaves doctors unprepared to act as mediators of suffering, dying, death, and bereavement.

3. INITIATORY SPECIALIZATION VERSUS VERTICAL BUREAUCRATIC "PROFESSIONALISM"

A Lakota healer explained to Frances Densmore the guiding principle of specialization in herbology: "In the old days the Indians had few diseases, and so there was not a demand for a large variety of medicines. A medicine man usually treated one special disease and treated it successfully. He did this in accordance with his dream. A medicine man would not try to dream of all herbs and treat all diseases, for then he could not expect to succeed in all nor to fulfill properly the dream of any one herb or animal. He would depend on too many and fail in all. That is one reason why our medicine men lost their power when so many diseases came among us with the advent of the white man" (1928, 323). There was, in the dissemination of knowledge and use of spiritual power, a basic similarity between members of the medicine society, but each possessed specialized knowledge within a loosely hierarchical system devoted to healing and defense against sorcery from rivals.[4] Members of the Ojibwa Midewiwin were situated in a loose hierarchy consisting of different levels of knowledge and control over spiritual power. They were taught a range of remedies at the time of their initiation by being introduced to the identification and uses of a number of plants. Advancement to higher "degrees" involved more extensive instruction, but in the meanwhile members had to be satisfied with "buying" information piecemeal from knowledgeable elders. At the same time, remedies were as much a result of personal inspiration as the carefully disclosed secrets of initiation (ibid., 322–23).

The permanent transitions imposed by colonialism throw into relief a basic area of contrast between biomedicine and indigenous healing. As Ernest Gellner writes, "The occupational and geographical mobility, the atomization of the population, the dependence of status on individual qual-

---

4. The social implications of Athabaskan spirituality at the time of early missionary efforts can be informed by the literature on the segmentary structure of North African tribes. Emile Durkheim (1933) used the ethnographic literature from North Africa to support a general theory of human progress, which described the early, simple form of the division of labor, exemplified by the nomadic tribesmen, as "mechanical," with great similarity among adjoining groups and among the individuals within each group. This was contrasted to "organic solidarity," the division of labor based upon social diversification of social units with complementary functions, typical of "advanced," complex, industrial societies. Segmentary societies in North Africa, the nomadic tribes with similar clan structures that occupied distinct territories, were examples of social cohesion based upon likeness, which, if we take his terminology (and ethnography) literally, would be more like the products of mechanization than the differentiated functioning of actual machinery. But Durkheim largely overlooks the vertical aspect of specialization, such as that of the medicine societies, which can be found even among hunter-gatherers.

ification rather than on group membership, all tend to erode clear-cut, sharply symbolized inequality" (1981, 93). Mobility, atomization, and individual qualifications are all present in biomedicine, but it is not sharp inequalities in indigenous societies that are eroded as much as self-reliance in situations of crisis. Bureaucracies and formally trained experts are imposed as care providers to replace local healers whose healing skills involve personal knowledge of communities and their members. The Lakota medicine man quoted above who attributes the decline of healers' power to the impact of new diseases does not perceive the tendency of biomedicine to replace those lacking formal qualifications and "certification." Biomedicine is associated with much greater formality in the instruction and organization of healers, with physicians deriving their knowledge and status from a standardized system of education and professional licensing. With the development of American medicine as an organized profession in the late nineteenth century, as Starr points out, "authority no longer depended on individual character and lay attitudes; instead, it was increasingly built into the structure of institutions" (1982, 20).

If biomedicine can be defined by its almost exclusive emphasis on biological processes in the diagnosis and treatment of disease, it can, at the same time, be considered "formal" because it has developed close associations with complex bureaucratic organizations. Educational and professional organizations are only the beginning of medical ties to bureaucracy. The professional authority of physicians increased greatly with the development of hospitals, institutions steeped in both hierarchy within the ranks of service providers (with high-prestige specialists such as surgeons and neurologists on one end of the scale and nurses, technicians, and support staff on the other) and control over providers and patients in the administering of treatment. In contrast to Gellner's basic model, there are usually sharper inequalities within bureaucratic organizations than in the indigenous communities they have been introduced to. The community-based knowledge of indigenous healing and sorcery contrasts with biomedicine's formal agencies based on wide networks of communication and record-keeping, which draw on non-native legislatures and bureaucracies for the rules by which they operate.

4. PERFORMATIVE VERSUS TECHNOLOGICAL AND COERCIVE LEGITIMACY

The expansion of formal helping agencies into Indian reservation communities, a development I will consider in more detail below, marked a profound disjuncture from the informal apprenticeship and initiation of local healers. Ultimately the greatest difference between the formal and community-based healing systems lay in the sources of legitimacy, defined in Weber's (1948, 78) classic exposition of the inner justifications and external means for establishing political domination. In explaining the sources of medical authority, legitimate domination can be understood as the social means of ensuring compliance with the requirements of healing intervention and, where it exists, developing trust in the healer and his or her methods.

The personal qualities of an accepted indigenous healer combine with his or her control of spiritual forces through natural remedies or ceremonial intervention. A patient's trust and compliance are based upon knowledge of the individual healer's abilities and reputation as someone able to "restore balance." Thus, on several levels, legitimacy is based upon "performance."[5] By "performance" I do not mean the actual ability to effect cures but the behavioral context in which healing takes place. This can include such subtle actions as displaying personal knowledge of the patient and his or her family and establishing rapport in a way described by the term "bedside manner." In its most dramatic form, it is exemplified by those indigenous healers who work without medicinal means, referred to variously as "shamans," "medicine men," "conjurers," or "jugglers," whose procedures include the apparent swallowing and regurgitation of poisons or spiritually powerful projectiles from the patient's body, summoning spirits for advice on causes and therapies, and drumming and singing over the patient to establish spiritual control. Legitimacy is based on a perception of the healer's ability to manipulate or become a vessel of sacred power. What is not often recognized, however, is that such control of the sacred can take place even in the interpersonal events referred to in formal systems as "counseling."

In establishing legitimacy, formal medicine has largely been able to dispense with the performative aspects of healing. It is able to draw upon the enormous prestige of science and technology to assure trust in its methods. There is more to this trust than the unquestionable accomplishments of biomedicine in reducing humanity's burden of disease. As Paul Starr points out, "Science worked even greater changes on the imagination than it worked on the processes of disease. . . . Once people

---

5. "Performance," as used here, is similar to Weber's (1948) concept of "charisma" but does not reside in the "spiritual musicality" of a gifted individual. To take the musical analogy further, the spirits themselves are not seen as mere instruments but as the real performers, with the "shaman" or medium a mere instrument.

began to regard science as a superior and legitimately complex way of explaining and controlling reality, they wanted physicians' interpretations of experience regardless of whether the doctors had remedies to offer" (1982, 18–19).

In some native communities, science and technology—not easily separated from the personal manners of physicians—are carefully scrutinized and compared, not always favorably, with the efficacy of indigenous methods. A collection of healing narratives I assembled from radio interviews broadcast by the Chisasibi Telecommunications Association between 1992 and 1994 makes it clear that there remains a strong undercurrent of skepticism among the James Bay Crees toward the healing abilities of biomedicine. A common theme in these narratives is the inability of doctors, using clinic facilities or prescriptions of medication, to effect cures of severe and/or chronic illness. An elder known to have the ability to heal using knowledge passed on from family members regarding medicinal plants and animals would often be reported as offering an alternative solution that brought about a spectacular cure. These narratives are interspersed with phrases like "She was alive, not dying like the doctor said" and "The modern medicine failed, so I wasn't going to use anything modern." These are indications that biomedicine has greater difficulty establishing legitimacy where it is in potential competition with long-standing indigenous healing systems, where local methods have been developed into new sources of identity or "tradition," where technology is not trusted without reservation, and where the professional status of physicians is not automatically a marker of prestige.

Biomedicine, however, does not depend upon trust and voluntary compliance to exercise control. Through its close association with bureaucracy, it can make use of the coercive powers of formal authority, not only in the guise of "total institutions," the hospitals that, in extreme cases, have the power to isolate patients in the medical environment, but also with more subtle rules and procedures: rules of confidentiality, which can give a physician control over a family reluctant to agree to treatment; the authority to define illness or insanity or to assess disabilities that may qualify patients for compensation—to mention only a few of the most direct examples of a physician's authority. Perhaps more important is his or her access to other agencies, such as in referring patients to social workers who, in turn, possess even greater authority as gatekeepers to institutions of enforcement. Biomedicine enjoys the advantage of being able to hand off coercive authority to others, being left relatively unscathed by reactions against it. Medical authority does not rest solely in trust or recognition of the moral qualities of physicians but ultimately in secondary relationships with institutions having recourse to state-sanctioned coercion.

5. CRISIS ORIENTATION VERSUS MEDICAL EVANGELISM

It cannot fairly be said that indigenous healing systems lack preventive action. Maintaining a productive relationship with spiritual forces to avoid illness or misfortune can be accomplished in simple ways, as through prayers, offerings, and amulets. Practical intervention can also take place, as in a recommendation given to me by a Cree woman in Mistassini, Québec, who suggested that at the onset of a cold, boiling and eating a whole, singed squirrel (including the broth) would prevent more serious illness. Such preventive measures, however, do not go on to involve a concern with altering behavior and belief, certainly not of those outside the local community, for a wider goal of human prosperity. The healer who rescued the French explorer Jacques Cartier and his surviving crew members from scurvy was responding to a crisis, but after this dramatic success did not extend his intervention to a campaign directed toward the nutritional practices of European sailors.

Despite its focus on science and technology, biomedicine has displayed a tendency toward selective cultural intolerance, and an almost evangelistic dissemination of belief, that act in ways analogous to movements of religious conversion. In each of the three phases of biomedical involvement in native communities—missionary intervention, federal control, and regional autonomy—we can see parallels between biomedicine and evangelical religion: First, both carry a conviction of access to vital knowledge. The salvationist doctrines of missionary Christianity and the scientific foundations of the biological orientation to health are sources of information not directly accessible to the experience of the uninitiated layperson, yet each is seen to have profound implications for human prosperity. Second, this conviction of truth implies the necessity to communicate "belief" and change human behavior where access to fundamental knowledge is lacking. Both missionary religion and biomedicine base many of their actions on an evangelical impulse to disseminate knowledge and alter behavior in order to promote human prosperity. Strategies of communication have varied greatly, ranging from passive conversion by example to the use of force and incarceration. At a time when missions and medicine were fully established in many native communities, the influence of religion and biomedicine was further reinforced

by "total institutions." Boarding schools and hospitals were parallel institutions through which cultural knowledge was communicated and
behavior closely observed and corrected. Third, missions and medicine
are universalistic in their communication of vital knowledge and encour-
agement of behavior that follows from it. The communication of knowledge and necessary behavior is not restricted by boundaries of race or
culture. Fourth, such human universalism is accompanied by a contrary
tendency toward cultural intolerance. Alternative local systems of belief
and behavior are either overlooked or scrutinized for susceptibility to
error. During the introduction of missions and medicine in the James Bay
region, for example, there was selective intolerance of Cree behavior seen
to be at odds with Western belief and practice (Niezen 1997). For different reasons, both missions and medicine obstructed practices associated with such things as shamanism, herbology, and a variety of other
healing techniques. Religious prohibitions centered upon behavior seen
to compromise spiritual salvation, while medical prohibitions isolated
behavior seen to compromise a biocentric conception of well-being.

MISSION PROGRAMS, FEDERAL INTERVENTION,
AND REGIONAL AUTONOMY

The earliest of the new approaches to healing made available to Indians
by missionaries was European humoral medicine. The Latin American
folk medicine transmitted through the missions of California, for example, was based upon a belief that a balance of "hot" and "cold" is necessary for health. This dichotomy did not necessarily refer to actual physical characteristics of heat and cold, but to a system for categorizing the
causes of illness and determining the appropriate treatment. Despite the
ready acceptance of this system by Indians as a supplement to their own
practices, it did lead to the first negative reaction of priests to the practice of sweat bathing, which produces a "hot" reaction thought to
adversely affect the body's equilibrium, especially in the treatment of similarly "hot" illnesses such as fever, rash, black urine, penis discharge,
"heartburn," and cuts (Walker and Hudson 1993, 78–79).

Also prevalent in European medical ideas, especially before the development in the late nineteenth century of the germ theory of disease, was
the attribution of disease and death to "sin" or the more ambiguous notion
of the "will of God." In its extreme expression, God was seen by missionaries as an avenger sending deadly epidemics as punishment for dis-
belief and sin. But such an explanation of illness could also take more sub-

tle forms. An 1804 report by Dr. José Benites, an army surgeon stationed in Monterey, explains, for example, that the causes of illness in the native population were a combination of bad habits and moral turpitude: "The causes of . . . diseases among the Indians are impure intercourse, filthy habits, sleeping huddled together, the sick with the others, and the interchange of clothing, passing the nights in dancing and gambling on which occasions they shout and exert themselves exceedingly" (cited ibid.). Implicit in such a description of the causes of disease is the idea that healing would involve not only the use of medicine but also moral instruction.

The development of biomedicine in the late nineteenth century, the revolutionary discoveries of the microscope as a window into the processes of the body and of microbes as causes of illness, and, eventually, the use of inoculations and other means to facilitate alleviation of human suffering were achievements that went far beyond anything missionaries had previously been able to offer. Biomedical views of disease and treatment became an important supplement to missionary ideas about the supernatural. Far from the mainly urban resources of biomedicine, some missionaries in remote reservation communities added medical intervention to their tasks, accepting the burden of bringing both spiritual salvation and bodily healing to the Indians.

During the early years of missionary efforts, indigenous healing was most significantly altered by spiritual reforms. The nonmedicinal healing of shamans was the focus of missionary efforts to eradicate practices seen to be antithetical to Christianity. "The Indian shaman," Axtell writes, " was the missionaries' number one enemy because he seemed to hold their potential converts in the devil's thraldom through errant superstition, hocus-pocus, and fear" (1981, 76). Sweat bathing, for example, may have occasionally violated the basic premises of European humoral medicine, but it was offensive to missionaries for a deeper reason: as a form of "blind idolatry" or "paganism." And, if it took a display of scientific understanding of nature to erode the influence of shamans and convince the potential converts of the truth contained in the Europeans' store of knowledge, medicine was a perfect vehicle for performing such a demonstration. "If the fortuitous administration of a cordial, the lancet, or baptismal water happened to rescue a native from the grave, his stock as a functional replacement of the medico-religious shaman would rise dramatically" (ibid., 71).

The scientific advances in biomedicine of the late nineteenth century broadened the scope for such lessons in medical truth. The introduction of biomedicine as an alternative to traditional healing began with the rudimentary application of knowledge and resources. Missionaries used medicine in much the same way as fur trade managers and anyone else working among the Indians with access to medicines and a basic knowledge of how to use them. Some, like Roger Vandersteene, an oblate priest living among the Cree of northern Alberta, took their commitment to developing health conditions among their congregations a step further and made personal commitments to change the health conditions of remote native communities. In Vandersteene's case it was the risks inherent in childbirth that most inspired his efforts toward local health reform. Responding to this need, he wrote to the Chicago School of Nursing and began obstetrical training to intervene in cases that had gone beyond the abilities of Cree midwives. He bought surgical tools, studied practical procedures, and, through his network of contacts in the medical profession, obtained drug samples and other medical supplies, some of which were not legal for him to possess. His reasoning in going beyond the laws of professional certification and practice was that, as his biographer Earle Waugh puts it, "necessity transcended the law" (1996, 108).

As the missions later became more successful and more committed to social programs, formal institutions were developed to disseminate the combination of spiritual and medical ideas and practices. Among the Crees of Fort George, Québec, for example, competing Anglican and Catholic denominations informally divided their institutional influence. From the 1920s onward, the Anglicans had been successful in establishing a congregation that included almost every family in the community. The Catholic mission, finding itself unable to erode Anglican influence, looked to the development of medical services as a way to establish a permanent presence. In 1930 a Catholic school and clinic were built, both of which were supervised by four "gray sisters." The school did not survive the community's deep-rooted suspicion of the Catholic mission, but the clinic, with three beds and a bustling outpatient service, seemed to answer a real need. The Canadian government was instrumental in developing this service, providing funds for a thirty-two-bed hospital that opened in 1950, full to capacity from the first day of its operation, mainly with tuberculosis cases. The provision of medical services was to make little difference to the success of the Catholic mission, yet the church was to remain active in the functioning of this hospital until 1970, when the federal government rebuilt it and definitively took over its staffing and administration (Niezen 1997; 1998, 50–55).

Figure 10. The 280-bed tuberculosis sanatorium at Ninette, Manitoba, 1929. (Western Canada Pictorial Index, Inc.)

A similar development of government-funded, mission-operated medical services occurred in many parts of North America. In the early nineteenth century, responsibility for the health of Indians was, ironically, in the hands of the War Department, which at the same time was principally responsible for the material means of destroying them, should the need arise. The actual dispensing of medical services remained largely a charitable undertaking of missions. The administration of Indian health was then transferred to the newly created Department of the Interior in 1849, where it stayed until being transferred to the Public Health Service in 1955. Until the mid-twentieth century, therefore, the health of the native population of the United States was officially under the jurisdiction of agencies mainly responsible for issues other than health, leaving missions an important part in providing services.

Increased government involvement in the provision of health care to native communities seems to have mirrored the common missionary goals of providing both humanitarian services and using the empirical success and technological power of biomedicine as a "civilizing" tool. A

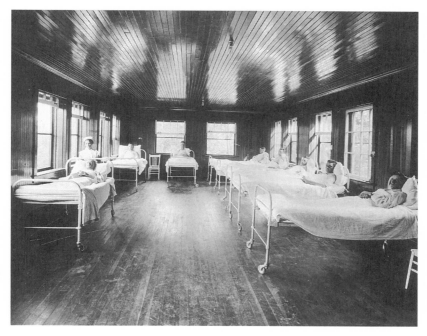

Figure 11. A men's ward of the tuberculosis sanatorium at Ninette, Manitoba, 1929. (Western Canada Pictorial Index, Inc.)

report from a Canadian Indian agent in 1912 already shows the link between native health services and the goals of assimilation: "A permanent medical officer at this point would be a great benefit to the Indians: nothing has a more civilizing effect upon them as a display of the white man's skill in healing, nothing convinces them more readily of the white man's interest in them" (cited in Young 1988, 90). This passage is explained by Young as one of the less obvious reasons for the federal government's assumption of financial responsibility for Indian health care: "Health services were seen as an integral part of the policy of total assimilation and elevation of Indians from 'wards of the nation' to full citizens" (1988, 90).

From the 1930s to 1970s tuberculosis sanatoriums (see figures 10 and 11) came to represent one of the most complete forms of control over the bodies and lives of native people. Crowded housing conditions in reserve communities made tuberculosis particularly virulent in the native population. The government responded with institutional isolation, in circumstances under which long-term healing was accompanied by cultural education. The sanatorium at Ninette, Manitoba, which treated both native and non-native patients, provided regular musical entertainment by a military band and access to a recreation room decorated with Christian motifs, complete with a library, upright piano, and a pool table. But, as in residential schools, the sanatoriums have a dark history that is only now beginning to emerge. In Manitoba the sanatoriums located near Ninette, Brandon, and Clearwater Lake are coming under scrutiny from native leaders concerned over the discovery of unmarked graves and stories of abuse from former patients. In September 1998, Grand Chief Francis Flett of the Manitoba Keewatinowi Okimakanak, an assembly of chiefs from twenty-six communities, called for an investigation of the former institutions, pointing to the issue's national importance: "Canadian society must know what happened to our people, to learn about the pain and anguish we suffered at the hands of people who were charged with healing us" (*Indigenous Times* 1998, 10).

At the same time that tuberculosis sanatoriums were functioning as closed medicalized communities, local health programs were also being developed. In the early 1960s, as part of the postwar expansion of native health care, the Canadian federal government launched the Community Health Worker program, a strategy of service delivery in reserve communities vaguely reminiscent of the training of local catechists or "lay readers" by some missionary groups. The main duties of community health workers involved sanitary inspection and health education under the supervision of more formally trained nurses. Another category of health worker created in the same period for service on reservations was the "lay dispenser," who was, Young reports, "given varying periods of training in first aid and basic drug dispensing to handle minor illnesses in those communities without nursing stations" (1988, 107). Although lacking in formal qualifications or professional licensing, such local personnel were a vital part of the acceptance of biomedical practices and services, especially through their educational, public awareness activities.

One of the ways biomedicine has permanently altered native healing has been by eroding the status of local traditional healers. In 1947 the anthropologist Clyde Kluckhohn urged the physicians attached to the United States Bureau of Indian Affairs to acknowledge the importance of Navaho and Sioux healers as prestigious notables in their societies and to develop collegial relations with them in the provision of health services. Such a step, however, has yet to be made and, as Bonnie O'Connor notes with regret, "will come with difficulty to the tightly hierarchical world of the health professions" (1995, 79 n. 16). Biomedical services were usually established as dominant, formally structured resources without ties to local healers. Largely because of the strict licensing and control of physicians in hierarchical professional organizations, it is difficult for them to recognize indigenous healers as "peers." Just as missionaries perceived "conjurers" as rivals and obstacles to their conversion efforts, physicians have tended to see native healers as, at best, amateurs without professional training or, in harsher judgments, as ignorant paraprofessionals endangering the health of their clients.

Biomedicine has also tended to replace the wider base of traditional knowledge possessed by those providing services within families. This was documented in a follow-up to the development of a "bush kit" program, which began in 1982 among the James Bay Crees. The provision of well-stocked medical kits, training of lay healers to supervise diagnosis and treatment in hunting camps, and a communications infrastructure linking remote camps to nursing stations through bush radios were all part of an innovative program designed to improve health conditions of Cree hunters and reduce the number (and expense) of air evacuations. Only five years after the implementation of this program, traditional healing had declined 9 percent as a strategy used to treat patients in remote hunting camps (Lavallée 1988; Niezen 1997, 29). There is more to be regretted in this trend than the loss of tradition and self-sufficiency. Some Cree healing strategies have practical advantages over biomedicine in that they draw on readily available resources in situations of extreme isolation, as in the use of tamarack resin to close and disinfect a wound or of a hastily constructed sweat lodge to aid an individual in surviving hypothermia after falling through the ice.

The Crees are responding to local perceptions of the importance of traditional healing knowledge by developing a process of piecemeal disengagement from Québec's health administrations and a simultaneous promotion of medical diversity that includes Cree practices. Regional autonomy has made it possible for the Crees to establish claims of medical pluralism. Formal autonomy was implemented through the 1975 James Bay and Northern Quebec Agreement, intended in part to allay Cree resistance to extractive industry in the north and to give the province of Québec greater control over its aboriginal population. Under the provisions of this agreement, schools and hospitals under federal jurisdiction were reshaped into regional native organizations, jointly financed by federal and provincial governments and operating according to Québec's policies and procedures. The Cree Board of Health and Social Services of James Bay, established under this new regime, was, in the first years of its existence, hampered by insufficient government funding, inexperienced administrators and care providers, and the imposition of rules and programs formulated and legislated in the south that often came into conflict with the Crees' geographical isolation and perceptions of healing. For the most part, cultural appropriateness was equated with native personnel, while the local impacts of services based upon a southern model (including the bush kit program) were largely overlooked.

But the attachment of the prefix "Cree" to such agencies as the new school board and health board raised expectations that they would truly reflect regional identity rather than merely exchange one form of external domination for another. Thus began the public scrutiny of administrative action. In the early 1990s the Cree Trappers Association began requesting that greater attention be paid to traditional healing in the medical services provided in remote regions. In response to this request, bush kits are being reexamined for their impact on traditional healing; Cree healing methods are being recorded and cataloged for possible inclusion in the bush kit program; and a manual of traditional medicine for use in the camps is being developed (Lavallée 1991; Elizabeth Robinson, pers. comm., 1995). The clearest example of administrative divestment occurred on 1 August 1994, when the Cree Board of Health and Social Services officially cut ties with the Centre d'Orientation l'Étape, a provincial establishment for troubled youth. The inappropriateness of existing services at this agency was highlighted by a failure to train and hire Cree youth counselors, despite a $300,000 annual budget to do so, and confirmed by a high incidence of runaways, which prompted the decision to intervene. After formal notification, the five Cree youths being kept at the Centre l'Étape were taken to a group home in Mistassini, then flown to a bush camp run by Chisasibi elder Robbie Matthew Sr., who volunteered to spend some time with them both as an informal counselor and as one who would introduce them to the forest lifestyle (Niezen 1998, 108–9).

Regional autonomy only provides the opportunities, not the incentives, to implement such pluralism. Were it not for the popular public sentiment that looked to the traditional practices of hunters and knowledge of elders, it is not likely that Cree administrations would have taken meaningful steps to reform the policies and procedures they inherited from the state. In chapter 5 we will see that the transitions favoring aboriginal self-determination do not in themselves mean that state agencies will be fully divested of control over the policy-making process, nor that the distinctiveness of local native cultures, or even "pan-Indian" movements, will be formally recognized by regional native governments.

SORROW AND FORGETTING

If there is one major failing of biomedicine among native North Americans, it is in its delivery of mental health services. A study led by Spero Manson (1985) concluded that rates of depressive disorder among Native American populations may be up to six times the rate for the general U.S. population. A 1990 report to Congress, *Indian Adolescent Mental Health*, by the Office of Technology Assessment, also found very high frequencies of depression, suicide, anxiety, substance abuse, and "conduct disorders" among native youth nationwide. Suicide, the most tragic and traumatizing manifestation of mental health problems, is particularly high for native adolescents, with 26.3 deaths per 100,000 population, compared to 10.0 per 100,000 in the U.S. general population. Suicide deaths for native ten-to-fourteen-year-olds are roughly four times higher than among all races in the United States (U.S. Congress 1990, 16). At the same time, the resources for dealing with this crisis are seen as being woefully inadequate: "While there are at least 397,000 children and adolescents in Indian Health Service (IHS) service areas, IHS funds only 17 mental health providers trained to treat children and adolescents, a ratio of less than one-half mental health provider to every 10,000 children and adolescents. In total, approximately 1 to 2 percent of IHS's budget is allocated to mental health services for Indians of all ages" (ibid., 1).

In Canada, a statistical profile of native mental health by the Medical Services Branch of Indian and Northern Health Services confirms the high incidence of a wide range of mental health problems in Canada's Indian and Inuit communities: "The mental well-being of many Native peoples is in jeopardy. Overall, Indians are four to five times more likely to die from accidents or violence, and two to three times more likely to commit suicide when compared to the total Canadian population. . . . Alcohol and substance abuse, family violence and sexual abuse are social problems which are currently demanding increased attention within many First Nations communities" (Government of Canada 1991, 57). The general finding for suicide is that "the population at greatest risk for suicide is Indian males between 20–29 years of age who are 4.6 times as likely to die from suicide as compared to Canadian males of the same age" (ibid., ii). The Medical Services Branch report goes on to observe that "the trend in this specific area has been the increase in the number of suicides, attempted suicides, as well as the severity of the attempt" (ibid., 46).

Alcohol and substance abuse are widely considered indicators of poor mental health, often interacting with other psychological factors such as depression, anxiety, and debilitating pessimism about the future. Although there is no reliable measure of rates of alcohol or substance abuse among First Nations peoples, a steering committee's report on the health of First Nations and Inuit peoples found that in Manitoba alcohol abuse was considered a major or serious concern in 86 percent of sixty communities surveyed (Nishnawbe-Aski Nation 1991, 10). Those who are witness to the havoc wreaked by self-destructive drinking find it difficult to describe what they see and even more difficult to find an explanation for it. Anastasia Shkilnyk provides a stark description of the immediate impact of binge drinking in the Ojibwa community of Grassy Narrows, Ontario: "A prolonged binge is like a tornado that tears across the landscape of the community, leaving devastation in its wake. During the binge, infants become dehydrated, children go hungry, women are swollen from beatings, young girls are raped. The consequences of this mode of drinking reinforce the perception of Indian drinking as pathological" (1985, 21).[6]

Mental health crises have reached the point in some native communities that they have become the single most important challenge faced by local and regional political leaders. A prominent example of widespread, endemic crisis can be found in the Nishnawbe-Aski Nation of northern Ontario, a political affiliation of some 28,000 people in forty-nine communities scattered through an area that spans the provincial boundaries, with Québec on the east and Manitoba on the west. In the ten years from 1986 to the end of 1995 there were 129 completed suicides in the Nishnawbe-Aski Nation, 103 (79.8 percent) of which were among young people ten to twenty-five years old. Twenty-one (20.4%) suicide victims were in the youngest age category of ten to fourteen years old. In comparative terms, the Canadian suicide rate for the highest risk category, males from ten to nineteen years old, was 13 per 100,000 in 1991, while the Nishnawbe-Aski suicide rate for this group was 32 per 100,000 in 1993 (Nishnawbe-Aski Nation 1996, 2–3). These suicide sta-

---

6. Kunitz and Levy (1994) in a study of alcohol use among Navaho men and women, which follows up on earlier research done by the same authors in the late 1960s, find that binge drinking of the kind described by Shkilnyk is among the most destructive of several patterns of drinking, none of which has an inevitably catastrophic outcome.

tistics for the native population of northern Ontario are, at more than twice the national rate, indicative of serious social problems, but they belie the fact that many of the suicides are concentrated in a few villages in which epidemics of self-destructive behavior occur in "suicide clusters." During these "clusters" there is an extremely high incidence of suicidal behavior and actual self-inflicted deaths. For residents of these communities, an apparently unbroken cycle of loss, grief, and confusion caused by a series of suicide attempts and completed suicides, often within single networks of friends and relatives, seems to defy both explanation and emotional endurance.

Histories of betrayal of native peoples leading to their loss of resources, political autonomy, and cultural continuity have been documented many times over, and unusually high frequencies of all indicators of mental illness have similarly been widely noted in native communities; but causal relationships between these two circumstances have rarely been confirmed. Solid connections between dispossession and depression are difficult to establish.

A step in this direction is taken by Shkilnyk's (1985) ethnohistorical study of the "social pathology" in Grassy Narrows following the government-imposed relocation of the community to a site that may have been "practical" but was inconsistent with Ojibwa spiritual beliefs and social practices. In a study of rapid social change in Chisasibi, Québec, following hydroelectric construction, trapline flooding, and village relocation, I found statistical evidence in social service records that communities relatively unaffected by megaproject construction had far fewer social service interventions and, on an individual level, those who maintained connections to the hunting lifestyle were comparatively untroubled with depression, family violence, or other indicators of "social pathology" (Niezen 1993). Similar findings have been presented in a global survey of mental health in low-income countries. Dam and resettlement projects, Desjarlais and his colleagues find, "mean not only a loss of home and the identity that comes from a sense of place; they can obliterate generations of cultural knowledge and effort" (1995, 138). There is, therefore, a reasonably clear connection between local histories of dispossession and high frequencies of mental illness, but there remain many strands that can go into an explanation of the more dramatic incidents of community-wide depression, violence, and self-destruction.

Part of the explanation for such crises lies in local histories of unresolved grief that are overlooked by formal helping agencies. One Nishnawbe counselor in Ontario pointed out to me that overt expressions of sorrow and anxiety among the people she works with do not often occur: "We don't say, 'I'm sick. You've got to help me. There's something wrong with me. I need help.'" Such reluctance to go outside oneself for help in the grieving process can be understood by looking at the difficulties some elders recall having faced when a family member died in a remote area of the forest. One such elder told me, "There was one time when we were traveling on a river that goes way up there, Pipestone River. I lost one of my brothers. He was about five or six years old. He was sick and we were trying to come this way, towards Wunnumin, traveling by canoe. But we had to spend the night somewhere [along the river], and that night he died. So it was up to us to make a burial, my parents and siblings who were there. There were a lot of people who had to bury their own family members because people were not together. They were scattered all over." Complications in the grief process have also occurred because of callous handling of deceased persons and their relatives in non-native society. Such was a pattern that one person I interviewed saw in the handling of those who die destitute in southern cities. A Cree nurse in Moose Factory told me about how the body of a man who had died after a life of addiction and destitution in Toronto had been returned to the community: "They opened the coffin, and there's a guy lying in there, wasn't even dressed, lying face down."

On a wider scale, unresolved grief was caused by the unreported deaths of many native patients in Canada who were sent to tuberculosis sanatoriums for treatment from the 1930s to 1970s. Unreported deaths and mass burials in Sioux Lookout were pointed out to me as having occurred during tuberculosis epidemics in the decades after World War II. In some cases, the families of patients who died of tuberculosis in sanatoriums far from the reserve communities were not informed of the deaths, nor were the bodies sent home to allow family and friends the closure provided by mourning and ritual parting. Such handling of the deceased, which portends darkly for the treatment of patients before they died, has also been reported in Manitoba. Following the discovery in the spring of 1998 of several unmarked graves in wooded areas near former sanatoriums at Ninette, Brandon, and Clearwater Lake, Manitoba, Eric Robinson, member of Manitoba's Legislative Assembly from Rupertsland, called on the provincial government to have the medical examiner do forensic examinations of the unidentified bodies in order to "bring our brothers and sisters home to rest in peace" (*Manitoba Keewatinowi Okimakanak Nations* 1998, 1).

The complications of grief in the northern native communities stem from a wide variety of sources: silence and stoicism that worked better for hunters than for those in the communities, the intensity of grief that follows from suicide, the collective emotional impact of death heightened by the technology of communication and dense settlement in villages, a recent history of unreported deaths in sanatoriums, and the desecration of bodies that can occur when a person dies in the anonymity of southern towns and cities. Taken together, these incidents and patterns in the emotional response to death and dying make unresolved grief a significant challenge for any mental health strategy in native communities.

But for all the difficulties one faces in trying to untangle the complex social and psychological background to phenomena such as rampant addiction or suicide clusters, one issue stands out above all others: The system in place for mental health intervention is not trusted, nor are there effective informal resources, such as counseling by elders, that can stop the downward spiral into self-destruction. LaFramboise makes the general point that "most psychological interventions have been culturally myopic and have not accepted assumptions or procedures that could be helpful to Indian clients. Treatment reports rarely account for the functional aspects of American Indian problems, nor do they recognize the efficacy of coping interventions that have been used for centuries" (1988, 393). LaFramboise's overview of the U.S. government's American Indian mental health policy finds that concepts like "mental health," "personality," and "self," are sources of concern to native people who expect more holistic, naturalistic, family- and community-oriented ideas guiding the therapeutic process (ibid., 392). This is confirmed by Theresa O'Nell's study of depression among the Flathead Indians, whose uses of English emotion-concepts such as depression and loneliness are imbued with Salish meaning. "Flathead depression," O'Nell writes, "encircles a broad semantic domain that extends well beyond narrowly defined psychological distress into the realms of moral development, social relations, history, and contemporary American Indian identity" (1996, 8). Those seeking effective ways to improve the well-being of native communities are faced not only with the daunting frequency of severe problems but also the possibility of radically different local perceptions of common psychological terms, and a professional helping system that tends to be medicalistic, individualistic, and does not often include local helping strategies or address the root causes of community dysfunction.

Theresa O'Nell can be credited with the surprising finding that Flathead understanding of depression and loneliness reveals a broad social concern with history and identity, which stands in stark contrast to the medicalistic focus on individual disorder. "Depression, as I encountered it on the reservation," she writes, "reflected far more than a troublesome condition affecting individuals. An essential part of a larger discourse on Indian identity, depression in individual narratives often resonated with one hundred fifty years of loss and betrayal and the moral imagination with which the Flathead Indians strive to make meaning out of that history" (ibid.). There is a sense, therefore, in which depression in native communities can come to represent a form of grieving for a lost tradition which, like other forms of bereavement, can reverberate with a sense of the positive value of suffering. It is no wonder, then, that medicalistic diagnoses often fail to resonate positively with those experiencing depression or loneliness in reservation communities.

The conclusion that a long history of betrayal and loss can be seen in local patterns of depression includes another possibility: the socially articulated experience of depression can result from a sense that significant markers of identity are still extant but unrecoverable, being in the possession of individuals unwilling to share their knowledge. In northern Ontario, the Nishnawbe communities hardest hit by epidemics of alcohol and drug abuse, family violence, and youth suicide seem at the same time to face the greatest complications in the renewal of native identity. In Pikangikum, there is a style of evangelical Christianity that has become increasingly vociferous in its opposition to "non-Christian" ritual, seeing it, as did the early missionaries, as associated with forces of evil and an explanation for the failures and crises faced by their communities. Although evangelical Christians are a minority in most native villages, their readiness to publicly denounce the (re)appearance of local rituals is enough to discourage knowledgeable elders from making an attempt to introduce them to new practitioners. They accentuate a fear that the spiritual energy being revived through the exploration of drumming, singing, dancing, or even the practice of herbology can be corrupted and used for the all-too-human will to destroy. Such concerns are only inflamed by a legacy of missionary declamations against the "instruments of the Devil" and the insidious "evil" of a wide range of curing and divinitory practices. There can be no denying the enthusiasm of those who are reviving the past, some Christian elders feel, but who can say where it will lead? Who knows what might happen if destructive powers become indiscriminately available, outside the restrictions of secrecy, apprenticeship, initiation, and, above all, outside the essential teachings of Christianity?

Such concerns are rarely overtly expressed but still find their way into attempts made by elders to address the problems faced by young people. And as one elder from Wunnumin Lake pointed out, such efforts at providing advice are not often met with success: "A lot of the time church people try to [change young people's behavior], but it doesn't help because they have a different teaching. . . . The school kids, with the language they use, have a difficult time understanding people teaching those things [from the Bible]." The lack of connection between elders and youth is often a result of differing spiritual interests. Christian elders sometimes expressed disappointment that they were not welcome to teach from the Bible to gatherings of youth, while elsewhere elders with knowledge of native ritual did not feel they could reintroduce their practices without stirring controversy.

While many elders expressed confusion and sorrow over their inability to communicate effectively with young people, the youth themselves were often very clear about why they had difficulty listening. In one case, elders who talked about the past were seen as hypocritical, willing to criticize young people for their behavior but unwilling to admit their own faults and to deal with them. A mental health worker in Pikangikum told me, "When I was growing up I used to see a lot of elders out drinking their home brew stuff, and all that. They used to bang on the doors, bust the doors down. What I notice is that they don't talk about anything they caused in breaking things. . . . They don't want to heal themselves in order to heal [others]."

In discussions about strategies for community healing, one of the most striking differences between elders and youth lies in perceptions of tradition. In several communities, informal efforts have been made to incorporate native healing practices as one available resource for counseling service clients. These practices have included pipe ceremonies, sweat lodges, vision quests, and powwows. For some elders, the use of the drum in particular is a reminder of pre-Christian sorcery. The impact of these concerns and the influence of elders voicing them varies from community to community. In Wahgoshig, an annual powwow is attracting increasing numbers of drummers and dancers, while sweat lodges and pipe ceremonies take place regularly without resistance from Christian elders. In Moose Factory there is a stronger base of opposition to traditional healing, but the community still has an informal network of "traditionalists," whose members gather occasionally for ritual observance. In Wunnumin Lake and Pikangikum, the youth have evidenced a great deal of interest in native spirituality, but the actual practice of ceremonies has been vigorously resisted by elders. Young people expressed frustration that this avenue of healing and cultural exploration had been blocked: "The elders, they're against the traditional stuff, the powwows and . . . the drumming. . . . They're very negative about it. . . . And they tell people that this is wrong, wrong religion you're doing. I don't know why. They should just respect each other."[7] According to one younger person, the elders themselves faced the greatest obstacles to healing because of their resistance to traditional ritual: "[The elders] are all still screwed up from way back. They don't really deal with medicine the traditional way. . . . They know it all." This expresses more than the usual remonstrances of youth; it reveals the frustration of those who share few experiences with elders while being blocked from exploring what they see as potentially the most meaningful aspects of their heritage. And at a time when the Christianity of elders ceases to have much sway over youth, and the old/new traditional rituals have become a form of cultural dissidence, many are left without means to deal with personal tragedy and bereavement.

It is difficult to say with any certainty how common this pattern of spiritual dissonance is in native North America as a whole, but it does suggest one reason behind the high incidence of mental illness in so many native communities. Complex local histories of assimilationist policies pursued by missions, government, and medical enterprises are significant aspects of the climate of confusion and low self-esteem in which mental health crises have occurred; and, perhaps more significant, the decline of local healing resources, largely through competition with biomedicine, is an obstacle to recovery when a crisis does occur. In some cases the purging of native healing and spirituality by the combined forces of religious and medical evangelism has been so thorough and rapid that a vacuum is created by the absence of locally meaningful strategies for dealing with the relatively new pathologies of reservation and urban life: alcohol and drug addiction, juvenile crime, suicide and its aftermath, family violence, and various forms of mental illness. These are problems claimed within the purview of formal healing through programs of psychiatric intervention, public health, and social services; but increasingly they have also been handled successfully by native healers who apply tra-

---

7. Another view, expressed by "traditional" elders, though not told to me directly, is that the young often drum and engage in other ritual activity when they are not pure and have not received the blessings and powers that entitle them to perform spiritually powerful actions properly. Such actions are seen in Ojibwa "medical" thinking as putting these young people at risk of harm or sickness (Jennifer Brown, pers. comm., 1998).

ditional techniques to modern forms of crisis. It is where formal medical systems and local religious groups have left room for traditional healers and spiritual leaders to function, where there is a choice of helping services ranging from the biomedical to the performative, that communities dealing with the suffering of a self-destructive youth have the best chances of recovery.

Hearing Voices

Gwich'in Athabaskan Perceptions
of Spirit Invasion and Recovery

Phyllis Fast

Late one night in December 1994 a young Gwich'in Athabaskan man ran in his stocking feet from his cabin to his grandmother's home about a mile away. The recorded temperature that day was −35° Fahrenheit. He was taken to the Gwichyaa Zhee health clinic and immediately given strong sedatives for which he had no current or previous prescription. He was then flown into the nearest urban center (Fairbanks, Alaska) to be hospitalized in order to receive psychiatric care. He told his mother and grandmother that during the months prior to this episode he had been hearing voices that had tormented him for hours on end. I had passed him on the street a few days before this happened and noticed heavy black circles under his eyes that made him look as if he had two black eyes. Apparently he had not been sleeping well.

His mother went to his house the day after the incident and found heavy-metal CDs in his player, a loaded gun on one side of his chair, and the Bible on the other. His grandmother made arrangements with one of the Episcopal ministers in Fairbanks to exorcise her grandson, a process for which the priest was known to have been very successful with other Gwich'in people suffering from similar troubles. Meanwhile, his mother began making plans concerning the house. It belonged to her, but she had moved out years before because she had been frightened by a series of supernatural events in the house, which she described to me in great detail. (One night she heard a sound in an empty room. She went to check, and something grabbed her by the throat. She felt herself being choked. She struggled. It stopped, and she saw no one there. She thought she had dreamed it, but her son confirmed that he had heard her making noise.) When her son was old enough to live on his own, he asked to move into the old house, haunted or not. She acquiesced. After the experience of her son's mental crisis, she had the house burned with all of its contents. In so doing, she was trying to ensure that no spirits could disturb anyone else who might occupy the building. The young man has moved back to Gwichyaa Zhee, and lives in relative independence from his family. He continues to take the medication as prescribed by his psychiatrist. Neither he nor anyone else in his family attend the local Episcopal church, and his mother considers herself to be an atheist.

Ritual cures by Gwich'in medicine practitioners were not readily available to the family for several reasons. For one, Christian missionaries since 1868 had forbidden the use of traditional religious practices in Gwichyaa Zhee. Also, while the mother knew, and in other contexts socialized with, medicine people, the social framework for asking for that kind of help required an investment of time and energy that she did not consider worthwhile. Her choice was based on a combination of her own social position in the village as a member of a family that had once considered themselves to be more white than Indian, and, further, as a woman with a university education: rather than make a social investment in Gwich'in traditions, whose adherents had marginalized her anyway, she simply had the house and its contents burned in order to prevent future spirit entry into the physical world.

This incident involves three cultural explanations of self-destructive behavior. The first is the mainstream medical diagnosis, which assumes the problem was caused by a psychological imbalance located within the body and that the cure would be medication. The second theory is the Christian belief in the Devil's influence on the human soul, for which the solution is prayer and purification of the body and mind of the afflicted. The Christian analysis locates the source of the trouble in a supernatural domain as well as the body of the victim. By contrast, the Gwich'in view (the third paradigm) postulates the presence of bad spirits in a specific geographic location, which invade the mind and body of the victim.

It is hard to tell from this case how effective any of these solutions are, as one of them is still in process and probably will continue for the duration of the man's life and the others have not been tried again, even though the voices persist. He is required to take the medication or lose potential benefits from the health care system, which includes free transportation ($150 per round-trip in 1994) to and from Fairbanks, where he has friends and family. Sometimes the free transportation includes an additional round-trip for a family member as an escort for the patient. Some people in Gwichyaa Zhee make it their business to volunteer to help their sick friends and relatives in this way. As a cure, the Western medical model is somewhat successful and provides economic benefits to a number of people, from the wages of the clinic personnel who now administer his "meds," to the escorts who check on him periodically to see if they can get a free trip because of him. The voices that torture the young man continue to molest him even under the dampening effects of the psychiatric medicine. Thus, in this case, the medical model has merely suppressed the condition rather than removed it; the other theories attacked the perceived cause, although their success is questionable.

Another Gwich'in man in Vashraii K'oo, Alaska, to the north, has been treated for similar problems since 1989. He has been in and out of hospitals several times and has become an alcoholic as well. He has been diagnosed as schizophrenic by his psychiatrist, and his family members try to help by making sure he takes his medications regularly and by checking in on him and comforting him. However, none of them try to prevent him from drinking. His mother also consults Gwich'in and other Native American medicine men whenever she gets a chance to ask for their help. She told me about two of their explanations. The first is that her son is a nascent medicine man himself who is hearing the voice-thoughts of shamanic spirits. One such consultant told his mother that in order to temper the voices he must seek shamanic training.

A second Gwich'in explanation from a different source suggested that the Vashraii K'oo youth is a victim of witchcraft. This person suggested that he or someone in his family has an enemy casting spells on him. This explanation is part of Gwich'in lore about *shan,* bad medicine. Moreover, his mother and her family are part of a volatile group of Gwich'in activists who antagonize many people in their home village of Vashraii K'oo. Hence, they are aware that they have made enemies. She did not tell me if she knew who might cause such trouble or if she had been instructed in counterremedies. In any event, he still hears the voices. In the meantime, this beleaguered young man also provides benefits to his family and friends in the form of free trips. His condition is deemed to be more complex than that of the other Gwich'in man due to the alcoholism. Thus, he is sometimes flown to treatment centers in Anchorage, Alaska, where there are long-term treatment programs for drug abuse and alcoholism. Anchorage is a larger city than Fairbanks, and while there are many more diversions, it is much more expensive than Fairbanks, so escorts are less willing to go there. As long as the escorts can find a place to stay in either Anchorage or Fairbanks, they can stay as long as they want. The airfare is not restricted to same-day travel. However, escort expenses, such as hotels, taxis, and meals, are not usually covered except on days of travel, if then. Thus, the escorts need other sources of money for trips to Anchorage, and few have that luxury. At least the medical solution brings with it economic and social benefits, and, unlike in urban centers, being crazy in Gwich'in does not stigmatize the patients as social misfits or frightening creatures.

The voices produce yet another side effect: they fuel Gwich'in gossip. In gossiping about the patients, coffee-table medicine people conjecture about, retell, augment, and invigorate Gwich'in lore. Ghost stories and explanations of witnessed events couched in magical terms are common in Gwich'in conversations. Thus, the existence of these patients contributes indirectly to keeping Gwich'in traditions alive. With respect to witchcraft, coffee-table gossips can point to any number of disputes between neighbors and recite many threats that include vague allusions to *shan* or other forms of witchcraft.

The voices these young men hear are explained by several somewhat discordant hypotheses. Some of the explanations originate from or at least concur with Gwich'in religious traditions. The Christian theory is similar to the Gwich'in models in emphasizing the supernatural, while the medical paradigm locates cause within the individual. Of all of them, the medical solution is the most successful in helping the patients to tolerate their conditions. The Gwich'in are induced to receive it as well for its economic component. The patients' families have used every solution offered, and they appear to be quite willing to try others as they are suggested. In the final analysis, however, none of the suggested remedies bring absolute peace to those who are suffering.

CHAPTER 5

The Politics
of Repression

The Indians' misfortune has been to come into contact with
the most civilized nation in the world, and also, I would add,
the greediest . . . [, and] to find masters in their instructors,
having enlightenment and oppression brought to them
together.

Alexis de Tocqueville, *Democracy in America*

Government authorities in Indian country during the late nineteenth century expressed views about the ceremonial practices of Indians in their
agencies that often combined paternalistic philanthropy with intolerance
and a readiness to use the powers of the state to eliminate "barbarous"
customs. Little or no effort was made to understand ritual symbolism,
the meanings of songs, or the importance of gatherings. In 1894 Superintendent Waugh described the Northern Ute Sun Dance as being in the
same category as horse racing and card playing, mere "imitations of their
former 'orgies'" that could only be considered "superstitious amusements" (cited in Jorgensen 1972, 23). Themes of sacrifice, suffering,
redemption, and spiritual awakening that often infused indigenous practices with a Christian flavor were overlooked in favor of the unfamiliar
sights, sounds, and smells that evoked derogatory condemnation. The
First Amendment to the U.S. Constitution protecting religious freedom
was not considered applicable to Indian ceremonies, for the simple reason that "religion," outside of Christianity, was rarely seen to exist in
Indians' lives. W. M. McKewen, Clerk in Charge of the Unitah and
Ouray Agency in Utah, was unreserved in his perception that Indians
were without religion: "I have yet to see an Indian who professes or has
any religious belief, or any idea of the Creator and the great truths of
Christianity" (Government of the United States 1886, 448). This is con-

sistent with the somewhat more tempered view of a predecessor at the same agency, J. J. Critchlow, who reported to Congress in 1872 that the Indians "seem to have no settled or definite notion in regard to religion, though they have a general notion that there is a supreme being or Great Spirit . . . [and] believe in an evil spirit who in some way has influence and control over the actions of men, but their notions, as with all barbarous and savage nations and tribes, are exceedingly vague" (Government of the United States 1872, 963).

According to some government agents in the late nineteenth century, therefore, Indians were, in religious matters, empty vessels who expressed, at best, only vague notions of higher spiritual powers and did not believe in submission to a unique deity. Concerns about satanism, which were common in the colonies of the seventeenth century, were generally replaced by the view that Indians lacked essential religious understanding.

But if this lack of understanding were true, then what meaning and purpose could one attribute to Indians' sometimes elaborate and striking dances and ceremonies? These came to be seen as actions that almost deliberately flouted the values of "civilization" and national unity. Even worse, they could be seen as disguised forms of political resistance: If Indians did not have religion, their gatherings must be either debased forms of amusement, or subversion.

The notion that Indians had only vague (if any) understanding of religion was commonly accompanied by an abhorrence of Indian ceremonial practices on moral grounds. The 1886 report of the Indian agent John P. Williamson, of the Yankton Agency, Dakota, is an example of the almost visceral distaste expressed by many agents upon encountering non-Christian celebrations: "Dancing continues on the reservation, much to the hindrance of missionary work, corrupting the young, detrimental to all, perpetuating the wild Indian yell, and in speech and song recounting the horses stolen and scalps taken from enemies in wars in the distant past[,] . . . producing an influence which leads them to believe that such a life is more to be preferred than a life of labor" (Government of the United States 1886, 317). Williamson's frustration in dealing with what he calls "these carnivals of vice" is exacerbated by his failed efforts at suppression: "For two years I have tried by all peaceful means to break up these dances, but have utterly failed. My police cannot do it. My board of advisers have [sic] worked to this end, but have accomplished nothing" (ibid.).

With the decline of Indians as a military threat, and their settlement on reservations, government authorities began to feel comfortable with the idea of using the powers of the state as a tool of civilization. "Strong and energetic measures should be adopted in future dealings with the tribe," stated W. M. McKewen. "They should be made first to understand their own insignificance and the power of the Government" (ibid., 448). The specific policies McKewen had in mind are not expressed, but these are less important than the fact that he bristles with confidence in stating his willingness to use "law and order" to change the "barbarous" practices of the Indians. A slightly less strident tone was taken by the Canadian Department of Indian Affairs in the same year, when it called for the Indians to be "justly treated and so firmly controlled that they will not be a menace to white settlers" (Government of Canada 1886, 1). Part of this control was oriented toward "benevolent solicitude for their welfare and education" (ibid., 5). In fact, as I will discuss in more detail, the solicitude being called for had already found its way into legislation of 1884–85 that made participation by Northwest Coast Indians in their Potlatch gatherings and *tamanawas* dances misdemeanor offenses.

The state was thus ready to intervene in native ceremonial practices, especially when these were perceived as running counter to the welfare of society—the peace and security of the frontier and the prosperity of the Indians themselves. An observation made by Steven Runciman on the suppression of European heresies seems to apply equally well to government responses to the prophetic movements of native North Americans: "Persecution involves the co-operation of the State. The Church by itself has only spiritual arms. . . . It is the State, not the Church, that persecutes and the State that should be blamed for the cruelties of persecution" (1947, 3). State intervention in the ceremonial and spiritual practices of native North Americans, with and without the use or threat of force, has left a legacy of suspicion and secrecy heightened by a sense that the pursuit of religious freedom remains incomplete.

THE GHOST DANCE RELIGION
AND THE SUPPRESSION OF PROPHECY

In all places and at all times humans are capable of radically reordering their perceptions of the universe, the meaning of virtue, and the way to salvation. In its extreme form, the world is seen to be approaching an inevitable upheaval, to be turned upside down in an apocalyptic reversal of things-as-they-are, including, above all, human fortunes and the rewards of righteousness. The expectation of a coming millennium—a term based upon the Christian expectation of the return of Christ after a thousand-year absence in Spirit—was a common theme of European heresy in the Middle Ages; and the persecution of Christian groups originating in heresies prompted many to seek refuge by emigrating to the New World.

Missionary activities and federal boarding school education influenced the prophetic traditions of native North Americans beyond exposure to Christian teachings. During the early period of missionary endeavors, prayer sticks and maps sometimes came to be regarded as "Great Books," sacred objects embodying both the perceived power of scriptural literacy and the integrity of indigenous oral traditions. In seeking to establish themselves as spiritual leaders, many Indian "prophets," including those who stressed a return to the traditional lifestyle, drew upon missionary teachings, combining elements from both the so-called pagan and progressive attitudes.

It was later in the history of prophetic movements in North America that the seeds of government and missionary education programs reached some degree of fruition and had practical consequences for the spread of prophetic revelation. The written word of religious instruction in this context was perhaps more important as an instrument of communication than a source of ideas about sacred power. The influence of practical literacy on the part of a literate native minority is fully evident in the Ghost Dance movement of 1890, which prophesied the imminent coming of an age when the dead would return, the whites would be eliminated in a cataclysm of selective destructiveness, and the lives of all Indians would be returned to a state of bounty and pristine purity. The prophet Wovoka, a Paiute of the Mason Valley in Nevada, placed great emphasis on the visionary quest but was fully aware of the communicative uses of alphabetic literacy, making good use of dictated letters to spread his doctrine.[1] One message was dictated by Wovoka to Cheyenne and Arapahoe delegates who had traveled to receive prophecies and confirm the rumors they had heard of the new visionary. The "messiah let-

---

1. Although Wovoka was the focal point of the spread of the 1890 Ghost Dance to the Sioux, earlier communication and transmission of prophetic legitimacy were at work in the establishment of Wovoka's credentials and in communicating the ideas of the dance to neighboring tribes. Wovoka's father, Tavibo, had been a follower of the prophet Wodziwob, leader of the 1870 Paiute Ghost Dance. Messianic movements of the eighteenth and nineteenth centuries established vast networks of communication resulting in connections and historical continuity between ritual complexes far apart in time and space (DeMallie 1991, xxi).

ter" was written by a young Arapahoe who had acquired an English education at the Indian school at Carlisle, Pennsylvania. The ethical precepts, prophecies, and ritual injunctions of the letter are all extremely
simple:

> You must not fight. Do right always. It will give you satisfaction in life. . . . Do
> not tell the white people about this. Jesus is now upon the earth. He appears
> like a cloud. The dead are alive again. I do not know when they will be here;
> maybe this fall or in the spring. When the time comes there will be no more
> sickness and everyone will be young again. Do not refuse to work for the
> whites and do not make any trouble with them until you leave them. When
> the earth shakes [at the coming of the new world] do not be afraid. It will not
> hurt you. I want you to dance every six weeks . . . then bathe in the water.
> That is all. You will receive good words again from me some time. Do not
> tell lies. (Mooney 1991, 781)

A similar Sioux delegation from the Standing Rock Agency in Dakota
had visited the prophet and returned to their homes in the spring of 1890.
The message they brought with them, that the Great Spirit had sent the
whites to punish them for their sins, and that the time had come for their
suffering to end and for the time of deliverance to be inaugurated, was
taken up with enthusiasm by the majority of the tribe within a few
months. This rapid spread of the movement was largely facilitated by
those who had experienced boarding school education. An Indian post-
master at the Pine Ridge reservation said that there was some talk about
the Ghost Dance by Indians from western tribes that visited the agency,
but that it did not excite much attention until numerous letters concerning the new prophet were received from tribes in Utah, Wyoming,
Montana, Dakota, and Oklahoma (ibid., 819). James Mooney's observation was that, given the fact that the various tribes were isolated upon
widely separated reservations, "the Ghost Dance could never have
become so widespread, and would probably have died out within a year
of its inception, had it not been for the efficient aid it received from the
returned pupils of various eastern government schools, who conducted
the sacred correspondence for their friends at the different agencies, acted
as interpreters for the delegates to the messiah, and in various ways
assumed the leadership and conduct of the dance" (ibid., 820).

The spiritual promises of the Ghost Dance had a powerful effect on
those whose treaties had been broken under the pressure of settlers, railroad construction, and the discovery of gold, whose reservation lands
had shrunk until few could successfully farm there and none could pursue buffalo, and whose rations provided by the government had been

cut back to the point of inducing slow starvation. An anonymous narrator who, during the enthusiasm of 1890, had escaped with about fifty other children from residential boarding school to participate in the dance, told the Sioux anthropologist Ella Deloria about the experience:

> All joined hands [in a circle]. Everyone was respectful and quiet, expecting something wonderful to happen. It was not a glad time, though. All walked cautiously and in awe, feeling their dead were close at hand. The leaders beat time and sang as the people danced, going round to the left in a sideways step. They danced without rest, on and on, and they got out of breath but still they kept going as long as possible. Occasionally someone thoroughly exhausted and dizzy fell unconscious into the center and lay there "dead." Quickly those on each side of him closed the gap and went right on. After a while many lay about in that condition. They were now "dead" and seeing their dear ones. As each one came to, she, or he, slowly sat up and looked about, bewildered, and then began wailing inconsolably. . . . The visions varied at the start, but they ended the same way, like a chorus describing a great encampment of all the Dakotas who had ever died, where all were related and therefore understood each other, where the buffalo came eagerly to feed them, and there was no sorrow but only joy, where relatives thronged out with happy laughter to greet the newcomer. . . . Waking to the drab and wretched present after such a glowing vision, it was little wonder that they wailed as if their poor hearts would break in two with disillusionment. (Nabokov 1992, 254–55)

The simplicity of the prophet's message was soon embellished. Mooney reports that miraculous powers were attributed to Wovoka: "It was claimed that he could make animals talk and distant objects appear close at hand, and that he came down from heaven in a cloud" (1991, 821). "Ghost shirts," made from buffalo hide and decorated with painted designs and long fringes, were worn by some of the men with the expectation that these would make them invulnerable to bullets. The rifles of the American soldiers would be useless. The time of the great transformation was at hand.

Most Indian agents in the Dakota region in October 1890 did what they could to suppress the Ghost Dance. Agent Wright of the Rosebud Agency observed that the dances were peaceful and that none of the participants were armed, but forbade participation anyway "on account of its physical and mental effect on the participants and its tendency to draw them from their homes" (ibid., 847). Inexperienced agents, such as D. F. Royer, locally known as "Lakota Kokipa-Koshkala," or "Young-man-afraid-of-Indians," acted rashly, unsuccessfully attempting to suppress the dance with the police and subsequently calling for military intervention. Agent Palmer of Cheyenne River reported that members of Big

Figure 12. The Arapahoe Ghost Dance of 1893. Photograph by James Mooney. (National Anthropological Archives, Smithsonian Institution)

Foot's band (the eventual victims of the Wounded Knee Massacre) were excited about the imminent coming of the messiah and could not be kept by the police from dancing. The reply to both agents from the War Department was that they should "use every prudent measure to stop the dance and . . . that military assistance would be furnished if immediate need should arise" (ibid., 848). Despite the continued absence of violence among the dancers, military intervention was invoked shortly after the following words were delivered to the dancers by Short Bull near the Pine Ridge Agency: "My friends and relations: I will soon start this thing in running order. I have told you that this would come to pass in two seasons, but since the whites are interfering so much, I will advance the time from what my father above told me to do, so the time will be shorter. Therefore you must not be afraid of anything. . . . We must continue this dance. If the soldiers surround you four deep, three of you, on whom I have put holy shirts, will sing a song, which I have taught you . . . [and] some of [the soldiers] will drop dead. Then the rest will start to run, but their horses will sink into the earth" (ibid., 788–89).

By mid-November 1890, more than three thousand troops had arrived in Sioux country, with headquarters established by General N. A. Miles in Rapid City, South Dakota, the center of the so-called disturbance. Upon the appearance of so many troops, many Indians fled their homes into the "bad lands," the rough, broken country in which the military was less mobile and would have more difficulty reaching them. But the ability of these groups of fugitives—which included women, children, and the elderly—to elude the military was limited, and within a month most had been persuaded to return to their homes in the Standing Rock, Cheyenne River, Pine Ridge, and Rosebud reservations.

The last bedraggled group in the badlands, consisting of about 120 men and 250 women and children, prepared to surrender to the Seventh Cavalry near Wounded Knee Creek on 29 December 1890. They were instructed to pitch their tipis on an open plain where they could be surrounded on all sides by the soldiers, and where four Hotchkiss machine guns could be trained on the camp. As the Indians were giving up their weapons one was said to have drawn a rifle from under his blanket and fired at the soldiers. The events that followed are reconstructed by Mooney, based upon interviews with survivors:

> From the number of sticks set up by the Indians to mark where the dead fell, as seen by the author a year later, [the first] volley must have killed nearly half the warriors. . . . The survivors sprang to their feet, throwing their blankets from their shoulders as they rose, and for a few minutes there was a terrible hand to hand struggle, where every man's thought was to kill. . . . At the first volley the Hotchkiss guns trained on the camp opened fire and sent a storm of shells and bullets among the women and children. . . . The guns poured in 2-pound explosive shells at the rate of nearly fifty per minute, mowing down everything alive. . . . In a few minutes 200 Indian men, women, and children, with 60 soldiers, were lying dead and wounded on the ground, the tipis had been torn down by the shells and some of them were burning above the helpless wounded, and the surviving handful of Indians were flying in wild panic to the shelter of the ravine, pursued by hundreds of maddened soldiers and followed up by a raking fire from the Hotchkiss guns, which had been moved into position to sweep the ravine.
>
> There can be no question that the pursuit was simply a massacre, where fleeing women, with infants in their arms, were shot down after resistance had ceased and when almost every warrior was stretched dead or dying on the ground. (ibid., 869)

The Wounded Knee massacre was precipitated by a fear of the consequences of Indian spiritual revitalization. The Ghost Dance was not seen as a source of inspiration and strength in the unbearable circumstances following treaty negotiation and abrogation, subsistence failure, and a new state of insecure dependency; it was a potential source of insurrection. The massacre was partly the culmination of a series of smaller efforts at suppression. Once the powers of the state were used without hesitation by inexperienced Indian agents to stop the dances, a pattern was established that led the government to more strident measures of suppression, measures that also led participants of the Ghost Dance to an increasingly radical eschatology, more imminent predictions of the coming Apocalypse, and greater resentment of government forces. But the events of the massacre itself show that there was more to military intervention than a perceived threat to the security of settlers. The Ghost Dance was a manifestation of difference, of resistance to "civilization," a refusal by the newly powerless to be dominated and reshaped. And it provoked in the soldiers of the Seventh Cavalry that destructive pursuit of symmetry that lies behind all so-called wars of extermination.

THE POTLATCH LAWS

In 1883, John A. Macdonald, the first Prime Minister of Canada, acting in his capacity as Superintendent General of Indian Affairs, defined the Potlatch in a way that revealed an abhorrence of waste more than a condemnation of non-Christian ceremony. For Macdonald, the Potlatch was "the useless and degrading custom in vogue among the Indians . . . at which an immense amount of personal property is squandered in gifts by one Band to another, and at which much valuable time is lost" (Government of Canada 1884, ix). W. H. Lomas, from the Cowichan Agency in Maple Bay, British Columbia, provides a firsthand observation of a large Potlatch on Valdes Island attended by over two thousand participants from such a wide area that they were speaking several languages. He was impressed by the peaceful nature of the gathering but condemns its profligateness: "One youth alone gave away over $400 worth of goods, being the savings of years, and all to earn the praise or flattery of a few old people, who will no doubt, be themselves entirely destitute in a few years" (Government of Canada 1885, 97). Prohibiting the Potlatch would therefore be a sure way to improve the prosperity of the Indians.

The legislation of 1884–85 that prohibited the Potlatch also targeted *tamanawas* dances for suppression. The term *tamanawas* has a broad meaning, derived from a Lower Chinook word referring to the supernatural power of both shamanic acts and the performances of the so-called secret societies, more specifically the winter ceremonials of the

Tsimshian-speaking groups involving "dog-eating" rites, and initiation ceremonies of the central-coast Kwakwaka'wakw and Nuxalk involving ritual cannibalism. According to Cole and Chaikin, both kinds of ceremony "were expressions of repugnance at practices unacceptable in human society, but were acted out in realistic ways horrifying to white society" (1990, 12). This included possessed novices taking bites from the arms and chests of witnesses and from human corpses.

To the Indian agents, missionaries, and other non-native observers, the symbolism of moral reversal inherent in the dances and rituals of secret societies was not at all apparent, reducing them to spectacles that, according to John A. Macdonald, "[are] disgusting and degrading to the Indians indulging in or witnessing it" (Government of Canada 1885, lv).[2] Even the symbolic aspects of such practices offended Euro-Canadian sensibilities. Legislation prohibiting the *tamanawas* dance was tabled and then passed, even though missionaries and Indian agents had been largely successful in encouraging modifications to the secret societies— the practices that aroused moral condemnation, such as mutilation of the dead, human or animal, had already been eliminated (Cole and Chaikin 1990, 19).

Officially banning the Potlatch was one thing; enforcing the law in the midst of Indian communities more or less united in their defense of "giving" was another matter altogether. A minority of Christian Indians opposed to the Potlatch was ineffective in bringing the law to bear upon those who continued the practice, even though activist non-natives did their best to deepen and exploit factional differences surrounding this issue. In 1898 a set of identically worded petitions signed by the people of Nisga'a, Tsimshian, and Haisla villages on the north coast, probably drafted by the Vancouver lawyer R. W. Harris, was sent to the Superintendent General of Indian Affairs, declaring that their "emancipation" from "the bondage of ignorance, superstition, and barbarism is impeded, and opposed by the custom of *giving away and destroying property*[,] . . . together with its preliminary, and supplementary rites and ceremonies at which the *bodies of human beings and dogs are frequently bitten and mutilated*" (cited in Bracken 1997, 179; italics in original). The rather terse reply from Secretary John McLean was that the department's policy was to let these "festivals" wane of their own accord (ibid.).

---

2. Macdonald's statement refers to the *tamanawas* in the singular, thus raising the possibility that missionaries and Indian agents included a range of secret societies' ceremonies under a single rubric, with moral repulsiveness as the basic common denominator.

Yet the "waning" and "death" of Potlatch ceremonies did not happen through the mere passage of a statute of prohibition. For nearly three decades a modus vivendi had been reached in which Indians more or less discreetly violated the law while federal officials were content to denounce the illegal practices in writing and pronounce them "nearly dead" without resorting to enforcement. Some officials and clergymen were so strongly against the outlawed ceremonies, however, that their patience eventually began to grow thin. They could no longer tolerate a contradictory situation in which practices that were supposed to be illegal and on their way to extinction were actually thriving. A dramatic shift in government practice took place beginning in 1913, when William Halliday, in charge of the Kwawkewlth Agency, began lobbying to permanently eradicate the Potlatch.

Halliday recommended that potlatching be made a summary offense so that prosecutions could take place before a magistrate and in the absence of a jury. Potlatch trials under this new regime could be handled by justices of the peace—and, under Canada's Indian Act, Indian agents had all the powers of justices of the peace. This meant that local Indian agents could prosecute their own "wards" without the usual encumbrances of legal accountability. In 1918 Canada's Parliament took up Halliday's suggestion by removing the word "indictable" and introducing the term "on summary conviction," a change in wording that gave to Indian agents the judicial power to enforce the Potlatch law.

On 21 October 1918, Duncan Campbell Scott, Deputy Superintendent General of Indian Affairs (a position that made him Canada's most powerful Indian Affairs administrator after the Prime Minister), sent a circular to agents in British Colombia advising them that, since the war in Europe had put extreme pressures on the economy, no "wasteful practice" could be countenanced and they were to take advantage of their powers to summarily convict those engaging in the "matter of the Potlatch." As Bracken comments, "In Scott's discourse, gifts are a form of waste, and waste has to be restricted, held in, contained—especially in time of war, which is a time of ultimate waste" (ibid., 210–11).

Ironically, Scott's rhetoric in mobilizing action against the Potlatch did not result in administrative action until the war was over. Halliday began his arrests in the Kwawkewlth Agency in January 1919, with the prosecution and sentencing of Likiosa and his brother-in-law Kwosteetsas to two months in prison after Likiosa married Kwosteetsas's sister with a lavish distribution of property. They were released on bail after their lawyer filed an appeal. In March 1919 four more potlatchers were arrested and arraigned, but instead of receiving a conviction they and seventy-three of their community members signed an agreement to obey the law from then on, and the Crown dropped its charges. In January 1920 the first jail sentences were handed down, with eight potlatchers from Alert Bay pleading guilty. Seven received two months in jail and one, an elderly man, received a suspended sentence.

The expectations of Indian agents that such strict measures would result in a cessation of potlatching activities were not to be realized. Herbert Martin, one of those who served time in prison for attending a Potlatch, remembers that after his two months in jail he and his fellow prisoners resumed potlatching not long after returning home: "They did not stop our ways. We came home. It was good. There were no more arrests [for a while]. After that [there was] a Potlatch in Fort Rupert. The Chieftains were afraid but we all went" (ibid., 215).

Arrests and prison terms were not the only results of government opposition to the Potlatch. In the course of shutting down a ceremony with police intervention many of the material artifacts intended for exchange or ceremonial usage were confiscated, destined for museums in Canada and the United States (see figure 13). One example is provided by Christopher Bracken's report of the aftermath of Potlatch suppression in which thirty-four people were arrested in the Kwawkewlth Agency: "Most of the articles confiscated in the aftermath of the Canmer Potlatch were sent either to the Victoria Memorial Museum in Ottawa or to the Royal Ontario Museum . . . in Toronto. They were not returned until 1979. In September, 1922, however, Halliday sold a number of articles to George Heye, founder of the Museum of the American Indian in New York. By the time McLean [the Secretary of Indian Affairs] reprimanded him for making this unauthorized sale, the property had been moved to the United States. It has never returned" (ibid., 215).

Despite repeated arrests, confiscations, and predictions of the imminent disappearance of the Potlatch, extravagant public acts of "giving away" continued to resurface, supported by a widespread resentment among native people against administrators' lack of understanding concerning their social lives and the symbolism and significance of "giving." The law did not drop from the statute books until Canada's Parliament passed a revised Indian Act in 1951. Although arrests had not been made since it became clear in the 1920s that the free use of the judiciary as a means of suppression was not having its desired effect, the fact that the law remained on the statute books for so long is significant testimony to the desire of many with authority over the native peoples of the North-

Figure 13. Confiscated masks in the parish hall of the Kwakwaka'wakw village of Alert Bay, British Columbia, photographed by W. M. Halliday in 1921 or 1922. (Royal British Columbia Museum, negative PN 12209)

west Coast to enforce unrealistic standards of cultural uniformity, to punish those who brazenly practiced ceremonies that came to symbolize radical difference and a denial of the thrift and progress of an expanding economy, of the virtues necessary to build a nation.

THE PEYOTE RELIGION AND ITS ENEMIES

Another style of intertribal religious reform was less apocalyptic than the Ghost Dance religion, less driven by the urgency of an anticipated universal transformation, more oriented toward individual communion with the spirit world and, correspondingly, toward individual improvement and redemption. But for all its relative quietism and incorporation of elements of Christianity within the framework of distinctly native styles of drumming, singing, paraphernalia, and symbolism, the Peyote religion was not less subject to organized repression. On the surface, one might assume that its opponents felt compelled to act against the ritual use of a hallucinogenic substance, but their motives seem to have run deeper than this, into the dangerous currents of national and tribal identities and the need of those in power to impose a uniform standard of truth.

Peyote (*Lophophora williamsii*) is a small, spineless cactus growing in the Rio Grande Valley and southward into northern Mexico, containing narcotic alkaloids that produce profound psychophysiological (some use the term "hallucinogenic") effects (La Barre 1989, 7). The Peyote religion, sometimes referred to as the "Peyote cult" or "Peyote way," is a very successful intertribal movement, a form of "voluntary association whose rite is one of singing, prayer and quiet contemplation, centered on Peyote both as a symbol of the spirits being worshipped and as a sacrament" (Slotkin 1956, 28). Prior to its diffusion among the southern Plains peoples during the second half of the nineteenth century, it was, for several millennia, used primarily by individuals as a medicine and source of visionary inspiration or, when used by a group, was taken to induce trance states during dancing rites. In this form, its use was more or less restricted to the area of distribution of the peyote cactus (ibid.).

The time and place of the transition from the "peyote complex" to the widely distributed intertribal Peyote religion are unknown. James Mooney (1897) first "discovered" the Peyote religion in 1891 during a wide-ranging research expedition to the Kiowa, Comanche, and Wichita Agencies in Oklahoma. After this, the literature on peyotism grew rapidly, especially as the religion itself spread to other tribes. The first full ethnography of peyotism, Weston La Barre's *The Peyote Cult,* was originally a doctoral dissertation, and, since its original publication in 1938, the book has gone into its fifth edition. The Kiowa-Comanche version of the peyote ritual described by La Barre is characterized by an "all-night meeting in a tipii around a crescent-shaped earthen mound and a ceremonially-built fire; here a special drum, gourd rattle and carved staff are passed around after smoking and purifying ceremonies, as each person sings four 'peyote songs.' Various water-bringing ceremonies occur at midnight and dawn, when there is a 'baptism' or curing rite, followed by a special ritual breakfast of parched corn, fruit, and boneless meat" (1989, 7–8). The Kiowa-Comanche version of the peyote meeting has become, with some variations from one tribe or community to the next, a widespread standard, to some extent facilitated by the process of ethnographic writing, which has been used as a guide to the performance of ceremonies in the absence of ritual experts.[3] One of the constants of these meetings, despite the variations in song and ritual, is the emotional response of participants: "At intervals older men pray aloud, with affecting sincerity, often with tears running down their cheeks, their voices choked with emotion, and their bodies swaying with earnestness as they gesture and stretch out their arms to invoke the aid of Peyote. The tone is of a poor and pitiful person humbly asking the aid and pity of a great power, and absolutely no shame whatever is felt by anyone when a grown man breaks down into loud sobbing during his prayer" (ibid., 50). There is also, according to an anonymous participant, an element of self-discipline associated with peyotism: "Peyotism isn't easy on you like the Bible is. It will be hard on you if you aren't ready for it. We call using it for kicks shooting yourself, because Peyote is loaded and can backfire. You have to prepare to use it. You must purify yourself, be free of alcohol and be in a humble, benevolent state of mind" (Smith and Snake 1996, 66).

Throughout its area of influence, the Peyote religion has encountered a broad base of opposition. Almost all categories of nonadherent, including educated and skeptical agnostics, committed Christians, and "traditionalists," have their own reasons for disliking peyote, including spurious arguments about its effects on the body, concerns about its spiritual effects—often stemming from the belief that it is satanic in origin—and fears that it will erode already fragile local traditions. Peyotists themselves have often tried to deflect such concerns with a broad ecumenicalism, welcoming both Christian and traditional elements in their meetings. Omer Stewart (1948, 6), for example, describes Ute Peyote leaders offering to combine Peyote meetings with Episcopalian Christian services: "The meetings were to be held jointly in the mission church, the white missionary conducting his usual Sunday morning services for the Indians who had congregated and spent the preceding night in a regular peyote meeting in the chapel. To prove their religion truly Christian, the Indians cite the Bible, especially Exodus 12, 8 concerning eating the feast of the Passover 'with bitter herbs.'"

David Aberle's (1991) study of peyotism among the Navaho includes an illustration of political suppression involving local-level factionalism

---

3. La Barre writes in the preface to the second edition of *The Peyote Cult* that his study "has been so far accepted as authoritative by Indians themselves that when new tribes acquire the peyote cult, I am told, they consult the book . . . for the proper ritual details" (1989, xi).

and resistance to "foreign ceremonies" by tribal leaders committed to upholding universal Christian truths.[4] In the 1930s the peyote movement was introduced to Navaho territory, first among Navahos living on the neighboring Ute reservation, then through sporadic meetings in the region near Shiprock, Arizona. By 1940 it had a wide distribution and had caught the attention of the Navaho Tribal Council, which, in its meeting of 3 June, approached peyotism as a serious problem that had to be addressed. The Navaho leaders opposed to peyotism at this time were Christians who felt strongly that this was a dangerous innovation that could only lead to spiritual and social decline on the reservation. The chairman of the Tribal Council, Jacob C. Morgan, a Navaho Christian missionary educated at the Hampton Institute, was the principal leader of opposition to peyotism. In the meeting of 3 June, the peyote issue was the first item on the agenda. The presentations by council members began with unequivocal opposition to peyotism, largely based upon what they had heard of the movement from other sources equally opposed to it. Aberle presents a summary of the views expressed: "Peyotism was regarded as foreign, as leading to extravagant expenditures for peyote, as accompanied by gross sexual misbehavior (especially since peyote was said to enlarge the prostate gland), as a cause of insanity and death . . . and as a danger to traditional Navaho religion. For some Christian Navahos, it was a threat to Christianity. The character of some peyote priests was castigated. Claims of the curative value of peyote were ridiculed, as were claims that it stopped people from drinking. . . . And there was anxiety that peyote would cause the birth of crippled, deformed, or otherwise unhealthy infants" (1991, 111–12). The meeting would have been one-sided, but for a brief statement by Hola Tso, the only person on the council who was a peyotist:

> He defended the cult. He asked for more evidence, for an analysis of the plant, and for medical testimony. He informed people that he had gone to a peyote meeting . . . and implied that he spoke with more authority than others present. . . . He said that he had quit drinking, and indeed had been forced to do so before the peyotists would admit him to a meeting, and listed other former drinkers who were now teetotalers. He said that the harm done by alcohol was obvious to all, and for this reason it was forbidden to Indians [in the Native American Church]. He implied that outlawing peyote could occur only if it were equally harmful, but acknowledged the Council's power to act. He

---

4. The following summary of the Navaho struggle over peyotism is an abbreviation of the contents in chapter 8 in Aberle's (1991) general study of the peyote movement among the Navaho.

implied that fear that peyote would damage Navaho ceremonies was exaggerated. . . . Hence he could not expect respectful treatment of peyotism in this meeting. (ibid., 112)

In the course of the meeting, Morgan drafted a resolution that, after peripheral discussion about making penalties more severe and including bans on other foreign ceremonies, was passed, with Hola Tso casting the only dissenting vote. Ironically, the resolution drafted by Christian leaders bans the "bean known as peyote" because of a concern, invoked several times, that "peyote is harmful and foreign to our traditional way of life" (cited ibid., 113).

Another unusual turn of events in this case was the defense of peyotism on the part of government. John Collier Sr., Commissioner of Indian Affairs and author of the 1930s "New Deal" in U.S. Indian policy, introduced into the *Congressional Record* a survey of the literature on peyote, totaling some four hundred published books and papers, the findings of which showed no adverse pharmacological, biological, psychological, or social consequences of peyote use. The Bureau of Indian Affairs consequently adopted a policy of noninterference with the religious practices of the Native American Church (Collier 1952, 503). Collier also expressed views favorable to peyote in the hearings reported in the 1937 *Survey of Conditions*. The Navaho Tribal Council's 1940 resolution prohibiting the possession and use of peyote placed Collier in a delicate situation. He strongly advocated Indian tribal government and equally recognized the importance of freedom in the practice of native rituals, the Peyote religion in particular; but the 1940 resolution involved a tribal government imposing restrictions on native ritual. Which set of rights was he to uphold?

His decision was that the tribal ordinance should be approved, that given a conflict between the principles of self-government and religious freedom, the reinforcement of political reforms should prevail. In 1944, however, Collier successfully established a policy of minimal enforcement, arguing that the use of federal employees to enforce a restriction of religious freedom would constitute a violation of First Amendment rights, and since Navaho police were paid with federal funds, they were off-limits to the antipeyote campaign. Only tribal employees paid with tribal funds could enforce the peyote ordinance, and the Navaho Tribal Council at that time did not have such control of the police payroll.

This position on enforcement seems to have spread dissatisfaction to all parties concerned. The peyotists objected to the mere existence of the ordinance, while those in favor of its enforcement sensed an intrusion into tribal sovereignty. Frustration on the part of antipeyotists built to the point where they began taking the law into their own hands. In 1947 night raids started taking place in which "a gang of anti-peyotists would descend on a peyote meeting and attempt to break it up, often trying to destroy the altar, seize ritual paraphernalia, and, it is said, to grab jewelry from peyotists. . . . In one case the peyotists were ready, tied up the raiders for the night, and continued the meeting" (Aberle 1991, 115).

Opposition to peyote remained strong. Arrests were made by police paid out of tribal funds.[5] But in 1956, as a result of pressure from peyotists, a new Tribal Council hearing took place. "There were," Aberle reports, "signs of a very small shift of attitude favorable to the peyotists. . . . Two non-peyotists spoke in favor of a laissez-faire policy for peyote. One . . . [who had been in the 1940 council meeting, now] said that there was no evidence that peyote caused death or moral deterioration, or even that peyotists ran about in the nude, as some alleged. There was, however, evidence that alcohol was deleterious, for anyone to see" (ibid., 119). Despite this example of a shift in opinion, the council voted (by a margin of fifty-four to five, with ten or twelve abstentions) only to amend the 1940 regulations so that confiscated peyote would have to be destroyed, a point not covered by the original ordinance.

The Native American Church has since concentrated on taking the issue to state and federal courts and state legislatures, with somewhat greater success. In collaboration with the American Civil Liberties Union, the church led a legal campaign that resulted in the repeal of a New Mexico law against peyote, as well as in having an Arizona law declared unconstitutional. California, however, managed to uphold its arrest of three Navahos in 1962 for possession of peyote under its Narcotics Law, which was then under appeal in the superior court. And throughout the twists and turns of legal and legislative debate, the Navaho tribal ordinance remained intact for decades, upheld by the courts' consistent recognition of Indian sovereign powers that have never been removed. With the continued growth of the Native American Church, and a shift in the balance of power in the Tribal Council between peyotists and nonpeyotists, a point has been reached in which freedoms granted under fed-

---

5. Thirteen arrests resulting in jail terms for peyote possession took place in 1954, at a time when the tribe was paying most of the police salaries, thus meeting Collier's objection (Aberle 1991, 116).

eral law are influencing decisions made by the Tribal Council. Testifying in hearings on the American Indian Religious Freedom Act Amendments of 1994 before the House Subcommittee on Native American Affairs, Peterson Zah, President of the Navaho Nation, acknowledged a "trickle-down" effect of federal legislation: "The tribe is . . . having to amend its tribal laws to accommodate the Native American Church members. So depending on what the Federal Government does, we will also have to coordinate the Act down at the local tribal level" (Government of the United States 1994, 61).

The Navaho suppression of peyotism takes us beyond a simple collision of assimilationist state and church policies acting to eliminate indigenous spirituality. In the Navaho case, the Tribal Council itself originally passed an ordinance prohibiting peyotism, and the government, under the leadership of John Collier Sr., acted to limit the implementation of suppression. Was this simply an anomaly? Was this an extension into Indian political behavior of the Christianizing efforts of the Carlisle school and other residential education programs? The 1940 ordinance cited the dangers of peyotism to Navaho traditions. Was this a cynical exploitation of concerns about loss of spiritual knowledge and continuity by those with little or no interest in cultural preservation?

Or did the Navaho Tribal Council replicate the actions of states in another way: was this an example of protonationalism, of the Tribal Council jealously preserving its symbols of identity and unity from competing transnational influences? Peyotism in the 1930s and 1940s was a dynamic intertribal movement, an early form of what has been called pan-Indianism, introducing supratribal symbolism and organization to those whose local traditions had been lost—or had lost their meaning. A reconstituted visionary movement began plucking thorns from the feet of those who could not find complete solace in either Christianity or local systems of knowledge and initiation. And to those in power on the Navaho Tribal Council in 1940, it seemed to stand in the way of their objectives of shoring up tribal unity and reconstituting a native political entity with new powers and opportunities. The intertribal Peyote religion was understood as a threat to tribal identity, an obstacle to nation building.

Despite Collier's support in the 1940s, the Native American Church has also faced opposition from state governments and the judiciary. In the early 1990s, recognition of the necessity of legal protections for members of the Native American Church was not uniform. While at least twenty-eight states had enacted legislation protecting the transportation, possession, and use of peyote for religious purposes, many others had not, leaving members of the Native American Church in a position of uncertainty and creating, at the very least, a climate in which Native Americans could be stigmatized and marginalized for their religious practices. At worst it fostered such feelings of insecurity as those reported by Robert Billie White Horse, President of the Navaho chapters of the Native American Church: "When we want to pray, we have to look up to see if someone is watching us. That means that we pray in fear. We'd like to be free of shadows that follow us" (Smith and Snake 1996, 70).

One such shadow was a 1990 Supreme Court ruling in *Employment Division of Oregon v. Smith,* which supported the denial of unemployment compensation to Alfred Leo Smith, a member of the Klamath Nation who was fired from his job with an alcohol- and drug-treatment agency in Roseburg, Oregon, for participation in peyote meetings. As Leo Smith remembers, "One Friday afternoon my supervisor called me into his office and asked if I was a member of the Native American Church. I said I was, and he asked if I used the drug, peyote. I said, 'No, but I do take the holy sacrament.' He told me not to, that it was illegal, and then checked up on me on Monday, asking if I had taken the drug during the Saturday night ceremony. Again I said no, but that I had partaken of the sacrament. So he said I left him no alternative but to fire me" (cited ibid., 68).

The Supreme Court decision in *Employment Division v. Smith* held that the First Amendment does not protect individuals who use peyote in Indian religious ceremonies. A significant implication of the decision, pointed to by Aberle, is that "although the Court held that under the U.S. Constitution states *may* enact statutes exempting from general legal prohibitions the use of Peyote for religious purposes, there is no *obligation* for state legislatures to do so, nor of state courts to afford relief" (1991, iii). Walter Echo-Hawk, staff attorney of the Native American Rights Fund, summarized his view of the implications of this decision: "After *Smith,* Indians can be imprisoned or discriminated against in the job place for worshiping God. It is hard to imagine worship by any citizen under a climate of such fears in the United States" (cited in Government of the United States 1994, 120–21). This decision made it clear that previous legislation protecting Native American religious freedoms was in some areas still ineffective, prompting a 1994 amendment to the American Indian Religious Freedom Act that provides greater uniformity in legal protection against discrimination and obstruction of religious practice to members of the Native American Church.

The hearings on the 1994 amendment brought out an aspect of state restrictions of Native American religion that remains unaddressed—the religious freedom of incarcerated Indians. Gaiashkibos, President of the National Congress of American Indians, stated, "As of today no legislative initiative has been offered in the House of Representatives to enforce the First Amendment rights of Native Americans who are incarcerated in prisons across the country. Just as other prisoners' religious practices are respected and honored, so too should the religious practices of our brothers and sisters be understood and respected" (ibid., 51).

This observation is supported by Elizabeth Grobsmith's study of Native American inmates in the Nebraska prison system. Her work is largely concerned with two interrelated themes: the struggle for spiritual freedom and the largely unmet need for appropriate therapy. Nebraska's native inmates have been at the forefront of efforts in recent decades to establish and protect the rights of religious freedom among incarcerated Native Americans. Sweat lodge facilities and spiritual activities in the prison setting are recent products of native activism. In 1974 a legally binding agreement, referred to officially as a Consent Decree, between Nebraska's state correctional system and Indian inmates, which regulates how Native Americans' cultural and spiritual needs are met in the prison setting, was implemented as an outcome of Indian litigation in an effort to limit the state's encroachment on religious freedoms. But, as Grobsmith stresses, prevailing attitudes of prison officials make these freedoms seem tenuous: "Ongoing battles between correctional authorities and Indian prisoners seem to indicate that the authorities comply with Native American requests only when forced to do so by the courts. Conversely, letting up on litigious behavior appears to result in a loss of privileges previously allowed" (1994, 177).

An example of unsuccessful litigation initiated as a result of spiritual restrictions in the Nebraska prison system involves the prisoners' access to peyote. In 1986 Dennis Tyndall filed a complaint against Gary Grammar, then-warden of a Nebraska penitentiary, because of the prison's failure to cooperate in allowing "a limited amount of peyote, subject to all adequate safeguards and necessary inspections by the Nebraska Department of Corrections employees, and [which will be permitted] to remain at all times within the custody of a Road Man [a ritual leader] approved by the Native American Church" (cited ibid., 67). A pretrial conference about the case, in which Grobsmith participated, illustrates some of the difficulties that can be encountered in litigating religious freedom:

> The discussion centered on whether or not we could use the word peyote during the trial. The plaintiffs argued that since Native American Church worship and peyote are inseparable, the term must be referenced. The defendants argued that since there was no mention of the substance in the decree, mention of it should not be permitted in court. My concern about how difficult it would be to discuss the use of peyote in prison without saying peyote met with little support. The judge ordered us to proceed to trial with no mention of peyote and in fact stated that if we used the word in our testimony, we would be declared in contempt of court. (ibid.)

Not surprisingly, the ruling in this case went against the plaintiffs, with the judge arguing that "the potential threat that peyote use in the prison poses to security, safety, and discipline weighs heavily in the balance" (cited ibid., 69), despite the fact that no evidence has ever been presented to substantiate a claim that peyote is a threat to institutional security. This decision makes it easier to understand the complaint often voiced by native social service professionals that the handling of offenders in the criminal justice system is oriented more toward "punishment" than "healing."

TRANSGRESSIONS OF SACRED SPACE

When Cree elder Robbie Matthew Sr. traveled from his community of Chisasibi, Québec, on the northern shore of James Bay, to Boston and Cambridge, Massachusetts, to spend a short time as a guest speaker at Harvard University, one of the things he noticed about this historic region was the predominance of monuments. The cannons left behind by retreating British soldiers in the war of independence standing next to a stone tablet commemorating George Washington's swearing in as commander of the American army were clear markers of historic, even sacred, space. "Maybe if we Crees had left things like this on our land," he later mused, "maybe then it would have been easier to show how important it is to us. Maybe if we could say, 'This is where our ancestors are buried. Here is a statue to show how important it is,' then today our ancestors might not be under all that water [as a result of hydroelectric construction]." This observation brings out one of the most essential and far-reaching differences between native and Euro-Canadian/Euro-American approaches to sacred space. For Robbie Matthew Sr. the inherent qualities of the land that influence human thought and emotion, including the presence in a specific location of ancestral remains, are enough to signify that it is imbued with sacred power. And, in an indirect way, the forest, as the source of inspiration for elders, is the main source of Cree values and spiritual teachings: "Without the forest, the Elders have nothing to teach," says Matthew. "Their learning comes from the forest. For them, that is their book and their blackboard; that is where they get their education." But in the southern cities, people seem to require physical evidence of spiritual presence: a marker or a monument. Material evidence of human achievement, separating the sacred from the profane, seems to be necessary before a location can attain public importance.

Robbie Matthew's perspective comes largely from witnessing first-hand the impacts of megaproject construction on Cree hunting territories: the relocation of his community from Fort George Island at the mouth of the La Grande River to a new, centralized village on the mainland, the loss of hunting lands through construction and flooding, and more specifically, the submersion of an ancient burial ground following the creation of a reservoir by the La Grande 2 hydroelectric facility. The installation of a memorial plaque at the dam site did little to alleviate the impact of human bones washing up on the shore of the La Grande River near the village of Chisasibi.

The Crees of northern Manitoba faced an almost identical situation beginning in the early 1970s, when Manitoba Hydro began construction of a hydroelectric megaproject on the Nelson and Churchill Rivers, causing wide fluctuations in water levels, which in turn eroded burial sites and exposed human remains. Rodney Spence, Chief of the Cree community of Nelson House, told of the impact of this development in a speech in Cross Lake on 25 June 1974 attended by Jean Chrétien, then Minister of Indian Affairs: "Some of our graveyards, camp sites, hunting and fishing and trapping grounds are already under water north of our reserve since the dam was [constructed]. . . . Next week our community is planning to pay our last respects to one of our larger grave sites . . . before it is also flooded. . . . I cannot describe the ordeal my people are going through as the result of this issue" (Mennonite Central Committee 1975, 151–52). In 1998, the same ordeal was being experienced as a result of the same hydroelectric project. At a site on the Nelson River approximately forty miles north of Cross Lake, a burial ground was exposed by fluctuating water levels, and some of the bones washed away. An offer by Manitoba Hydro to relocate the burial site was rejected by the Cross Lake Band Council. Councillor Nelson Miller, in phone calls and memos to Manitoba Hydro, pointed out provisions of the Northern Flood Agreement, signed by Canada, Manitoba, Manitoba Hydro, and the Northern Flood Committee, which promises funding of "mitigatory measures" to protect sacred sites (Government of Canada 1977, Article 7). Manitoba Hydro responded with a small project in which the remains were reburied in a ceremony officiated by a Cross Lake elder, and boulders were transported by boat to secure the shoreline along the graveyard. Meanwhile, other eroding burial sites are being discovered with some regularity in the months without snow cover. The preferred location for burials on the land was once small peninsulas overlooking the river, places now eroding more quickly than anywhere else. Some of these destroyed sites contained the remains of people still remembered by elders in the community. The land is slipping away, literally taking with it the blood and bones of the ancestors and, by extension, one of the few remaining connections the people of Cross Lake have with their past.

Such destruction of burial sites as a result of extractive industry in northern Canada is part of a larger picture of land use conflicts between native peoples and non-native resource developers that have occurred throughout much of the history of European settlement in North America. These situations can be traced to the early perceptions of land expressed by settlers, and to the ways they used land, which largely overlooked native patterns of land use and attachment to sites of spiritual significance.

William Cronon points to several far-reaching differences between Indians and colonists of New England in their approaches to land and resources. Indian villages, Cronon points out, were not fixed geographical entities, either in the northern forests, where a seminomadic hunting and fishing way of life followed the seasonal fluctuations of natural abundance, or in the region south of the Kennebunk River, where agriculture supplemented by hunting, fishing, and gathering was more common. The English approach to land, by contrast, was much more concerned with improving it by labor, with little concern about waste or depletion. Traders and merchants, as has always been their tendency, saw much of the world around them as potential commodities. Stands of two-hundred-foot-tall white pine, for example, were of strategic military importance because of their ideal use as masts and were therefore highly profitable to harvest. But changes in the land did not result exclusively from the extraction of "merchantable commodities." The typical non-native New England household in the seventeenth century burned thirty to forty cords of firewood each year, equivalent to an acre of forest (1983, 120), a pattern that was more responsible for forest depletion than commercial lumbering. A wilderness that could be discovered, cul-

tivated, conquered, tamed, and owned—this was what settlers throughout the New World commonly perceived in their efforts to build new
lives for themselves while expanding the frontiers of civilization.

Cronon's account adds clarity to a wide range of policies and programs affecting indigenous peoples both on the frontier and in the more
recent development of ambitious, complex megaprojects, but for our
purposes it also provides insight into the obstacles native peoples of
North America have faced in their attempts to have land itself recognized as sacred and inviolable. A widespread ethnocentric bias that asso-
ciates religion with buildings, altars, shrines, and monuments has been
a source of numerous conflicts arising between native peoples and
governments concerning control over sacred sites and the free exercise
of native religion. Raymond Apodaca, coordinator of the American
Indian Religious Freedom Coalition, had this to say about government-
sponsored uses of land: "The federal government not only has failed to
protect American Indian religions and religious practitioners from
encroachment, but has, in fact, itself been a participant in or the major
perpetrator of gross and unnecessary interference with Native American
religions and the use and protection of sacred sites. In numerous
instances, for example, the development of forests and other public lands
for recreation or resource development have [sic] been placed above the
needs of Native American religions and practitioners and sacred sites
have been desecrated and damaged or destroyed" (Government of the
United States 1994, 78).

Perhaps the best-known instance in which an indigenous people were
dispossessed of sacred land is the appropriation of the Black Hills from
the Sioux in the 1870s. It is not difficult to understand what made the
Black Hills stand out as a locus of sacred power. The site of an ancient
geological upheaval that pushed the rocky strata far above the surrounding semiarid plains, the Black Hills were, before the gold rush of
the 1870s, a place of tranquil beauty. The peaks of this landform trapped
the clouds that elsewhere swept across the plains, giving the region its
own climate and encouraging a dense vegetation that gave the hills, from
a distance, their dark appearance and their name. In summer, the hills
were a preferred site of spiritual observance: pipe ceremonies, sweat
lodge ceremonies, Sun Dances, and the gathering of medicinal plants.
Adolescent boys, as part of coming of age, would embark on vision
quests, preparing themselves for the experience under the guidance of an
elder, removing themselves to an isolated spot, naked and without food,
waiting in conditions of extreme physical privation for the appearance

of a guardian spirit, suffused in the power of *wakan,* the general animating force of the universe.[6]

Article 2 of the 1868 Fort Laramie Treaty designated the Black Hills as part of Sioux reservation land. This allocation was undisputed as long as the hills were considered by settlers to be without resources and not suitable for farming—useful, in other words, only to the Indians. But the Dakota frontiersmen, restless for new opportunities, were soon spreading rumors of gold in the Black Hills, and in 1874 the army sponsored an expedition, led by General Custer, to determine whether the rumors had any merit. Undaunted by the prospect of trespassing on unceded territory, and observing few indications of Indian presence, Custer's party had time to consider their surroundings. A reporter for the *Bismarck Tribune* was inspired by the hills' majesty and floral richness and wrote to his readers: "No wonder the Indians regard this as the home of the Great Spirit and guard it with jealous care" (quoted in Lazarus 1991, 75), a statement that suggests a broad public awareness of the hills' spiritual importance to the Sioux. The expedition did find gold among the scenic riches of the Black Hills, instantly sparking an influx of prospectors. By the following spring, the news had generated enough excitement to encourage several hundred miners, who defied both the Sioux and army patrols protecting the reservation boundary. The army faced difficulties in performing this task, not the least of which was, as Edward Lazarus points out, the fact that "its officers and men empathized with the miners and were reluctant to take the harsh punitive measures that might discourage the gold rush" (ibid., 79). This, in turn, was part of a more general problem of political will: "What the country lacked, what perhaps any democratic country subject to the pressures of popular opinion would have lacked, was the will and self-discipline to curb its own people" (ibid.). The culmination of this tacitly approved invasion by prospectors was unilateral action by the Grant administration for U.S. occupation of the Black Hills, formalized by a statute on 28 February 1877.

It took a century for the Sioux grievance over the appropriation of the Black Hills to be taken seriously, and for Congress to authorize the court of claims to review the case. In 1979 the court ruled that the Sioux

---

6. There is a vast literature on Lakotan belief and ritual, including John Neihardt's classic rendition of Black Elk's autobiography, *Black Elk Speaks* (1979). A useful short summary of Lakotan belief and ritual is provided by DeMallie (1987); and an overview of visionary practices and interpretations can be found in Irwin (1994).

were entitled to an award based upon an annual interest rate of 5 percent on a principal sum of $17.5 million, starting from the year 1877.
This was not, however, the end of the Sioux's legal battle. In 1980 the
Supreme Court reviewed the case in *United States v. Sioux Nation of
Indians* and decided by an eight-to-one majority that the tribe was due
compensation for the "taking" of the Black Hills, awarding a settlement
of $105 million. Having secured this material victory against the lawyers
of the Justice Department, the Oglala Sioux refused to accept the award,
demanding the return of their sacred land, refusing to give up that claim
in exchange for any amount of money (Prucha 1994, 388–90).[7]

The destruction of sacred sites in the interests of "development" is
not limited to nineteenth-century westward expansion. The most prominent recent example of government encroachment on Native Americans'
sacred sites can be found in a dispute between the Yurok, Karok, and
Tolowa Indians of Northern California and the U.S. Forest Service. In
1972 the Forest Service prepared a management plan for a 67,500-acre
area of the Six Rivers National Forest of northwest California, which
called for the harvesting of 733 million board feet of timber over an
eighty-year period, the construction of two hundred miles of logging
roads, and the paving of a six-mile segment of road between the communities of Gasquet and Orleans. This plan overlooked the importance
of sites in the area for the spiritual practices of Native American tribes,
who had for centuries gone to the High Country for religious purposes,
communing with spirits, attaining spiritual and curative power, and performing ceremonies of "world renewal." The road plan called for construction within a mile of several sacred areas—rock outcroppings
referred to officially as Chimney Rock, Doctor Rock, and Peak 8.

In a legal battle that eventually went to the Supreme Court, *Lyng v.
Northwest Indian Cemetery Protective Association,* the Court determined in 1988 that the First Amendment did not prevent the government from permitting timber harvesting and road construction near
sacred sites. The argument in support of this ruling was that government
actions did not cause an individual to act in opposition to his or her religious beliefs, and that any other decision would amount to a "diminu-
tion of the Government['s] property rights" (Loesch 1996, 355). Thus,
in the *Lyng* case the Indian plaintiffs proved that road construction
would drastically alter the High Country in which sacred sites were

---

7. At the time of writing, this grievance remains unresolved, with the Oglala Nation
continuing to pursue its claim for the return of the annexed Black Hills territory.

located and would thereby destroy their religion, but were told that the Constitution did not protect them from such consequences of government land use. Following this decision, the relevant criterion in determining violations of religious freedom under the First Amendment became whether or not a government action coerces an individual into violating his or her beliefs. The effect of government action on the ability of a particular group to practice its religion became irrelevant to issues of constitutionality (ibid.).

The *Lyng* decision provided an impetus toward legal reform. In 1994 an amendment to the American Indian Religious Freedom Act included a provision for "the management of federal lands in a manner that does not undermine or frustrate traditional Native American religions or religious practices" (Government of the United States 1994). The amendment provides for a process of negotiation with Indian tribes to "identify appropriate land management procedures" in order to arrive at Sacred Sites Protection Agreements (ibid., 191). The issue that remains is whether the government will enter into such negotiations in good faith, or whether the value of the land in question and the corresponding "compelling public interest" will lead to adversarial politics and further destruction of sacred sites. As Steve Brady of the Medicine Wheel Coalition for Sacred Sites of North America remarked, "I suspect that Native American (Indian) religious freedom and right will still be in the criminal courts, litigation and legislative process in the next millennium, even though it is a constitutional right and more importantly an indigenous human right" (ibid., 158).

The two major themes that run most consistently through government suppression of native North American spirituality are "subversion" and "waste." Together, these are a corollary of the notions that Indians lack basic religious understanding and sentiments—that their ceremonies are thus meaningless, misguided, subversive, and/or damaging to health and hygiene, and the land they claim as sacred can only be thought of as not being put to good use. Even the Navaho Tribal Council's suppression of the Peyote religion represented an effort to establish national-tribal unity and uniformity with the tools of a new political order. The Indians' "carnivals of vice" or "superstitious amusements" are seen as inversions of Christian morality. This morality is no longer engaged in a mortal struggle with the powers of darkness but in an equally rousing struggle to secure the supposed virtues of civility and nationhood.

Native Spiritual Traditions and the Tribal State

*The Oklahoma Choctaws
in the Late Twentieth Century*

Valerie Long Lambert

It is well known that the late twentieth century has been an era of nation building for tribes in the United States. On reservations and tribal trust lands across America, tribal leaders have built elaborate, centralized bureaucracies and multi-million-dollar businesses. They have expanded their citizenries even as they have hardened the boundaries around these citizenries by strictly enforcing formal criteria for tribal membership. Finally, with favorable rulings from the courts, as well as by outright purchase, tribal leaders have expanded tribal territories, in most cases far beyond the boundaries laid out for them during the reservation period.

How have native spiritual traditions fared in this new age of nation building? Have the transformations of the past several decades nurtured these traditions, providing new opportunities for their practice and proliferation? Or has the new era robbed these practices of their power and meanings, reducing their popularity in the new Indian nations? Helping shape the answers to these questions, particularly within tribal territories, are the new tribal governments, or "states." To pursue a question raised earlier in this volume about the Cree and Navaho tribes, to what extent have the new tribal states provided room for, or even promoted, native spiritual traditions, creating the kind of pluralism existing among the Cree (see above and Niezen 1997); and to what extent have these states, like the Navaho tribal governments of the 1940s, failed to provide room for—or even inhibited—such practices?

This issue can be explored by considering the case of the Oklahoma Choctaws, a tribe of over one hundred thousand. Using material from seventeen months of anthropological field research that I conducted from the fall of 1994 to the spring of 1996, as well as my personal experiences of growing up in Oklahoma and as a member of this tribe, I will explore the puzzle of why, in the context of an intensive period of nation building that transformed the tribe during the 1980s and 1990s, the Choctaw tribal state adopted a position of hostility toward native spiritual traditions. The clearest and most trenchant expression of this hostility is found in the public speeches of Hollis E. Roberts, a man who was four times reelected to the tribe's highest office. What explains Roberts's repeated efforts to frame himself and the new tribal state as hostile to native spirituality? More than that, what explains the emergence and tremendous growth of a movement in this Indian nation against what is called "Choctaw traditions," a movement that reached its peak in the mid-1990s? My research suggests at least three possibilities. While each reflects the uniqueness of the Choctaw case, these also uncover larger events and processes that may be helping to shape the future of native spiritual traditions across the United States.

The first way of understanding the Choctaw tribal state's hostility toward native spirituality is to see it as part of a larger strategy that the tribal state, and Roberts in particular, may have used to launch and sustain the period of rapid and extensive nation building of the 1980s and 1990s. By framing the tribal state as hostile to native spirituality, Roberts may have been trying to exploit regional stereotypes of Indians (and stereotypes of Indian culture) in marketing tribal economic development projects. In the region that includes the Choctaw homelands, these stereotypes have long associated native spirituality with backwardness. In the late 1970s, in one of his first moves as tribal chief, Roberts began planning and carrying out a series of development projects. At that time, Roberts, who had earlier served as a representative to the Oklahoma State Legislature, began self-consciously crafting an image of the new tribal state, an image he marketed to potential investors and business partners, as well as to the population of the new tribal territory as a whole. Less than 10 percent of the population of the new tribal territory of Choctaw Nation, it should be pointed out, is Choctaw.

Roberts's campaign was enormously successful. By the mid-1990s, revenues of tribal businesses had grown from zero to over $150 million per year. He had also made the tribe the region's largest employer. At least partly responsible for this successful nation-building is the image with which Roberts clothed the new tribal state: that of a major business corporation or, to use Roberts's words, a "Fortune 500 company." In this image the tribal state was professional, efficient, and reliable; it was, to use the words of the former chief yet again, "modern."

This image, or more accurately, the way Roberts chose to market this image, informed and may even explain the derogatory comments he and other members of the Choctaw tribal state made during the 1980s and 1990s about native spiritual traditions. By opposing the tribal state to native spirituality, Roberts may simply have been seeking to publicly oppose the tribe (as a corporation) to the associations of backwardness that accompanied popular ideas about native spirituality in the region, in order to align the tribal state (and the tribe as a whole) with modernity. For an opportunist such as Roberts, the strategy might have seemed superior to other, simpler methods of associating the tribal state with modernity because of the possibility, if not the probability, that the tribe's development projects would by extension be considered backward simply (and only) because they were tribally owned and operated. By adopting this hostile stance, Roberts might have been taking what he saw as a preventive measure. Viewed in this light, the antagonism of the new tribal state toward native spirituality might be understood as a part of a larger strategy of turning racist stereotypes on their heads in the age of tribal nation building.

A second explanation for this antagonism focuses on the Choctaw people rather than their leader. It is possible that the position of the tribal state is simply a reflection of the views of the Choctaw people in the late twentieth century. If so, comments from Roberts and other members of the tribal state that restate or emphasize the official tribal position on native spirituality can be understood as efforts to court the favor of the Choctaw citizenry.

The argument for this second explanation derives from the history of this tribe, particularly tribal members' relationship to that history. It is well known that the Choctaws, as one of what was called in the nineteenth century the "Five Civilized Tribes," adopted Euro-American customs and practices with not a small amount of zeal. In fact, by the end of the nineteenth century, little remained of what might be called Choctaw spiritual traditions.

Very importantly, Choctaws were forced to reflect upon this part of their history, as well as their relationship to this history, in the 1970s when leaders of a pan-Indian movement urged Indians to observe "remembrance of their traditions." At that time, a relatively small number of Choctaws began what they called searching for the spiritual traditions of their tribe. Others—the vast majority, in fact—rejected the quest out of hand. A quasi debate over native spirituality, a debate that helped create a movement against what were termed "Choctaw traditions," continues to the present. This movement reached the height of its popularity during the tribal elections of 1995. What brought the movement to a head was a rumor that began circulating late in the electoral season: that, if elected, the challenger in the race for chief intended to "bring back Choctaw traditions."

From this debate and from the movement against Choctaw traditions, there emerged a hegemony that may bring us closer to understanding why, through four of his five tribal elections, Roberts marketed himself and the tribal state as hostile to native spirituality. Reflecting an American preoccupation with authenticity, the view that had gained enormous popularity among Choctaws by the end of the twentieth century was a view that considered it impossible, even absurd, for tribal members to practice native spiritual traditions because the "authentic" tribal traditions, the traditions of the precontact past, were unrecoverable. As such, the quest for spiritual traditions was quixotic. If Roberts, who echoed popular opinion enough to win two terms on the Oklahoma state legislature and five terms as Choctaw chief, was the politician he appears to have been, he may very well have opposed native spirituality primarily, or perhaps only, to increase his popular support.

A third way that the development of the institutionalized hostility toward native spirituality might be explained is as an unintended consequence of a campaign strategy that Roberts's staff used to procure a second, third, fourth, and even fifth term for their candidate. During election years, which for chief occur every four years, Roberts's staff made their candidate's many successes in creating and managing the tribe's economic development projects and tribal businesses the centerpiece of his campaigns. In this connection, during the early 1980s and again in the mid-1990s his staff contended that Roberts's program of economic development made the race for chief no less than a choice between the past and the future. A vote for Roberts, they insisted, was a vote for the future; it was a vote for "progress" and for "moving forward." A vote for the challenger, they said, was a vote for the past, or more specifically, for remaining "stuck in the past." More than that, they told the Choctaw people, a vote for the challenger was a vote for backwardness, economic dependency, and continued powerlessness.

Against this backdrop, it happened that during Roberts's first bid for reelection the challenger was one of the few Choctaws who had responded favorably to the call for native spiritual resurgence that had been issued only a few years earlier by leaders of the pan-Indian movement of the 1970s. Very simply, the interest in Indians and tribal affairs that had prompted this young man to run for the tribe's highest office had several years earlier prompted him to become involved in the pan-Indian movement's quest for resumption of native spiritual traditions. The fact that few Choctaws had responded favorably, if at all, to this quest may have been something Roberts and his staff exploited to their political advantage. If, for example, in their effort to discredit this man they constructed his quest (and therefore his person) as quixotic—a technique Roberts and his staff also used in the elections of 1995—they may have unwittingly abetted, or even initiated, a movement in southeastern Oklahoma against native spiritual traditions.

Moreover, as a related, unintended consequence, the fact that the challenger in the early 1980s happened to support native spirituality during a campaign that associated him with the past and backwardness may explain how native spirituality itself came to be associated with backwardness—and opposed to modernity—in southeastern Oklahoma. The subsequent antagonism of the new tribal state toward native spiritual traditions might also be so explained as an unintended consequence of a specific reelection campaign from the early 1980s that defined the new leader and his administration in a particular way.

Since the 1970s it has become increasingly difficult to ignore the role of tribal states in shaping reservation-based practices. The new legal and political context of the era of Indian self-determination has inextricably associated the study of Native Americans with the study of Native American tribal governments. Understanding and explaining trends in native spiritual practices during (and beyond) the late twentieth century must begin with the kinds of questions raised elsewhere in this volume about how and why some tribal states have developed policies that support the continued practice of these traditions. The policies of what the Choctaw people have dubbed the Hollis Robert era (1978–96) (and the era itself) may never be fully understood. The same is no doubt true for another interesting puzzle that the Choctaw case presents: why, under the leadership of Roberts's successor, Greg Pyle, who became Choctaw chief in June 1996, the Choctaw tribal state developed and adopted policies that support native spirituality and native spiritual resurgence.

CHAPTER 6

The Collectors

In an anthropology museum the nation could at last prove,
not only that it possesses culture, but that it has the power to
minoritize other cultures. For . . . not only is it said that a
healthy nation has a culture; it also has minorities.

Richard Handler, *Nationalism and
the Politics of Culture in Quebec*

The first exploration and "scientific" study of "primitive" societies in
the nineteenth century were often motivated by a geographical imperative to fill blank spaces on the map and to establish a corresponding
national presence in spaces perceived as devoid of civilization. The
geographical appetite in the expanding powers of Europe and America
were important impulses behind exploration and scholarship.[1] But for
nineteenth-century scholars of the American Indian these blank spaces
were as much cultural as geographical.[2] American Indian religion in particular came to be understood as a source of exploratory challenge, full
of esoteric knowledge and fragile secrets. It comprised a vast, differentiated landscape uncharted by the civilized observer. A sense of urgency

---

  1. As Edward Said notes in his study of orientalist scholarship, "Geography was essentially the material underpinning for knowledge about the Orient. All the latent and
unchanging characteristics of the Orient stood upon, were rooted in, its geography" (1978,
216).
  2. Henry Schoolcraft (1851–60) and Lewis Henry Morgan ([1851] 1962) were among
the first to describe Native American peoples from firsthand experience in the mid-
nineteenth century. With the establishment in the late nineteenth century of such institutions as the Bureau of American Ethnology, the Smithsonian Institution, the Peabody
Museum at Harvard University, and the Field Columbian Museum of Chicago, many more
ethnologists were active, and only several of those who left a detailed record of their activities are discussed here. Of these pioneering researchers, this chapter deals with Frank
Hamilton Cushing and Alice Fletcher, while James Mooney is discussed in chapter 5. Other
notable early studies of Native American spirituality and ceremonies were completed by
Franz Boas (1897), George Dorsey and H. R. Voth (1901, 1902), James Owen Dorsey
(1894), James Swan (1868), and Voth (1901, 1903).

was encouraged by the understanding that this landscape was scheduled for destruction in the interests of prosperity and improvement. In a land that by the late nineteenth century had given up most of its geographical mysteries, Indian custom and mythology became some of the new preferred loci of exploration.

The first anthropologists, or "ethnologists" as they called themselves, to study native societies systematically and at first hand in the late nineteenth century shared a tragically flawed assumption: that native peoples confined to reservations by the westward expansion were destined either for extinction or assimilation into American society. The powers of Progress and Improvement were seen to be such that no primitive race could survive intact. The most humane outcome of this inevitable march of civilization was seen to be the Indians' adaptation to their new circumstances, by their learning how to live as useful citizens in American society: how to be farmers or ranchers, how to ply a trade, how to use money and understand the value of work—by their learning to disappear as Indians. This humanitarian gloss on the situation was more or less confined to what we might call "Victorian America," the intellectual, political, and mercantile elite of the eastern seaboard. The closer one came to actual native communities whose land was coveted by those who perceived a wasted potential, the more did naked self-interest lead to calls for further removal of the Indians, with little or no thought to what was to become of them; and certainly when thought was given to this problem the solution was usually uncharitable.

The reality of this frontier situation is precisely what led to either/or assumptions about Indian disappearance by those with genuine, sympathetic interest in native cultures. First and foremost, though, this presumed imminent disappearance provided a strong impetus to the sponsorship and conducting of research. Ethnologists in the late nineteenth century undertook their expeditions, usually under the auspices of the Bureau of American Ethnology (a research branch of the Smithsonian Institution), driven by the idea that they were to record the customs and beliefs of people destined for upheaval. They became engaged in what has been referred to as "salvage anthropology,"[3] the collection and presentation of data in order to preserve for posterity the cultures of disappearing peoples.

3. Clifford (1988) provides a variety of discussions on the place of "salvage" anthropology in defining tribal identities within the limited framework of "decline" and "resistance."

In the frontier situation of the Americas, several things combined to produce an almost insatiable appetite for the permanent acquisition of artifacts. Objects and observations were seen as imbued with information, often temporarily inscrutable facts that could eventually be illuminated through the methods of science. "Primitive" peoples were therefore the unwitting guardians of the secrets of human origins, the rise of civilization, the sources of human diversity. A new origin myth, legitimated by science rather than ancestors, was hidden in the tales, customs, and artifacts of "savages" soon to be obliterated, it was assumed, by the forces of civilization. Ethnological and anthropological societies were established to coordinate efforts to fill the voids in scientific knowledge of American Indians.[4]

Once under way, collecting became a mission in itself, driven by the urge to complete the gestalts of material and ethnographic collections, to bring by almost any means the entire range of facts and artifacts into possession, into the reach of observation and science. To the collectors in the field it usually mattered little that they were not to be individual "owners" of the objects they gathered. The goal of collecting expeditions was to leave with a sense of completion, to appear competent in the eyes of sponsors from the East, to meet the vague demands of science by digging, bartering, labeling, boxing, and transporting anything remotely of interest, anything with the slightest possibility of revealing permanent truths about impermanent human societies.

One of the most striking features of early collecting expeditions was the extent to which ceremonies, shrines, and grave sites were desecrated by researchers eager to obtain coveted items. Violations of sanctity were usually committed unintentionally, but as Ronald Grimes (1986, 314–15) points out, desecration involves discounting or ignoring sacredness, whether intentional or not: "It is, we might say, a ritual blunder even though the perpetrators may deny that they intended to violate or to engage in a ritual act. . . . It seems to arise in two sorts of circumstances: when one is ignorant of ritual consecration or refuses to admit the sacred as a relevant category." The circumstances in which early ethnological collection and observation took place seemed to have favored desecration of sacred places and rituals for three principal reasons: (1) a hurried approach to collection, in which the fact that many ethnologists did not thoroughly

---

4. The literature on anthropologists as collectors is sparse, but a number of useful studies have been written by Hinsley (1979, 1983, 1992, 1994), Parezo (1985), and Schindlbeck (1993).

study the language or participate in the daily life of the community easily led to violations of the sacred through ignorance or misunderstanding; (2) the scientific pretenses of many researchers and the scientific imperatives of gathering objects and information, which commonly led to a refusal to acknowledge the sacred as relevant to their work; and (3) the strong impulse for researchers to complete a collection that would otherwise have an aggravating missing item and perhaps provoke the disapproval of sponsors and supervisors, which led some to intentional desecration, since these collectors cared less for the consequences of their actions in the field than for their successful return (usually to Washington) with an impressive cargo of manufactured items, skeletal remains, and/or notebooks.

Collecting activities under the auspices of the Bureau of American Ethnology came in three basic forms: ethnographic observations made by taking notes and sketches of routine activities, ceremonies, and narratives of informants; collecting activities involving purchase, exchange, or theft in order to acquire manufactured items; and the disinterment and removal of human remains. Each differs in the goals, strategies, and uses of the material gathered, even though some projects combined all three activities.

Professional collecting has left a complex legacy fraught with moral ambiguity. Libraries, archives, and museum collections are often sources of data for those interested in understanding or restoring indigenous traditions. But a common thread running through much of the early research expeditions to Indian communities has been the violation of sacred places, objects, and practices. In many native communities of North America, the tension between faith and science had far greater implications than a mere shift in epistemology; scientific intrusions brought with them the possibility of radical spiritual disruptions and, eventually, concerted efforts toward reform and redress.

ETHNOLOGICAL COLLECTING

Most intellectual histories of anthropology understandably emphasize the leading figures, whose innovative ideas served as reference points for many others in the discipline; but in the early studies of native North Americans the most significant activities were far more prosaic. The successful ethnologists in the late nineteenth century and early twentieth century were above all single-minded, well-organized collectors. Ethnological collection involved the gathering of information about language, subsistence strategies, ritual activities, myths—anything that could be recorded on a page but not physically transported in a crate. As with material artifacts, preference was given to observations considered rare and "authentic"; anything thought to have been tainted by "civilization" was hardly worth the effort of noting.

Not all early ethnographers working among native peoples were quite so narrow in their approach. James Mooney, for example, stands out as an imaginative and impassioned observer of Indian ceremony, spiritual revitalization, and the wider social conditions forcing changes upon the Plains way of life. His detailed record of the Ghost Dance religion, connecting the various strands of this phenomenon to a wide range of other prophetic movements in North America and Europe, and which includes an unprecedented study of military repression, makes a strong case for Indian self-determination and spiritual freedom.[5] As Raymond DeMallie writes in his introduction to *The Ghost-Dance Religion,* "Mooney's distinctiveness among his colleagues at the Bureau of Ethnology was an unfailing interest in such new developments as the Ghost Dance and a willingness to treat them as legitimate cultural expressions, not mere perversions of influences from civilization" (1991, xviii).

Many other anthropologists in the nineteenth and early twentieth centuries, however, remained focused on the picturesque details of Indian lives, on collecting detailed, on-the-spot ethnographic data, without considering the consequences of intrusions and desecrations among their Indian hosts. The earliest ethnographic observations of the late nineteenth century were rarely informed by theoretical or methodological reflections. Facts were usually seen to be obtainable in the same way as artifacts: one paid an informant or local assistant to provide material to the "experts," who would then engage in the routines of scrutinizing for authenticity, packaging, preserving, and categorizing. In the prescribed procedure, members of such expeditions were to remain in the external encampment and interview through interpreters the Indian men who forayed from the village to meet them. Information and artifacts would usually be exchanged for "trinkets." Rarely did members of the party venture beyond their tents.

One researcher refused to follow this usual pattern and succeeded in influencing the way later ethnologists in native communities did their work. On 19 September 1879, an ethnological expedition that included

---

5. As the son of Roman Catholic Irish immigrants, Mooney would himself have been subject to prejudice and discrimination. His personal background probably contributed to his unusually empathetic understanding of Indian peoples.

the twenty-two-year-old assistant curator of the National Museum, Frank Hamilton Cushing, arrived on the outskirts of Zuñi. This pueblo was descended from the group of villages that comprised the fabled Cíbola, the "kingdom more magnificent than either Mexico or Peru" (Gutiérez 1991, 42) that Fray Marcos reported in 1539, which relocated to the relative security of the mesa tops at the time of the Pueblo Revolt in 1680, soon to descend from these strongholds into a single settlement near present-day Fort Wingate. Despite its illustrious history and the resilience of its inhabitants and their culture through centuries of domination and resistance, Zuñi pueblo in the 1870s was understood by some observers to be earmarked for extinction, under pressure from imminent railroad construction and settlement, making it imperative for the new Bureau of American Ethnology to sponsor a collecting party in order to study and salvage the customs and artifacts of the Indians in their "primitive state" while it was yet possible. What made this site particularly appealing to Cushing was its potential to yield a rich harvest of observations. In a letter written to his cousin in 1884, Cushing compared his ethnographic appetite to that of a bee indiscriminately searching for honey, and went on to describe his obsession in more prosaic terms: "I have to have knowledge of savage life, and it matters less to me where I find it, than it does in what measure I find it. Zuñi, therefore, while I confess it to be a patch of thorns in the side of a civilized being, is attractive to me because of the satisfaction it gives to my craving after savage lore and life" (cited in Hinsley 1983, 56).

Within a week of his arrival in Zuñi, Cushing was to break the tacit rules of the usual pattern of researcher/informant exchange. His youthful efforts to recreate the life and artifacts of the Indian found their way by analogy into his ethnographic collecting in Zuñi. "If I would study any old, lost art," he wrote retrospectively, "I must make myself the artisan of it . . . and anxiously strive with my own hands to reproduce, not to imitate, these things as ever strove primitive man to produce them" (cited in Green 1990, 6). Similarly, he strove early on to make himself the artisan of Zuñi custom, in this case using as his principal tool the reproduction at a personal level of their entire way of life, most obviously by dressing himself in Zuñi clothing (as he appears in figure 14) and learning the language as quickly as his diligent efforts would allow.

Jesse Green describes Cushing's boldness in first gaining admittance to the pueblo:

> Soon realizing how much hostility and mistrust his activities were arousing and how little he could learn under those circumstances, Cushing took the

Figure 14. Frank Hamilton Cushing with a Zuñi delegation in Boston, Massachusetts, 23 March 1882. (Courtesy Museum of New Mexico, negative 9146. Photograph by James W. Black)

unprecedented step of leaving his tent and moving in with the Indians. This was a distinct departure from conventional behavior; while many respectable people . . . had "gone among" the natives to negotiate with them, trade with them, educate them, convert them, or even study them, no scientist hitherto had actually crossed over to live with them. It was a move evidently greeted without enthusiasm either by Cushing's colleagues or by his new hosts, whom he had neglected to consult beforehand. "How long will it be before you go back to Washington?" the Zuni governor, or secular chief, wanted to know, upon discovering the unwanted guest in his home, and was dismayed when Cushing answered, "Two months." (ibid., 4)

Cushing's efforts did not result in instant appreciation of their superior worth or scientific value. His immersion in Zuñi life made him a bit of a curiosity among both the Zuñi themselves and his colleagues in the sponsoring institutions. Greater value was often attached to the work of those able to produce in quantity, with little regard to problems of language or the reliability of sources; and because of the time it took Cushing to immerse himself in Zuñi life, and the division of his commitments between leadership among the Zuñi and his ethnological activities, his literary output was sporadic. Neither the derision of his colleagues nor the entreaties of his sponsors could induce Cushing to consistently produce reports during his periods of residence at Zuñi.

With time, however, it became apparent that Cushing's approach to ethnological collection had distinct advantages. He was, for one thing, able to observe at first hand the activities and ceremonies that attracted scholarly interest. His material, when he did produce it, was rich in detail and possessed the additional advantage of coming from an individual recognized as a trained observer. For better or worse, increased dedication by ethnologists to particular societies came to be standard practice, as research over a longer time frame was seen to add richness and detail to the work of science. The ethnologist was no longer a temporary interloper camped on the outskirts of the village. He or she became an active presence in the life of the community. From this new vantage point the observer had more opportunity to witness and record the rare and secret occurrences of ceremonial life—but at the same time was more likely to violate their sanctity.

Some of Cushing's earliest observations of Zuñi ceremonial life were made in clear violation of the Zuñi expectation that sacred dances were not to be recorded. The first event in which the Zuñi expressed extreme displeasure at his sketching and writing was the Water Dance, an all-day event that attracted Cushing's eye with the dancers' masks and embroidered clothing. Recording this event on paper proved to be more controversial than he expected: "When I took my station on a house-top," Cushing writes in his autobiography, "I was surprised to see frowns and hear explosive, angry expostulations in every direction. As the day wore on this indignation increased, until at last an old, bushy-headed hag approached me, and scowling into my face made a grab at my book and pantomimically tore it to pieces" (1941, 47). He insisted, in spite of this obvious display of disapproval, on continuing with his work, bolstering himself with the thought that "the sketching and note-taking were essential to my work" (ibid.). He was much later to discover the extent to which his recording activities disturbed the community. After he had persistently and blatantly ignored the Zuñi's numerous stern requests to desist from taking his notebook to ceremonial events, a council of chiefs was called to discuss the possibility of getting him to stop or, if all else failed, to dispose of him without provoking retaliation from "Washington." It was decided at this council, according to Cushing, to kill him as a sacrificial victim (symbolically a Navaho) in an upcoming Knife Dance. Cushing, unaware of the council, duly insisted on observing the dance with his notepad in hand. At an intermission in the dance, two masked clowns singled Cushing out from his vantage point on a terrace. "Soon they began to point wildly at me with their clubs. Unable as I was to understand all they had been saying, I at first regarded it all as a joke . . . until one shouted out to the other, 'Kill him! kill him!'" (ibid., 65). Cushing drew his own hunting knife and, after a standoff, was relieved to see the dancers seek out and kill a dog as an alternative to the sacrificial "Navaho." He surmised that with his daring composure he had elevated his standing in the community. "Never afterward was I molested to any serious extent in attempting to make notes and sketches," Cushing says, concluding that this was an important turning point in his career as an ethnologist (ibid., 67).

What Cushing took to be a greater tolerance from his hosts could simply have been a result of his own change in approach to observation and greater command of the Zuñi language, which would have allowed him to better communicate his intentions and the potential uses of his work. As he participated more knowledgeably in Zuñi culture, he also came to share a commitment to the sanctity of ceremonial secrecy, placing himself in a dilemma in which his professional obligations could not be met without betraying personal trust. His early observations, however, provided a public justification of a form of ethnographic desecration, an example of professional resistance to secrecy and sanctity. "From the Zuni standpoint," Green (1990, 7) points out, "the notebook and sketch pad represented a particularly objectionable form of intrusion. With a kind of prophetic wisdom, they feared that copying things down and taking them away in a book was a way of stealing the spirit out of those things." For Cushing and his contemporaries, however, ethnological collecting seemed to possess its own justification: "savage life" was threatened with disappearance, and anything "genuine" that could be noted or gathered would stand as evidence of an earlier and vanishing way of life.

Self-justifying collection dominated research on native North Americans in the first decades of the twentieth century, even though the work of Franz Boas and his students brought about a radical change in the basic assumptions of anthropology, replacing the loose conjectural approach of evolutionary history with a more rigorous method based on more carefully defined boundaries for ethnographic research. Boas stressed the wholeness of cultures and the distribution of such things as language, myth, and the techniques of material culture without the imposition of preconceived evolutionary comparisons. Understanding the distribution of traits took precedence over determining their origins. Boas considered cultural features as inherently unstable, constantly undergoing modification through invention or diffusion from the influence of neighboring groups. The laws of human development were therefore not likely to be found, buried as they were beneath the flux of social life. But historical study on a smaller scale was still important, patterns of human life still possible to be determined (after the ethnological record had been made more complete), the practices and beliefs of single groups reliably studied, and the distribution of features carefully mapped. Boas was confident in the ultimate value of detailed local studies, explaining that "when we have cleared up the history of a single culture and understand the effects of environment and the psychological conditions that are reflected in it we have made a step forward, as we can then investigate in how far the same causes or other causes were at work in the development of other cultures" (1982, 279). The ethnological approach pioneered by Cushing, involving intensive fieldwork in one or several related communities, could therefore be given a new legitimacy (although Boas condemned Cushing's work as unreliable) as the best way to provide the initial information necessary for a classification of cultures according to areas of trait distribution.

Clearing up the histories of specific cultures, however, did not automatically result in any drastic innovation in field method or an overall improvement in relations between the ethnographer and his or her subjects of study. The particularism advocated by Boas and his students resulted in, if anything, an approach of radical induction in which the specific findings of field observation had to be completed before ideas about them could be generated and tested. What is more, this process of scientific recording had to be completed before the culture and technology of civilization were borrowed by or imposed upon indigenous societies, thereby obliterating original patterns of distribution. As with earlier ethnological research, there was a race against time and "civilization."

Field researchers inspired by the short-term goal of mapping and organizing the distribution of traits through accumulated studies of particular societies were usually enthusiastic, persistent, hardworking, and occasionally ingenious, ruthless, and myopic in their gathering of ethnographic material. By the first decades of the twentieth century the study of native North American societies routinely involved expeditions to study Indian life close at hand. Paul Radin, a student of Boas whose distinguished career spanned the first half of the twentieth century, was among the most gifted and perverse of these collectors of Native American language, folklore, and religion. His goal was nothing more than the complete description of Indian lifeways, without even an overarching scientific rationale. Ethnology, for Radin, "need properly have no purpose, any more than a description of the civilization of Greece or England has a purpose, over and above that of being a specific account of a given culture" (1933, xii). His purpose, therefore, was little more than the collector's sense of gratification upon possessing a unit of coveted items; but as a first step it was necessary "to discover some means whereby we can best obtain a complete account of an aboriginal culture" (ibid., xi).

Radin discovered such means in the controversy surrounding the introduction of the Peyote religion among the Winnebago of Nebraska and Iowa. As we have seen, in this religion Christian and native symbolism are combined in a ceremony in which peyote is consumed to stimulate visions, to contact spirits and receive revelations through the powers of the sacred plant. In the summer of 1908 the Peyote religion had been brought to the Winnebago from Oklahoma in a movement that, in its turbulent success, resembled many Christian conversion movements. In many native communities in which peyotism developed, local symbols and ceremonies were sometimes included with the new use of peyote. But the Winnebago movement of 1908 was intolerant of the existing ritual order. Like conversion movements elsewhere, the Peyote religion among the Winnebago, led by the charismatic Road Man John Rave, was built upon a sharp break with the past, with a categorical rejection of the rituals many sensed had lost power in the new life on reservations.

What Radin found as he entered the field was a sharp division between "peyote-eaters" and "pagans," which resulted in an "atmosphere of conflicts and dissensions, where all men's minds were unusually disturbed and perturbed and where feelings and emotions ran high" (1945, 36). To Radin's credit, a detailed description of his introduction to the Winnebago tribe and his strategy for securing a narration of the Medicine Rite is included in his introduction to a translation of the narrative published in *The Road of Life and Death*. Radin's first translator, Oliver Lamere, introduced him to his father, who expressed interest in helping Radin secure an account of the Medicine Rite, "the greatest and most sacred [of] all Winnebago ceremonies" (ibid., 37). The elder Lamere was a member of the Peyote religion; and Radin assumes this was an important part of his motivation in trying to find someone who would expose the secret knowledge of the Medicine Rite to the anthropologist: "undoubtedly he was . . . interested in dealing a deadly blow to the members of this society who were, naturally, the most bitter foes of the peyote-eaters. To induce a member to divulge the secrets of their Rite would, he felt, constitute such a blow" (ibid., 38). This view was seconded by John Rave, who "felt that the publicizing of the [Medicine Rite] would do much toward disclosing its wholly ridiculous character" (ibid., 40).

Eventually three former practitioners of the rite were found who agreed to recount the Origin Myth of the World, the most sacred myth of the tribe, known only to members of the secret society. The three elders who agreed to recount the myth, however, were fearful of the lack of privacy on the reservation and would not recite it where anyone might hear and possibly even summon retaliation from the rival group. So it was agreed that the best place for the "interview" would be a hotel room in Sioux City, Iowa, some twenty-five miles away. Radin was an extremely gifted linguist who, in his first days on the reservation, had mastered the difficult sounds of Winnebago and immediately displayed the ability to write down entire stories and read them back. In his hands, the narrations in the hotel room in Sioux City proceeded smoothly, beginning at midnight and continuing for five hours, until daybreak. When it was over the four men shook hands and caught some sleep before returning to the reservation.

By the next afternoon, news of the trip by the three elders and the anthropologist to Sioux City had already spread throughout the reservation, and the exposure of the Origin Myth of the World was public knowledge. Radin, however, seems to have been unconcerned. He even satisfied the curiosity of those who wanted to hear the Origin Myth, without considering the impact this would have on members of the Medicine Rite or on the wider "atmosphere of conflicts and dissensions" in the reservation. As Radin reports, "The younger peyote-eaters and the older ones who had not belonged to the Medicine Rite soon began pressing me to read to them the text of the Origin Myth. There seemed to me no reason for refusing, and, after discussing the matter with the older men, it was arranged that if those interested would gather at the elder Lamere's house there would be a public reading" (ibid., 39). Not surprisingly, Radin seems to have stirred up hostilities on the reservation. He does not provide details of the aftermath of his first stint of fieldwork among the Winnebago but, in passing, considered it fortuitous that he had to return to his professional obligations in New York, "as time was thereby allowed for some of the antagonism toward my work to abate before I returned the following summer" (ibid., 40).

On his return, Radin used the same strategy of soliciting converts among the "peyote-eaters" to disclose secrets of the rival Medicine Rite. "I told all my numerous and friendly peyote acquaintances exactly what

I wanted and exhorted them to be on the alert for any Medicine Rite member who had recently joined the peyote-eaters" (ibid.). This time he was even more fortunate in his choice of informant. Jasper Blowsnake was a very recent "convert" to peyotism who had previously been an uncompromising opponent of anything to do with peyote. He had detailed knowledge of the Medicine Rite and was willing to recount it to the ethnologist, without remuneration, over a period of two months, working six hours a day. At one point, the narrative Jasper Blowsnake recited points explicitly to the importance of secrecy and the consequences of exposure: "This, too, remember. Never tell anyone about this Rite. Keep it absolutely secret. If you disclose it, the world will come to an end. We will all die. . . . Only misery and catastrophe would result from such conduct. . . . Into the very bowels of our grandmother Earth, must we project this information, so that by no possible chance can it ever emerge into daylight. So secret must this be kept. Forever and ever must this be done" (ibid., 265). The death of Radin's father a short time after Jasper Blowsnake's narrative was complete seemed to give Blowsnake second thoughts about the Medicine Rite's loss of power. When Radin returned from the funeral to begin the task of translation, Blowsnake left the reservation in fear and refused to resume an undertaking that he felt had already resulted in tragedy (ibid., 44). Later, responding to a vision during a peyote meeting that instructed him to finish his work on the Medicine Rite, Blowsnake changed his mind and returned to his task. He and Radin dedicated another three months to polishing and translating the narrative. Radin then returned to Washington to work for the Bureau of American Ethnology. Blowsnake, according to Radin's apparently secondhand account of the sequela to his work, was "ostracized for half a year by the pagan members of the tribe, many of whom were his relatives and his former colleagues in the old rituals" (ibid., 45).

It is difficult to say with any certainty how common this kind of ethnographic desecration has been in studies of spiritual systems. It almost certainly occurred more frequently in the first fifty years of collecting expeditions, when anthropologists were still genuine strangers, their powers of observation, recording, and translation still considered remarkable, their persistent curiosity more provocative of detached interest than timeworn irritation. There is also some truth to the widespread concern that Indian ritual systems were eventually to disappear under pressure from evangelism and legal prohibition; in many cases they did vanish, at least from the outsider's gaze, but were continued surreptitiously, usually without a broad base of community participation, with secrecy built upon secrecy. Nothing was left visible to interest those looking for genuine "pagan" traditions.

By the late 1960s, when Vine Deloria Jr. wrote his famous satirical critique of researchers in a chapter of *Custer Died for Your Sins* entitled "Anthropologists and Other Friends," the most obvious objection to their activities was not desecration but an overharvesting of trivial, obscure material. "Over the years," Deloria writes, "anthropologists have succeeded in burying Indian communities so completely beneath the mass of irrelevant information that the total impact of the scholarly community on Indian people has become one of simple authority" (1969, 87). Few would argue that Cushing's observations of the Kachina Dance or Radin's translation of the Medicine Rite were trivial, yet their activities show that researchers driven by the obsession to collect are prone to lapses in judgment. Some of the first studies of native spirituality are testimony in themselves to deep hostilities caused by the simple act of placing secret, sacred words and deeds into the permanent and public medium of writing.

DESECRATION AND THE GROWTH OF MUSEUMS

The first systematic ethnological observations of native North Americans were closely tied to the collection of material artifacts; the things people made were the most tangible remnants of practices that were extinct or soon to disappear. Products of lost ways of life that could be taken hold of, possessed, admired, were still able to evoke the mystery of those who, in the minds of many Euro-American observers, had to give way to civilization. Some Indian artifacts had special popular appeal for those who did not care to venture into the frontier, providing material confirmation of popular stories from dime novels and histrionic journalism. Simple weapons and tools could reveal to these observers the simplicity and harshness of the lives dependent upon such devices for survival; and sacred objects, such as the altar gods of the Hopi or the buffalo skulls used in Sun Dance ceremonies, may have invoked the prejudices of those who could see only the dramatic waywardness of those living without Christian enlightenment.

It was, as Henry Rowe Schoolcraft stated in a lecture to the inaugural meeting of the Board of Regents of the Smithsonian Institution in 1846, the task of museums to preserve the full array of artifacts or "objects of curiosity" produced by each "tribe and nation" in the country before they disappeared under the tide of settlement. "It is essential to the purposes of comparison, that a full and complete collection of antiquarian objects, and the characteristic fabric of nations, existing and ancient, should be formed and deposited in the [Smithsonian] Institution" (1846, 12). The precise nature of the comparison intended by Schoolcraft is unclear, but his plan was certainly ambitious, covering the complete range of objects and observations that could be collected "valley by valley" from each Indian tribe and deposited in a new "museum of mankind." The museum was intended essentially as a memorial to extinct and disappearing tribes of the "Red Race."

It seems clear that Schoolcraft's ideas were widely shared, generously funded, and taken up with alacrity by ambitious and disciplined collectors at the Smithsonian and elsewhere. The Peabody Museum of Archaeology and Ethnology at Harvard University, founded in 1866, began modestly with a collection consisting of "crania and bones of North American Indians, a few casts and crania of other races, several kinds of stone implements, and a few articles of pottery" (G. Dorsey 1896, 79). Three decades later George Dorsey described the condition of the Peabody, with a new five-story building, as "crowded" (ibid., 81), an indication of the exponential growth of its collections. An initial survey of Peabody Museum expeditions to the American Southwest between 1869 and 1957 reveals that for this museum alone, the activity in this one culture area involved the collection of 200,613 objects in the course of forty-one expeditions.[6]

Among those most active in the collecting expeditions to the Southwest was again Frank Hamilton Cushing, whose activities in the field spanned the entire range of ethnological inquiry. Cushing's acquisition of artifacts during his first years among the Zuñi was every bit as ambitious and insensitive as his observations of ritual. In January 1881 he visited a series of twenty-nine ruins near Zuñi, and he followed this up with a trip, accompanied by a soldier from Fort Wingate, to a set of shrines at a nearby spring to collect a cache of ceremonial objects. As Nancy Parezo points out, Cushing was probably unaware of the continuing spiritual importance of these sites: "Like other early anthropologists, Cushing at first mistakenly thought that objects placed in isolated shrines had been discarded. These materials had the added benefit that they could be collected at no cost" (1985, 767). But professional collectors who removed objects from shrines did not always act in a state of

---

6. I gathered this information from the Peabody Museum's accession records.

ignorance. A letter dated 15 January 1883, from V. Mindeleff to John Wesley Powell, describes the preparations taken for the removal of objects from active shrines among the Hopi:

> On January 3rd we received information from our interpreter "Tom" of a deposit of bowls etc. as offerings on graves. So Mr. Cushing and I went on a little exploring trip. We found the point described and saw a number of Mopue graves with specimens of the modern pottery and basket work laid on them. The locality appeared to be the site of quite an extensive ruin. We found also a sacrificial shrine—recently used as evidenced by the newly painted images deposited on the rocks—the contents of which we proposed to add to the present collection. We shall not venture to take possession, however, until the trading is finished in order to avoid any bad results to our work that might follow in case of discovery. (cited ibid., 770)

Even professional fieldworkers were sometimes so possessed by the "collecting bug" they could not restrain themselves from the theft of exotic objects, items that exerted a powerful attraction because of their use in communicating with the gods.

In the collecting activities of Alice Fletcher, an ethnologist working under Frederic Putnam at the Peabody Museum during the late nineteenth century, we can find an unusual combination of museum collecting and social reform.[7] Her commitment to public service was tied to a firm belief that Indians were rapidly succumbing to the greed of settlers, and that the only way to reverse this process was to assimilate them as rapidly as possible into "American" society. One way, it was believed, that this would be realized was the General Allotment Act of 1887, sometimes referred to as the "Dawes Act" after the senator from Massachusetts who sponsored it, which involved dividing reservation lands into private holdings, or allotments, the idea being that this would encourage Indian families to become industrious farmers pursuing a lifestyle essentially similar to that of their white neighbors. In 1883 the Commissioner of Indian Affairs invited Fletcher to work as a special agent in charge of land allotments among the Omahas, with the material incentive of five dollars per allotment plus expenses. Fletcher worked with great dedication, earning a half-admiring, half-derisive private comment from her friend and field assistant E. Jane Gay, who called Fletcher "Her Majesty" because of her dress and demeanor as she sat at the board table, which brought to mind the image of Queen Victoria writing decrees. In one year Fletcher distributed

---

7. The following discussion of Alice Fletcher's collecting owes a great deal to documents provided by Kimberly Arkin and to her 1998 senior thesis on this topic.

75,931 acres in 954 separate allotments, with 50,000 acres of the Omaha reservation left to be sold to white settlers. (In figure 15 she is depicted conducting the same activity among the Nez Perce.) Thirteen years later, when Fletcher returned to the Omaha reservation, she became aware that the social benefits intended by the Dawes Act had not been realized, that, in the words of Fletcher's biographer, Joan Mark, "the Omahas were not farming their land themselves but were leasing it and living on rental income. . . . It was a demoralized people who were left to cope with every temptation that local whites could offer, especially alcohol and credit. . . . Among even the best intentioned white people, the Indians found themselves having to face 'misunderstanding and a contemptuous sort of pity'" (1988, 265).

For Alice Fletcher museum collecting had some of the same potential to hasten the process of "civilizing" Indians as allotting land had. She saw the removal of significant objects from Indian hands to be placed in museums as a philanthropic act, one that gently removed attachments to a disappearing life and made room for a new era. Fletcher's accessions for the Peabody Museum during 1884 and 1888 include roughly 175 objects, housed in the museum as a loan from the Omaha tribe. By far the most significant items she and her close Omaha collaborator Francis La Flesche collected were the Tent of War and the Sacred Pole of the Omahas.

Fletcher herself was very much aware of the significance of the Tent of War: "The sacred tent of war was vital to the autonomy of the tribe. Without it war and chieftainship were impossible. It gave rank to the tribe among other tribes and caused the Omahas to be feared as enemies and consulted as friends" (Peabody Museum 1884, 411). The tent included ceremonial articles that were sometimes taken into battle, including two war pipes, a staff upon which the elder in charge of the tent leaned when calling men to the ceremonies of the tent, a Sacred Shell containing fourteen human scalps, and the "Sacred Pack" (the mystery of which was not revealed to anyone besides the Omaha chiefs) used in ceremonies when honors were being conferred upon warriors. At the time that the Sacred Tent was acquired by Fletcher and La Flesche for the Peabody, it was clear to them, and to many Omahas, that the tent and its contents represented a way of life that had passed, and that there was little likelihood that proper guardianship could be provided for them. Beliefs associated with the tent, however, were still strong: "If an unauthorized person, an animal, or even an inanimate object such as a tent pole came into accidental contact with the objects, the offending being or thing had to be cleaned ceremonially to prevent supernatural

Figure 15. Alice Fletcher working as an allotment agent on the Nez Perce reservation in the early 1890s. (Idaho State Historical Society)

retribution for the sacrilege" (Hall 1997, 103). The 1890 *Annual Report* of the Peabody Museum makes it clear that these objects were seen to represent an all but extinct way of life: "Since, largely through [Fletcher's] efforts, the people have become citizens and been brought to civilized ways, these objects can no longer form part in the ceremonies of the tribe, and they were given up to her keeping as an acknowlment [*sic*] of the adoption of the new life the people are to lead" (Peabody Museum 1890, 91). Alice Fletcher herself saw the hereditary chief, Ma-hin-thin-gae, who put the Sacred Tent into the keeping of the museum, as having an "extraordinary degree of mind and character," to which she adds, "These noble traits lie at the base of the act that has gently laid these articles among the historical remains of the Indian race; a race of the past, whose only future lies in the possibilities of American citizenship" (cited in Peabody Museum 1884, 412).[8]

8. Nearly a century later, in 1975, the error of this assumption is revealed in a letter from the anthropologist Richard Moore to Stephen Williams, director of the Peabody Museum: "While working with the Omaha tribe at Macy, Nebraska, I have heard many members of the Tribe tell how much they wish these Objects could be returned. Many feel there is a curse on their Tribe so long as these Objects are not in the Tribe's care" (Moore 1975).

Even more significant as a symbol of a "vanishing race" collected by Fletcher was the Sacred Pole, referred to by the Omahas as the "Venerable Man" and described by Fletcher and La Flesche in *The Omaha Tribe* as symbolizing "the unity of the tribe and of its governing power[,] . . . an object they could all behold and around which they could gather to manifest their loyalty to the idea it represented" ([1911] 1992, 217). A story of the origin of the pole gathered by Fletcher and La Flesche from its hereditary keeper, Yellow Smoke, points to its central place as a symbol of supernatural authority:[9]

> A great council was being held to devise some means by which the bands of the tribe might be kept together and the tribe itself saved from extinction. This council lasted many days. Meanwhile the son of one of the ruling men was off on a hunt. On his way home he came to a great forest and in the night lost his way. He walked and walked until he was exhausted with pushing his way through the underbrush. He stopped to rest and to find the "motionless star" for his guide when he was suddenly attracted by a light. Believing that it came from a tent the young hunter went toward it, but on coming to the place whence the light came he was amazed to find that it was a tree that sent forth the light. He went up to it and found that the whole tree, its trunk, branches, and leaves, were alight, yet remained unconsumed. He touched the tree but no heat came from it. . . . When the young man returned home he told his father of the wonder. Together they went to see the tree; they saw it all alight as it was before but the father observed something that had escaped the notice of the young man; this was that four animal paths led to it. These paths were well beaten[,] and as the two men examined the paths and the tree it was clear to them that the animals came to the tree and had rubbed against it and polished its bark by so doing. . . . It was agreed by all that the tree was a gift from Wakon'da and that it would be the thing that would help to keep the people together. With great ceremony they cut the tree down and hewed it to portable size. (ibid., 217–18)

The spiritual power attributed to the Sacred Pole was also apparent from the description of it given by Alice Fletcher in a letter to Frederic Putnam: "It is very old, a queer looking thing, encrusted with a hide with paint and fat, the annointings of the people during a long period" (1888). She adds that "the Washington folk are quite excited over our

---

9. Francis La Flesche's father, Joseph La Flesche, agreed to accept for himself any divine punishment that might follow the revelation of the stories about the Sacred Pole. Almost as soon as the transcription sessions were over, Joseph La Flesche fell ill with a fatal illness and died several weeks later in the very room in which the recording sessions had taken place (Hall 1997, 103). The fact that Francis La Flesche pursued his studies of Indian religion unabated is an indication of his dedication to ethnology and his remoteness from traditional beliefs.

securing all these things, it is a great thing for science" (ibid.). Putnam seems to have agreed, and in the 1890 *Annual Report* of the museum he congratulated Fletcher on her success in acquiring the Sacred Pole and accompanying Sacred Pipe and scalps of noted enemies of the tribe, pointing to their collective overall importance as "an emblem of power and authority" (Peabody Museum 1890, 90).

The official understanding of this event, as expressed by Robin Riddington (1992, 3) who was active in the pole's repatriation to the Omaha in 1989, is that "Fletcher and La Flesche placed the Sacred Pole in the Peabody Museum for safekeeping in 1888."[10] Although subsequent accounts create the illusion that, after four years of lobbying by Fletcher and La Flesche, Old Yellow Smoke finally parted with the object because he was swayed by the logic of the two anthropologists and the evidence of fading traditions, immediately after La Flesche obtained the object Fletcher wrote to Putnam, "Francis when here last month secured the sacred pole from the Hunga gens. This is a great prize. It cost us $45 and it is cheap" (cited in Arkin 1998). Without the Sacred Pole, as Fletcher was aware, the Omaha had little basis for legitimate, culturally sanctioned tribal government. Removing the foundation of the Omaha's tribal identity made the work of turning them into equal "citizens" infinitely easier; the Omaha would no longer have traditional ways to which they could return (ibid.).

Museum collecting, for Alice Fletcher, was more than merely a process of preservation; it was symbolic of inevitable transformations. By giving up the sacred objects for which they had responsibility, Omaha leaders were understood to be ushering in a new era in which these relics of the past no longer had a place. And, reading between the lines, we can assume that Fletcher saw collecting activities as actually facilitating Indian acceptance of civilization and citizenship.

At no time did research institutions such as museums, universities, and the Bureau of American Ethnology have a monopoly on artifact collection. At the same time that professional expeditions were being sponsored throughout the continent, many private collectors used their wealth and leisure to indulge themselves by seeking out exotic Indian objects. Some had practical reasons for acquiring such exotica. Objects of native wor-

---

10. To the Peabody Museum's credit, complaints by Omaha Tribal chairman Doran Morris about the public display of the Sacred Pole resulted in the pole's removal into storage in 1988, and further lobbying by the Omaha resulted in the pole's repatriation in 1989, a year before the Native American Graves Protection and Repatriation Act of 1990 required the museum to return it (Riddington 1988).

ship, for example, were shipped to Europe by missionaries to document the need for their work (Feest 1992, 8). Most collectors, however, were wealthy hobbyists attracted by the romance of owning concrete products of Indian life. One such collector, George Heye, was to go far beyond those merely interested in the strange, beautiful, and picturesque. His obsession began, as he recalls, when he saw an Indian woman working on her husband's deerskin shirt in a mining camp in 1897: "That shirt was the start of my collection. Naturally, when I had the shirt, I wanted a rattle and moccasins. And then the collecting bug seized me and I was lost" (cited in Wilcox 1978, 43). Heye went on to devote the rest of his life to amassing his collection, not only looking for exotica but paying equal attention to commonplace objects of daily use, disdaining only potsherds as specimens not worth acquiring. He built his collection by commissioning field collectors, ranging in status from professional anthropologists to tourists whose travels he paid for in return for the "souvenirs" they brought back from the remote corners of North and South America. In 1916 his collection acquired official status as the Museum of the American Indian, Heye Foundation, and in 1922, having been delayed by the First World War, it opened its doors to the public. Within only a few years it had exhausted all available space in its original building at Broadway and 155th Street in New York; and in 1926 a separate research and storage facility was constructed in the Bronx to house the continuing flow of artifacts and those working on them (ibid., 47).

What might have been the cumulative impact on native spiritual systems of this intensive, sustained effort of acquisition? The use of sacred articles in native spiritual systems varies greatly, as do the consequences for native communities of their removal by collectors. Algonquin hunters of the sub-Arctic, whose spiritual relationship with game animals is grounded in simple forms of ritual communication and personal forms of magic such as drumming and the use of amulets, were not significantly disrupted by the loss of spiritual items; but those, like the agricultural peoples of the Southwest, whose prosperity had been seen to depend upon public rituals and objects endowed with sacred powers that affected an entire community could be deeply troubled by the loss of sacred objects. The Hopi, for example, "objected vehemently to the trading of ceremonial paraphernalia and other objects currently in use. Sacred material was alive, and taking it away from the pueblo would diminish its living substance, leaving the pueblo weaker and less able to survive" (Parezo 1985, 769). In 1938, in an event that presaged some of the present concerns with repatriation of objects of "cultural patrimony," the Museum

of the American Indian returned a medicine bundle from its collection
to representatives of the Hidatsa in a formal ceremony held at the
museum. Vincent Wilcox (1978, 78) reports that, according to the
Hidatsa who took it upon themselves to trace the medicine bundle to
the Heye collection in New York, "the loss of the bundle was responsible for the long and serious drought from which they had been suffering. Return of the bundle was done in exchange for a medicine horn.
The drought is reported to have ended shortly thereafter." It is likely that
many objects with similar power attributed to them were acquired by
private collectors and subsequently lost in a network of purchase and
exchange or housed in museums unwilling to negotiate for their return.[11]

Besides the loss of sacred objects to professional and hobbyist collectors, their inclusion in museum displays has been widely perceived as
another, perhaps more insidious form of desecration. As part of the 1988
Calgary Winter Olympics festivities, the Glenbow Museum attempted
to promote the northern region's cultural heritage with an exhibit originally intended to be called *Forget Not My World,* in which artifacts,
some of them sacred objects, from museum collections in the United
States and Europe were to be displayed, at a cost of $2.6 million. The
Lubicon Cree of Northern Alberta responded with a public boycott of
the show, writing to museums that were approached to lend artifacts and
providing information that outlined the irony of a situation in which the
Alberta government and sponsoring oil companies were establishing a
self-promotional display of native artifacts, supposedly in celebration of
native cultures that were at the same time being adversely affected by oil
development megaprojects in the North. The European Musea and the
International Council of Museums supported the Lubicon boycott, writing a resolution that asked museums to consult with members of groups
whose artifacts they intended to represent in museum displays, and to
avoid including artifacts whose display might be detrimental or offensive to the groups they represent (Carter 1994, 214; Goddard 1991,
143–44).

---

11. Rosita Worl (1998) reports that the Tlingit of southeast Alaska have to some extent
resisted the loss of ceremonial objects, even in the absence of a legal system that recognizes communal ownership of property. Despite widespread economic hardship in their
communities, they have refused to sell their remaining clan objects to unscrupulous art
dealers who occasionally arrive, cash in hand, attempting to negotiate purchases. Offers
for the Tlingit's Whale House objects reportedly have reached $6 million, but the clan
leadership has consistently thwarted efforts to secure sales through individual clan members who have claimed possession of the ceremonial objects.

Native peoples' objections to displays of sacred objects become more understandable in light of Christian Feest's (1992, 7) definition of collecting "as a process by which samples of a complex whole are removed from their meaningful and functional context in order to be preserved under artificial conditions and within a new frame of reference." Moreover, if we take into account Curtis Hinsley's (1992, 15) observation that "the very recontextualization or ordering of objects as a 'collection' constitutes an act of authority over the artifacts and their makers," native peoples' resistance is fully to be expected. Museum displays can involve a complex form of desecration in which objects once important for human prosperity are publicly shown to have been appropriated by a dominant institution, in which sacred power is nullified or distorted by the objects' altered use in a misguided attempt to enlighten, and in which the mystery and secrets of spiritual action are laid bare outside of a meaningful context to the curiosity, apathy, and occasionally even derision of the museum-going public.

BONES AND SPIRITS

Displaying some form of respect for the remains of the dead is a human universal. Every society acknowledges the loss of life in ritual and, wherever possible, gathers human remains together in places that become imbued with sanctity through the memory or sometimes the tangible presence of Spirit. Native peoples everywhere have attached importance to ancestors as sources of knowledge and mythical heroism, and grave sites are natural reminders of their influence. Even though the sites themselves have not always been designated with markers or monuments, and even though ancestors may not be remembered individually, those who venture there are usually aware of, if nothing else, a sanctity that makes itself felt in the presence of the dead.

Those who visit grave sites with scientific pretensions, however, seem to be immune from perceptions of social meaning beyond the bones themselves. Grimes (1986, 316), for example, makes a revealing summary of his experience with osteological collection: "Most digs that I know anything about are not noted for their air of sanctity but rather for their sweat, bawdy humor, and iconoclasm. . . . We approach grave sites in a state of ritual ignorance; we may not even know . . . how to display respect." Science is somehow exempt from the perception or understanding of the sacred, even in the manipulation of human remains. Archaeology began with a scientific model of detachment that influenced the behavior of those working in native burial sites, one consistent with the medicalization and institutional suspension of mourning in the process of dying that developed in nineteenth-century Europe and America.

This is not to say that the collection of bones always proceeded with scientific regularity. There was, as in most forms of research, plenty of room for untidiness, especially in the early expeditions in which method was not yet fully defined. F. W. Hodge (1931) claims to have observed conduct in an expedition directed by Cushing that calls into question the professionalism of his collecting activities: "Under Cushing's directions all the collections from the Zuñi sites were in charge of Charles A. Garlick, a kind of camp foreman who paid little attention to them even when sober. . . . I well recall that in packing the skeletal material for shipment to Washington, he did not hesitate to discard any bones that did not readily go in the cases!"

And, as with the acquisition of artisanal objects, there were nonprofessional collectors of human remains who pursued their activities under questionable circumstances. In congressional hearings on a law that would establish the National American Indian Museum, Senator Daniel Inouye of Hawaii explained how, in the nineteenth century, the army surgeon general issued directives to his troops to acquire skeletal remains from burial grounds and the battlefield: "Sacred Indian burial grounds were desecrated, recently killed Indians were stripped of their flesh, and their skulls and remains were shipped to Washington" (U.S. Congress 1987, 1). Senator Inouye, as will be discussed below, introduced legislation to create the National American Indian Museum in large part to address the discovery that skeletal remains acquired in this manner were part of the Smithsonian Institution's osteological collection.

No matter what their degree of professionalism or iconoclasm, the greatest impact of osteological expeditions has been quite simply the removal of human remains from burial sites to the inaccessible storage facilities of research institutions. In roughly one hundred years, from the mid-nineteenth century to the mid-twentieth, hundreds of thousands of human remains were uncovered, labeled, boxed, shipped, accessioned, and stored for possible future examination. Today, of the 300,000 items of human remains stored in federal institutions in the United States, 99 percent are of Native American origin (Bowman 1989, 149). Throughout the process of collecting this astonishing number of remains, surprisingly little attention was paid to whether or not grave sites were active. The goals of science were put before all else. In a usually tacit and occasionally explicit rationalization that seems to be invoked in many cases of questionable institutional ethics, it was understood that the rights and dignity of the few could be sacrificed for a greater service to humanity.

Such universal benefits of osteological research are invoked by Jaymie Brauer (1992, 38) in an impassioned defense of her profession: "In this age of multiculturalism, there is a global move toward the universal rights of a common humanity. Understanding the past, how we lived and adapted to the world, is key to determining the direction of our survival as a species." Brauer points to several advances in osteoarchaeology that hold much promise for wide service to humanity, including those in molecular genetics, epidemiology, and forensics. The return of osteological collections to those interested in recovering tribal remains would therefore result in an "irrevocable loss of unique scientific information" (ibid.).

For those to whom institutional bone collections represent the appropriated remains of ancestors, there is a hollow ring to this argument. Native American protest against the behavior of archaeologists took place in the early mobilizations of the Civil Rights movement. In 1971, members of the American Indian Movement (AIM) disrupted a dig outside Minneapolis–St. Paul. The issue, as Grimes (1986, 305) points out, was a simple matter of respect: "Even though there were no burials at the site, the symbolism of the confrontation was important to A.I.M. members who felt the excavation was proceeding without consideration of Native values and beliefs." The indignation of many who see the remains of recognized ancestors being stored and manipulated without consent is expressed by Gerald Vizenor: "These bone barons protect their 'rights' to advance science and careers on the backs of tribal bones. The tribal dead become the academic chattel, the aboriginal bone slaves to advance archaeological technicism and the political power of institutional science" (1986, 322). He goes on to argue in a more even tone that "the power of academic institutions and the freedom demanded by archaeologists and anthropologists to conduct their research has been the loss of tribal rights, and the rights of human remains" (ibid., 325). No scientific benefit to humankind, if we take this view further, can justify the violation of rights that has occurred in the desecration of burial sites. A future in which science proceeds without ethical limitations should be of greater concern than a future without the discoveries it might achieve.

REPATRIATION

If we define repatriation in a broad sense, as the return of knowledge and material to those from whom they originated, one of the most enduring accomplishments of ethnological collecting will have been enabling the recovery of traditions for some tribes attempting to redefine an identity. The repatriation of written accounts of language, mythology, or ritual is possible simply by finding and consulting the relevant documents. McIlwraith's (1948) two-volume ethnography of the Bella Coola (Nuxalk) Indians of British Columbia, the research for which was conducted from 1922 to 1924, is an example of a document resulting from classic ethnographic research methods being used as a reference for cultural preservation; Stutwinii, writing on behalf of those among whom McIlwraith worked, expressed strong appreciation of his ethnographic legacy: "We are thoroughly grateful and thankful for the writings of T. F. McIlwraith. His recording of our history continues to affect our people today and will lead to better understanding tomorrow. We have been given a tool with which to rebuild and renew that which was almost lost or forgotten" (1992, vii). Not every community looking to the practices of its ancestors, as represented by ethnographers, for spiritual renewal is fortunate enough to have comprehensive, reliable documents to refer to. Accurate information reflecting a consensus of opinion among active members of a community is probably much less common than what Vine Deloria Jr. describes as "the popular drivel that increasingly comes to represent Indians" (1991, 460).

But of course more difficult repatriation issues stem from the bones and objects that are not part of the public domain, that are "owned," prized, and protected by institutions. A bill introduced to Congress in 1987 by Senator Inouye, the National American Indian Museum and Memorial Act, was part of an effort to address the need to repatriate objects acquired from Native Americans and Native Hawaiians through questionable means. This bill was to transfer the substantial Heye collection, floundering without adequate storage or exhibition facilities in New York, to the Smithsonian Institution and, at the same time, establish museum facilities on the Mall in Washington, D.C., and in New York City devoted to the history and culture of Native Americans. While offering tremendous opportunities to both the Heye Foundation, holding the largest, most valuable collection of Native American artifacts in the world, and the Smithsonian Institution, with its unparalleled location and facilities, Senator Inouye shrewdly included a demand for repatriation in the legislation for the proposed museum. In his introduction to the legislation he pointed out the questionable means by which many items in both museum collections were acquired, in particular the Smithsonian's collection of human remains. One of his goals was therefore to "assure the repatriation of those remains that could be identified as being associated with a particular tribe or specific region of Indian country, and a proper resting place for those remains of Native Americans that could not be so identified" (U.S. Congress 1987, 2). The bill, signed into law in November 1989, requires the Smithsonian Institution to follow procedures for identifying remains, provide an inventory, and consult with native leaders concerning the action to be taken with them.

In November 1990 another piece of legislation, the Native American Grave Protection and Repatriation Act (NAGPRA), applied the obligations established for the Smithsonian Institution to all federal agencies and museums receiving federal funding. Museums were required to prepare an itemization for human remains and associated funerary objects and more general "written summaries" for unassociated funerary objects, sacred objects, and "items of cultural patrimony." NAGPRA requires repatriation when federally recognized American Indian and Native Hawaiian groups can make a case for right of possession of human remains and cultural items that meet the loose criteria established for "sacred objects" or items of "cultural patrimony" (Thomas 1991, 10).[12] The Smithsonian Institution, for reasons that are not fully clear, is specifically exempted from NAGPRA, and Senator Inouye's intention to rectify this situation within a year of the law's passage has not been fulfilled. The Smithsonian has, however, established its own "Policy on Native American Human Remains and Cultural Materials," which, as of February 1995, has led to the return of approximately two hundred items from its collection of human remains (Saum 1995, 47).

Repatriation of museum holdings has in some instances led to positive change in relations between native peoples and museum workers, with dialogue over the return of objects resulting in more detailed knowledge about the social context in which objects are used. Exchange of information can lead to fuller understanding by non-native "experts" of sacred objects and their places in ritual observance. The Hopi tribe, for example, made a request to Harvard University's Peabody Museum of Archaeology and Ethnology for the return of a set of wooden sunflowers that were, according to the claim, culturally and religiously significant. To museum personnel the idea that these objects were not simply

12. "Sacred objects" are defined in NAGPRA as "specific ceremonial objects which are needed by traditional Native American religious leaders for the practice of traditional Native American religions by their present day adherents" (U.S. Congress 1991, 11), while objects of "cultural patrimony" are defined as "having ongoing historical, traditional, or cultural importance central to the Native American group or culture" (ibid.).

decorative but had ritual importance was questionable; and in order to see for themselves the "sacred" quality of the sunflowers, cultural anthropologist Anne-Marie Victor-Howe and assistant museum director Barbra Issac traveled to Walpi, Arizona, to attend a Hopi flute ceremony, a sixteen-day event in which the sunflowers are used to request rain and the warming of the earth before harvest (Yemma 1997, 9). Their observations confirmed the Hopi claim, led to the repatriation of the objects (not, however, as "sacred" but as objects of "cultural patrimony") and resulted in a sharing of knowledge about the artifacts, the significance of which was not understood outside Hopi society. And although the museum no longer has the sunflowers in its collection and so cannot apply this new knowledge, it does have an educational tool that can be used to improve communication of the contemporary significance and vitality of Hopi ritual to the public.[13]

Although almost everyone involved in repatriation hearings or negotiations would agree that in some circumstances particular objects, notably skeletal remains, need to be returned to specific claimants, especially those who can claim lineal descent from the victims of desecration and removal, there is still much room for debate as to how rigidly NAGPRA policies and those of the National Museum of the American Indian and other individual museums should be implemented. William Sturtevant, in a critique of the loose language in the National Museum of the American Indian's Collections Policy Statement, expresses concern that overzealous repatriation could lead museums to act in opposition to the public good: "The museum commits large amounts of taxpayers' money to the dispersal and potential destruction of collections, rather than their accumulation and preservation for the benefit of future generations" (1991, 30).

Some of the most compelling evidence of the importance of repatriation, however, comes from those whose ancestral remains have been returned. Vine Deloria Jr. (1992b, 596) reports what was told to him by medicine men who conducted reburial ceremonies: "In these ceremonies the spirits of the people whose remains were being returned appeared. They asked surprisingly practical questions for spirits. Some wanted to know if it was possible to get the indelible ink removed from their bones. Other said their remains had no feet or no head and they wondered at the kind of people who would remove these parts of the body and what

---

13. I am grateful to Galit Sarfaty (1997) for bringing this example of repatriation to my attention.

they thought human life was." Such experiences support Vizenor's point that "bones are not properties in the same categories as precious stones and metals, or abandoned sea treasure" (1986, 321). The current entanglements of museums in the process of repatriation also fully confirm this observation.

Dialogue or Diatribe?
Indians and Archaeologists
in the Post-NAGPRA Era

Michael Wilcox

> NAGPRA is an unmitigated disaster for archaeologists, bioarchaeol-
> ogists, and other physical anthropologists concerned with the study
> of human skeletal remains. This is because NAGPRA puts ethnicity
> and religious belief on equal footing with science and thus provides a
> mandate for claims of affiliation by virtually any interested
> party. . . . It is simply a fact that knowledge of most pre-contact abo-
> riginal cultures of the New World would have vanished without a
> trace were it not for archaeology (and the occasional presence of a
> Western observer to record information about them). We are all los-
> ers if, for reasons of political expediency, native Americans rebury
> their past.
>
> G. A. Clark, "NAGPRA and the Demon-Haunted World"

The responses of archaeologists, like that quoted above from G. A. Clark, and
of museums to NAGPRA may be quite surprising to many people who are
unfamiliar with the legislation and the academic professionals who have been
affected by it.[1] Both museums and archaeologists in North America have
assumed the professional responsibility for representing Native Americans to
the general public through research and education. The violent opposition to
NAGPRA reveals both a level of professional insecurity and, in a larger context, questions about the relevance of museums devoted to representations of
the primitive. On a more basic (and tragic) level, NAGPRA has forced the
people who represent Indians in journals, annual conferences, and glass cases
to meet living, breathing, fully modern Indians with educations, opinions, and
voices. Usually, it is for the first time.

In fact, the "salvage of the savage" and the representation of primitive peoples depends on and is embedded in a colonial narrative of Western scholarship as both savior and steward of "the Indian." The resulting scholarship has

---

1. G. A. Clark is Distinguished Research Professor of Anthropology at Arizona State
University and chair of the Archaeology Division of the American Anthropological Association.

served the purposes of each profession; as a "science," Americanist archaeology has insulated itself from a general trend in the social sciences toward critical self-reflexivity and appealed to a larger pool of National Science Foundation funding. Likewise, the prospect of forced deaccession threatens the relationship between wealthy benefactors and museum administrators. Museums are heavily invested in the collection and reproduction of "exotic" people and objects. In fact, the representations of Indian people as static, stone-age anachronisms depends on an essentialized and simplistic understanding of who Indian people are. Any dialogue between Indians and museums would threaten the role we play in the narrative of American history and collapse the social and temporal distance that separates us from modernity. After all, who wants to go to a museum to learn that Indians hold jobs, buy Pampers, and watch MTV?

The dialogue between archaeologists and Indians has not been much better, particularly in the American Southwest. During the 1960s, archaeological theory shifted its focus from the classification and description of artifacts to the "scientific" study of long-term cultural processes (Willey and Sabloff 1993, 152). Borrowing heavily from the evolutionary framework of Leslie White (1960) and the ecosystems models of Julian Steward (1955), "processual archaeology" viewed all human culture as an adaptive mechanism. In this approach, environmental stresses, population pressure, and technology interact in varying degrees to determine *universal* processes and laws of human behavior (Cordell 1984; Binford 1962). The interplay of these variables moves prehistoric cultures along an evolutionary continuum away from or toward a conceptual state of equilibrium; and Indian cultures become a data set for the scientific study of the past.

This approach also redefined the relationship between ethnographic information and archaeological research. There were methodological challenges raised by the interpretation of "static" artifact assemblages using the scientific method; the lack of observable patterns of behavior led to the creation of behavioral archaeology (Schiffer 1976) and the application of decontextualized "ethnographic analogies" to discover universal patterns of human behavior. Here, the professional and theoretical divergence of social anthropology and the new archaeology had a profound impact on the relationship between living native peoples and archaeologists. While "ethnohistory" gained acceptance within social anthropology, historical explanations were thought to contribute little to the illumination of universal laws and processes. If ethnographic data was to be applied to archaeological information, it would have to be drawn from a shrinking pool of "unacculturated" peoples still living in "traditional" communities, untainted by the modernization of the Western world. The history and lives of living Indians were no longer relevant to the research interests of archaeologists; the process of acculturation had rendered us theoretically irrelevant. To archaeologists, the real Indians were long gone.

The language of archaeology has reinforced a separation of Indians and our past. The process by which archaeology was elevated from a hobby to an academic field involved the development of a professional jargon and vocabulary. Archaeologists interpret general patterns of artifacts in a typological aggregate; similarities in technology, dwellings, settlement patterns, and artifact assemblages are considered "archaeological cultures." At any museum in the American Southwest, one can find a book about "the Anasazi" or "the Hohokam." One such book proclaims, "The roots of the Anasazi are not entirely clear. They were preceded by foragers who lived in the Southwest between 6000 B.C. and the time of Christ. Known as the Archaic or Desert Culture, they entered the Southwest as it was being vacated by big game hunters at the end of the Ice Age" (Houk 1992, 4).

These "cultures" assume the character and behavior of ethnic groups or races. Archaeologists have interpreted changes in patterns of refuse materials or technology as periods of migration and replacement. These simplistic explanations have helped create a past that curiously reiterates removal and replacement as both natural and universal. The past that has been invented by archaeologists obscures the relationships between Indian people and our own ethnohistory while reinforcing the self-affirming narrative of colonization. The creation of these cultures has also made the demonstration of "cultural affiliation," a key concept in repatriation, extremely difficult to prove.

In the context of NAGPRA, the demonstration of cultural affiliation must be proven for claims to be filed for the return of "sacred and ceremonial items, funerary objects," and "objects of cultural patrimony"; these categories and the relationship between archaeological cultures and living, changing Indian communities are determined by archaeologists and museum personnel. In a final, yet consistent indignity, Indian people must demonstrate connections to a past that has been created by a professional and theoretical dialogue that has explicitly excluded them. Cultural continuity must be proven in the language and by the terms of archaeologists themselves. Indians are asked to demonstrate our relation to the static cultures that archaeologists and museums have affirmed, reproduced, and codified in professional journals.

Items that the museums classify as "utilitarian" are excluded from repatriation. Museums and archaeologists insist upon defining value and meaning for Indian people despite the fact that the meanings and values of their own cultural patrimony are constantly redefined and recreated. On display in any number of Colonial American museums are "utilitarian objects" such as rifles, clothing, cookware, and so on. Their meaning has changed through time to reference a set of ideals told and retold in the narrative of American history. At a recent auction at Christie's in New York, John Kennedy's golf clubs, his ashtray, and other utilitarian items were auctioned (valued) at several hundred times their original price. But to Americans, these objects have a transcendent meaning because of their location within a historical context and cultural system. They are not merely clubs: They represent something deeply meaningful to Americans, a tangible connection to cultural ideals and hopes. They reference a period of history in which America was redefined, recreated, and reframed. Indian people are as dynamic a group as other people, and our relationship to our past and the material culture of our ancestors takes on new meaning precisely because we have played such a minimal role in telling our own story.

Perhaps it has come as some surprise to many museums that there has not been a wholesale flood of objects and mass reburials of priceless artifacts. This is where the break in communication between academics and Indians is most poignant. Despite the greatest fears of museum personnel, not all Indian people have the financial and human resources to deal with repatriation. Most archaeologists are completely unaware of the pressing issues facing Indian people in the past century, and many more just don't care. Survival, termination, relocation, the building of schools and roads, and the fighting of court battles over water and land rights, health care, and education need to be taken care of first.

Few archaeology classes even talk about native cultures of today except as anecdotal impediments to one's career path or research objectives. Likewise, the archaeologists who do care about Indian people can expect professional marginalization and resentment if they "advocate" themselves in a manner that opposes the research interests of their peers. When Indian people assert political sovereignty, affect democratic processes, and enact legislation, we are immediately labeled as antiscience, as religious zealots who disrespect the sanctity of science. For Indian people, repatriation is about respect. The return of objects and ancestors helps to affirm our presence as a people and allows us a greater voice in the telling of our own story on our own terms. The past we wish to rebury, Dr. Clark, is yours, not ours.

CHAPTER 7

Apostles of the New Age

One of the persistent delusions of mankind is that some sections of the human race are morally better or worse than others. . . . A rather curious form of this admiration for groups
to which the admirer does not belong is the belief in the superior virtue of the oppressed: subject nations, the poor,
women, and children. The eighteenth century, while conquer-
ing America from the Indians[,] . . . loved to sentimentalize
about the "noble savage." . . . It begins only when the
oppressors come to have a bad conscience, and this only hap-
pens when their power is no longer secure.

Bertrand Russell, *Unpopular Essays*

During the fifth annual meeting of the Circle of Elders of the Indigenous
Nations of North America on October 5, 1980, at Rosebud Creek, Montana, a resolution was passed that defined a new and powerful source of
spiritual compromise and erosion. Unqualified, self-appointed spiritual
practitioners with mostly non-native followers were identified as a source
of major concern. Above all, the handling of sacred objects, such as pipes
and eagle feathers, without proper initiation, instruction, and discipline
was subject to condemnation. As stated in the resolution, "These individuals are gathering non-Indian people as followers who believe they
are receiving instructions of the original people. We, the Elders and our
representatives sitting in Council, give warning to these non-Indian followers that it is our understanding this is not a proper process, that the
authority to carry these sacred objects is given by the people, and the
purpose and procedures is [*sic*] specific to time and the needs of the people" (cited in Churchill 1992, 223).

In 1984 at a meeting of the American Indian Movement at Window
Rock, Arizona, this call for action was taken up as a cause, resulting in
a warning to self-styled spiritual charlatans: "We Resolve to protect our

Elders and our traditions, and we condemn those who seek to profit from Indian Spirituality. We put them on notice that our patience has grown thin with them and they continue their disrespect at their own risk" (cited ibid., 228).

Native spirituality is being pulled in opposite directions by popularizers and preservationists. The preservationists see a new enemy of native spiritual integrity, one that is perhaps more insidious than legal suppression or Christian evangelism. It is difficult to combat because it works in the opposite direction, popularizing rather than rejecting, generating enthusiasm rather than censure. A radical shift has taken place, from selective or universal prohibition of native spiritual practices to their celebration as a solution to individualism, alienation, rampant technology—all the perceived ills of postindustrial society. In this process some see a serious dilution of the original meaning of spiritual guidance. Vine Deloria Jr., an outspoken critic of a range of trends in Indian-white relations, targets the use of tribal religious traditions for personal enlightenment as a source of well-intended cultural abuse: "Bookshelves today are filled with pap—written many times by Indians who have kicked over the traces and no longer feel they are responsible to any living or historic community, but more often by wholly sincere and utterly ignorant non-Indians who fancy themselves masters of the vision quest and sweat lodge. Lying beneath this mass of sentimental slop is the unchallenged assumption that personal sincerity is the equivalent of insight and that cosmic secrets can be not only shared by non-Indians but given out in weekend workshops as easily as diet plans" (1994, vii).

The development of a mass audience outside the native community, hungering for authenticity but uninformed and indiscriminate in its tastes, is seen to have placed an enormous strain on the integrity and cultural viability of many forms of native spirituality.[1] Radical innovation and lack of basic skill by practitioners with doubtful qualifications are seen almost everywhere in the communication of native spirituality to non-native audiences. "Plastic medicine men," "spiritual thieves," "New Age circle jerks," "spiritual colonizers"—such strong language reveals the emotions felt by those who perceive the sanctity of their traditions violated by acts of appropriation and deception.

Who are these cultural thieves and assassins so strongly denounced by native elders, activists, and intellectuals? What community could have

1. An overview of this audience and its organizations in Europe, described under the heading "Indian hobbyists," is provided in Taylor (1988).

aroused such indignation in a quest for spiritual understanding? The most common term is the "New Age movement," derived from a commonly held expectation of an imminent era of global healing and spiritual harmony for humankind. The New Age movement is, however, impossible to define and difficult to describe. It is not unified by a single formal organization, membership, or common body of beliefs. It therefore does not meet any of the criteria commonly used to describe a social "movement," and the term in this case is not formally precise. It embraces such diverse styles of belief and practice as spirit "channeling"; palmistry; the use of trees, stones, or crystals as sources of sacred power; and, of course, selected and adapted versions of native spirituality. Despite this diffuseness and variety it does have what can be called an audience—a more appropriate term than "congregation"—loosely united through networks. The New Age movement's ideas, and news about the organizations developed for sharing and ritualizing them, are communicated through print media. Spiritual autobiographies and simplified ritual systems often become runaway bestsellers, making the publishing industry the most important venue for a diverse, creative, and highly profitable body of spiritual ideas and recipes for self-help and inspiration. Journals and Web sites on the Internet cater to more focused interests and act as staging points, attracting audiences to workshops and weekend retreats.[2]

The emotional and intellectual yearning of non-native participants and observers of native ritual have sent native spirituality in two directions. The need for formal recognition and the honest desire to share local traditions with a wide and eager audience have resulted in a trend toward universalization, new styles of observance that can include the merely curious and bring together a diverse assembly of participants and spectators with an emphasis on spectacle and performance. But for those who want to maintain a community focus, who understand spiritual power as a force that may respond unkindly to the presence of the uncommitted, there is a perceived need for exclusivism.

Those who promote popular native religion in New Age circles often do so out of the conviction that ritual and visionary traditions were not

---

2. The reasons behind the popularity of alternative religions, including those that might be included under the rubric of the New Age movement, are even more diffuse than the composition of their membership. Charles Lindholm provides the general observation that "self-transcendence, no longer found in intimate personal relationships and long absent in the central institutions of the society, will be sought elsewhere," such as in experimental religions (1990, 188).

intended for secret societies or exclusive groups of initiates, that there should be no social barrier to the dissemination of these teachings, and that they can be used creatively in conjunction with other enlightened faiths to help individuals in their quest for healing and personal growth. The New Age author Brooke Medicine Eagle, for example, sees "actualization" as being hindered by the spiritual confusion created by the secrecy and exclusivism of native spiritual leaders. This view emerges partially from her version of the history of conquest: "When the white Europeans came, the Native peoples of the Americas, rather than being an allied and unified family confronting the people who came in boats and asking them to either learn the ways of harmony or get back on their boats, were instead fighting and warring among themselves" (1991, 239). Such disunity, according to Medicine Eagle, was the real reason behind the pillaging, destruction, and disease that accompanied the European occupation; and the lasting legacy of this catastrophe is a deep and prolonged spiritual need in all people of the Americas: "So the different peoples, both Native and non-Native, all joined in this great disharmony, this continental war, and thus became one people in need of regaining peace and a sense of the sacred, a way of harmony with All Our Relations" (ibid., 240). One significant result of the "continental war," for Medicine Eagle, is that many native spiritual leaders today are too much concerned with rigid preservation and exclusivism and have lost their trust in the power of Spirit: "They feel that they themselves must police the sacred ways[,] . . . a very pompous and burdensome place to put oneself" (ibid., 24). Medicine Eagle's solution to the perceived hegemony and abuse of trust by elders is to largely exclude them from the search for enlightenment, borrowing instead from various sources and traditions to suit individual inclinations. "One of our major lessons is that, although our elders can be of assistance, they are not the source of spiritual wisdom, nor the judges of it. Each person must call fervently—or, as the Sufi say, 'pound relentlessly on the door of God,' and awaken within themselves that golden cord of connection" (ibid., 142).

Based upon these arguments, the conflict between preservationists and popularizers seems to revolve around two basic issues: preservationists object to the absence of connection, especially by self-styled leaders, to historic or existing native communities, while popularizers oppose what they see as exclusivism and secrecy, which stand in the way of global understanding. Second, preservationists try to retain the integrity of traditional models of belief, behavior, and observance, while popularizers argue for the simplicity of basic teachings and the value of combining them with other religious traditions to achieve personal fulfillment and a universal harmony of the enlightened.

Ironically, an audience appreciative of native spiritual traditions has developed after centuries of organized suppression and intolerance—an audience seen by many as a serious threat to the integrity and continued vitality of what remains of these traditions—and the fact of its development raises a number of questions. How did this well-intentioned community develop in the first place? How did a Euro-American audience emerge that is sympathetic to native spirituality to the point of seeing it as a source of truth in its own search for understanding? When the most prevalent attitudes toward religion among non-natives were marked by racism and intolerance, what led to a cultural change of perception in which "traditional" Indians came to be regarded as keepers of sacred knowledge? To address this issue fully would require a survey of American and European cultural history over the past several centuries. To simplify the discussion for the reader, I have selected for consideration several key thinkers, "wild men of ideas" whose thoughts represent a shift from organized Christianity toward an individualistic theology that finds the clearest manifestations of the sacred in "nature." Ralph Waldo Emerson and Henry David Thoreau can be considered forebears of the New Age movement, with their eclectic idealism and anticlericalism grounded in contemplation of nature. With nature religion established as a prevalent form of spirituality in American culture, it required one more step, exemplified in the work of Gary Snyder, Pulitzer Prize–winner for poetry in 1974, to represent the Indian as an embodiment of human life in harmony with Mother Earth, and Indian spirituality as an important source of enlightenment for anyone seeking to establish a more meaningful connection to the natural world.

There are two sides to the irony inherent in an audience that appreciates native spiritual traditions even while it is seen by some native leaders as appropriating and destroying them. Once we have understood the cultural origins and impulses of the audience itself, we are left with the problem of tension between this audience and prominent leaders in the native community. The popularists' accusations of exclusivism and traditionalists' concerns about authenticity are the most commonly voiced opinions, from opposite sides of the controversy, but are these issues the only sources of division between them? When, later in this chapter, we look more closely at the New Age movement's systems of belief, in particular its diverging conceptions of misfortune and redemption, we will see more clearly that the movement is radically different

from any form of indigenous spirituality. The contrast is sharpened even
further when we consider the implications of the New Age's reliance on
published text as a primary source of inspirational wisdom, while preser-
vationist native traditions continue to be more fully grounded in symbolic and oral representations of visionary experience.

WILD MEN OF IDEAS

To those at all familiar with the impact of radical evangelism and western expansion on North America's native peoples, the apparent enthusiasm with which New Age practitioners and their admirers have
embraced native spirituality would appear to be a paradox. Is this a
reversal of the historical trend toward domination and directed transformation of indigenous cultures? Where does this unusual and widespread impulse to imitate and try to benefit from native rituals come
from?

Some argue that the intellectual origins of the New Age's embrace of
native spirituality are located much earlier than the pan-Indianism and
local cultural revivals of the 1960s and 1970s. Alice Kehoe looks back
the furthest, to writers in the ancient world who visited or heard about
northern tribespeople, for that first impulse in Western culture toward
romantic admiration of those with simple lifestyles living in harmony
with nature: "With no change in the basic thinking, 'Indian' has replaced
the Classical 'Scythian' as the label for the fabled Naturvolker. Cultural
primitivism, constructed as the opposition to civilization with its dis-
contents, has been part of Western culture for close to three thousand
years" (1990, 207).[3]

It is not possible, however, to find the literary origins of popular native
spirituality in the ancient world. Although there is a strain of distant
admiration for people living in harsh lands, buffeted by nature but content because of their simple needs, this did not lead to a rejection of
ancient spiritual ideas or a voluntary exchange of lifestyles. Even this

---

3. Ancient writers, however, were not at all consistent in their judgments of the Scythi-
ans or of other lesser known groups who presented radical cultural contrasts to classical
civilizations. Ovid's horror of the people to whom he was sent in exile, described by him
as *inhumani,* wild, savage, as laughing at his Latin and talking maliciously of him in his
presence (Lovejoy and Boas 1965, 336), results in condemnation rather than distant admiration. Ovid conflates his description of harsh savages with the severity of their environment: "The natives ward off the evil cold with skins and stitched trousers, and of their
whole body the face alone is exposed. Often their hair tinkles with pendant icicles and
their beards shine with a frosty covering" (cited in Lovejoy and Boas 1965, 335).

muted and inconsistent respect for other lifestyles is not a consistent theme in the historical writings of the Western world.[4] For many centuries, reflection on the relative virtues and vices of savages all but disappears as a form of narrative. Apostolic simplicity replaced the lifestyles of natural folk as the alternative to domination by the state. After the fall of Rome and before the discovery of the New World, Christian heresy was the almost exclusive medium of resistance to the expansion of civilization and orthodoxy.

If there is a literary antecedent to New Age spiritualism and its efforts to derive benefit from the sacred places, rituals, and beliefs of Native Americans, it is to be found in a nineteenth-century body of literature that glorifies nature rather than the Indian, and individualism rather than the religious community. Ralph Waldo Emerson is an important predecessor to the loose spiritual eclecticism of the New Age, above all because of his radical, noninstitutional Christianity, grounded as much in a vague appreciation of nature as in the Scriptures. The young pastor of the Second Church of Boston who resigned his post in 1832 because of a conviction that the sacrament was meaninglessness, found in nature a true place of worship:

> At the gates of the forest, the surprised man of the world is forced to leave his city estimates of great and small, wise and foolish. The knapsack of custom falls from his back with the first step he makes into these precincts. Here is sanctity which shames our religions, and reality which discredits our heroes. Here we find nature to be the circumstance which dwarfs every other circumstance, and judges like a god all men that come to her. . . . The incommunicable trees begin to persuade us to live with them, and quit our life of solemn trifles. Here no history, or church, or state, is interpolated on the divine sky and the immortal year. . . . These enchantments are medicinal, they sober and heal us. (1926, 381)

Emerson's combination of nature spirituality and individualism went beyond anticlericalism into anticongregationalism: "You can never come to any peace or power until you put your whole reliance in the moral constitution of man, and not at all in a historical Christianity" (1995, 124). Rather than calling for a reordering of the faith into a new, more meaningful community of believers resisting a hierarchical priesthood, Emerson found solace in reclusion: "The finished man is he who in the midst of the crowd keeps with perfect sweetness the independence of

---

4. Ibn Khaldun's respect for Bedouin tribespeople is a notable exception, from the Islamic world rather than the Occident, to the absence of "cultural primitivism" in the Middle Ages.

solitude" (ibid., 89). Emerson dispenses easily with church and congregation, but retains a Calvinistic flavor in his search for individual moral perfection.

Emerson's longtime friend and protégé Henry David Thoreau can be credited with sharpening and emphasizing key aspects of his ideas to the point where a new and more influential form of nature spirituality emerged. Thoreau's biological and botanical observations are more rigorous, grounded in scientific knowledge and attention to detail, and they build on Emerson's general sense of awe toward the grandeur of the natural world with attention to equally thought-provoking, spirit-stirring minutiae.

In *Walden,* Thoreau's indisputable masterpiece (but not so regarded in his own lifetime), his ability to closely observe the world around him becomes the backdrop of his famous experiment in simplified living, self-examination, and harmony with nature. During two years and two months, starting in 1845, he built and lived in a shack beside a New England pond, closely observing and recording his surroundings, the successes and failures of his subsistence activities, and the effect of solitude on his thoughts. One conclusion he draws from this is the salutary effect of isolation in nature: "The most sweet and tender, the most innocent and encouraging society may be found in any natural object, even for the poor misanthrope and most melancholy man. There can be no very black melancholy to him who lives in the midst of Nature and has his senses still" (1981, 202). Such sentimentalism was combined with an uncompromising rejection of large industry that spoke more powerfully to later generations than to his own contemporaries. Those who do not read *Walden* closely might not be aware of the proximity of his cabin to a railroad (today a commuter line into Boston), allowing him a contrast between his own usual tranquillity and the invasion of the senses and the natural world brought about by manufacture: "The whistle of the locomotive penetrates my woods summer and winter. . . . [carrying] timber like long battering rams going twenty miles an hour against the city's walls. . . . All the Indian huckleberry hills are stripped, all the cranberry meadows are raked into the city" (ibid., 190–91). The tranquillity of nature is offset by the noise and destructiveness of an encroaching civilization.

Thoreau's experiment in self-sufficiency also granted him time to reflect on his inner state and explore the relative strength of various strands of religious philosophy. He arrived at an anticongregationalism more uncompromising than Emerson's, flavored with influences from

Buddhism, Hinduism, and even Zoroastrianism, expressing the view that the sincerely religious man should "let 'our church' go by the board" (ibid., 186), and advocating in its stead solitude, contemplation, and the occasional "forsaking of works": "Sometimes, in a summer morning, having taken my accustomed bath, I sat in my sunny doorway from sunrise till noon, rapt in a revery, amidst the pines and hickories and sumachs, in undisturbed solitude and stillness, while the birds sang around or flitted noiseless through the house, until by the sun falling in at my west window, or the noise of some traveller's wagon on the distant highway, I was reminded of the lapse of time. I grew in those seasons like corn in the night, and they were far better than any work of the hands would have been" (ibid., 188).

Thoreau's moment of contemplation is, however, far from a literal interpretation of Buddhist doctrine. The reality he sees is not illusory or transitory without the intervention of human destructiveness. Meditation for him is the internalization of sensory experience. Expansion of the soul comes from patient attention to plants, animals, birds, insects, and the incessant natural rhythms in woods, fields, and waters. His biocentric mysticism goes further than Emerson's more conservative and puritan contemplation of nature, moving away from the gloom of their Calvinistic inheritance in a celebration of the sublime in immediate perceptions, in what Catherine Albanese suggests is an almost apocalyptic emphasis on purification and individual perfection in a fully realizable paradise of the natural world: "Paradoxically, to turn to nature meant to share something of what was happening in the great revivals of the era, when men and women said they received new hearts and spirits, knowing themselves now perfect and without blemish" (1990, 94).

The nature spirituality of writers like Emerson and Thoreau has had a distinct influence on the literary origins of the New Age movement. The spiritual essays and autobiographies of nineteenth-century transcendentalists who rejected organized Christianity describe the authors' initiations into the secret wisdom of Nature, and underscore the importance this has for anyone who desires spiritual growth. These ideas were taken up with alacrity in the spiritual explorations of the 1960s and 1970s. The expression by Emerson and Thoreau of a need for simplicity in life and a spirituality linked to the natural world, however, did not portray the Indian as a living exemplar of this ideal. Indians were significant only as those "whose pipe and arrow oft the plough unburies" (Thoreau 1981, 27); and Thoreau's moose-hunting excursion on the Penobscot River with an Indian guide recounted in his essay "The Maine

Woods" evokes more distaste for "sport" than perception of spiritual meaning in the pursuit of game. A telling remark in "A Week on the Concord and Merrimack Rivers" indicates that Thoreau shared Emerson's perception of the Indian as culturally extinct: "Town records, old, tattered, time-worn, weather-stained chronicles, contain the Indian sachem's mark, perchance an arrow or a beaver [pelt], and the few fatal words by which he deeded his hunting grounds away" (ibid., 52). What neither Emerson nor Thoreau engage in, therefore, is an attribution of spiritual enlightenment to Indians. The first inhabitants have been defeated, their lands appropriated, and they remain only as relics to remind us of the passage of time and the power of civilization.

Indigenous ritual and visionary practices do not become attached to the nature spirituality of a wide American audience until the pan-Indian movement of the 1960s, in which a popularized model of Plains religion was widely identified as a universal ideal, which, at the same time, stimulated the interest of a broad spectrum of native youth in their own local traditions. Many who were marginal to the teachings and experience of rural native communities, living isolated in the cities, found new avenues for understanding their identity. And others, mainly non-Indians, pursued the idea that indigenous forms of nature spirituality could be adapted to the inclinations and needs of those seeking alternative forms of enlightenment.

Such is a central theme in the work of Gary Snyder, a graduate in anthropology from Reed College who devoted his life to poetry as the preferred medium for expressing his vision of life in harmony with the natural world. He spent his early career writing mainly for offbeat journals, until winning a Pulitzer Prize for poetry for *Turtle Island* in 1975, which gave his work a much wider readership. In prose pieces and interviews he makes explicit his views on the dangers of modernity—environmental degradation, political hegemony, emotional apathy, and confusion—and the need to revive an archaic sense of harmony with the natural world and community values in order to restore our full humanity. The central concerns of Snyder's work are very close to those of Thoreau, interposed with a century of industrial expansion and a heightened awareness of tribal ways of life.

There is an apocalyptic flavor to his environmentalism, a sense that human abuse, if unchecked, will lead inevitably to global destruction: "The foolish tinkering with the powers of life and death by the occidental scientist-engineer-ruler puts the whole planet on the brink of degradation" (Snyder 1990, 19). Survival and meaningful human growth, stressing spiritual rather than material gains, depend upon a restoration of human acceptance of the organic world. He "seeks to recover," as McLean notes, "a poetry that could sing and thus relate to us: magpie, beaver, a mountain range, binding us to all these other lives, seeing our spiritual lives as bound up in the rounds of nature" (1980, xiii).

Seeing a correspondence between external and internal landscapes compels Snyder to explore a variety of cultural solutions to the tainted human relationship with the natural world. Buddhism, for example, has mastered intellectual and meditative disciplines, often combined with rigorous outdoor life, that can benefit anyone pursuing spiritual goals. It has the important disadvantage, however, of being tied to monastic traditions that stand in the way of applying this heightened awareness to a natural human community. It is important to integrate spiritual training into communities in which everyone is involved, without divisions of priest and layperson, disciple and master. "What we need to do now," says Snyder, "is to take the great intellectual achievement of the Mahayana Buddhists and bring it back to a community style of life which is not necessarily monastic" (1980, 16).

In Native American cultures he sees a source of natural wisdom that can be used to recreate a social order that reflects the principles of nature, that accommodates the wild qualities of human life. Native hunting lifestyles, for example, teach an etiquette that is mindful of the sacred qualities of animals and the importance of "killing and eating with gentleness and thanks" (1990, 21). The disposition toward both frugality and generosity in their dealings with the natural world is a quality of the "primary peoples" that all can learn from. With no suggestion of irony, Snyder says that all inhabitants of the Americas can learn from the primary peoples. Once native wisdom becomes available, Americans can learn how to cease acting and thinking like invaders, rediscover the land and become, in a broad sense, truly "native."

Native Americans in general are a source of wisdom, instructing us in the ways of pursuing spiritual training in a community setting: "They have, throughout Turtle Island, an ancient and clarified sense of what a right path is. And some of those societies, not all of them maybe, were actually living like a Zen monastery—a whole society *on the way*. . . . A whole social transmission is more to be desired than a monastic and esoteric transmission" (1980, 68).

Within native societies, instruction in the "right path" was widely accessible. But for those outside the society, says Snyder, the problem of accessibility remains: "American Indian spiritual practice is very remote and extremely difficult to enter, even though in one sense right next door, because it is a practice one has to be born into. Its intent is not cosmopolitan. Its content, perhaps, is universal, but you must be a Hopi to follow the Hopi way" (ibid., 94).

Social exclusion is not the only barrier to the broad accessibility of primary wisdom. Snyder writes of native cultures almost exclusively in the past tense, as though they are delicate artifacts such as those described by Emerson and Thoreau. These artifacts, however, form one of the few avenues to our understanding of their ability to thrive in harmony with the wilderness. For Snyder, most Indians today are rootless, sharing in the mobility and degradation of modern life. Others, still living in a natural way, mainly in Canada and Alaska, are isolated from those who might profit from their knowledge.

Such limitations are actually a source of opportunity for the critical, enlightened artist. Cultural artifacts can be examined for their worth and held out to a needful and appreciative audience. The logic of the literary elevation and sanctification of native practice excludes the living representatives of existing peoples and situates the writer as a cultural broker.

The implications of literary cultural mediation are every bit as significant for native spiritual traditions as the legacy of legal suppression. The transformation of symbolic, private forms of expressing visionary experience in Plains spirituality into ethnographic or inspirational texts implies a radically altered context for socialization and ritual expression. At the same time, the production of sacred text is not controlled by sanction or approval from a native audience, making it possible for literary license to take the place of, and come into conflict with, local perceptions of authenticity.

THE ORAL AND THE WRITTEN

The struggle between preservationists and popularizers can largely be understood as stemming from the opposing inclinations of oral and literate spirituality. With the development in this century of ethnographic scripturalism, an important transition took place, from private experience with restricted oral expression to the documentation of visions in inspirational records. The suppression of native ritual in the nineteenth century created a situation in which the sharing of ritual knowledge and visionary experience was for some an acceptable way to preserve traditions that were seriously threatened. The perception of overwhelming legal and cultural forces coming to bear on local practice and systems of knowledge encouraged the production of intercultural artifacts, new records of dreams, visions, and spiritual biographies that transformed personal knowledge into written text (Irwin 1994, 168).

At the time of colonial contact, native societies of the Americas possessed exclusively oral traditions, many of which have persisted through the era of missionary influence and residential education, and many features of which have been maintained to the present day. In a study of Plains visionary traditions based upon early ethnography, Lee Irwin points to the private nature of dream and vision experiences, and the tension between restrictions on verbal interpretation and the need to translate spiritual encounters into communicable form. The problematics of dream sharing were overcome in part through expression in song: "Unlike the tendentious 'Word' in the Judeo-Christian-Islamic tradition, these dream songs are of a private revelatory nature; words of power are not to be discussed or debated, only *used* to invoke their sources" (ibid., 165). Other forms of expression, says Irwin, other alternatives to the spoken report, were enactments of dream contents "combined with the making of physical icons or visionary objects and with the recreation of visual imagery and actions. The translation of the experience into verbal form is done rarely and cautiously, if at all" (ibid., 166). The principal reason for such restrictions in expressing visionary experience, says Irwin, stems from the potential of spoken words to transmit and diffuse personal spiritual power: "Speaking of a dream or vision means sharing the knowledge and empowerment contained in the vision. Such a sharing could mean the loss of that power or knowledge" (ibid., 172). Plains visionary traditions are not only grounded in nonliterate forms of communication—verbal representation is itself restricted by caution in expressing supernaturally charged experiences.

Even at a time when native visionary traditions were in creative ferment, writing was often resisted as a form of spiritual expression. Exceptions can be found, as in the Hudson Bay Cree religious movement of 1842–43, in which the prophet Abishabis had used the Reverend James Evans's phonetic syllabic writing system, copying texts on birch bark and eventually using a fur press to print hymns and easily remembered words about the Great Spirit, which were then sewn between deerskin covers (Brown 1996, 31). Ambivalence toward scriptural literacy, however, is a more common feature of prophetic movements in native North America. Borrowings from Christianity were usually in the guise of acceptance of the apocalyptic tradition in a return to the past, a tendency that has led many such movements to be called "nativistic." The strength of the conservative attitude, the importance they attached to resisting Euro-American domination, were consistent with a rejection of scriptural writing as a source of sacred power. Writing was not worshiped in and of itself; its value was primarily in its use as a tool of communication.

Indigenous hieroglyphics were one of the means by which visions with important consequences could be reported to a wide audience. In response to a vision, the Delaware prophet of 1762–63 drew a map of the soul's progress in this world and the next upon a piece of deerskin parchment about fifteen to eighteen inches square. This map he called "the Great Book of Writing." He traveled from village to village holding the map before him as he preached, pointing to images on it and giving explanations (Wallace 1969, 119). Heckewelder, a missionary who spent fifty years among the Delawares, reported that in order to maintain the impression of his doctrine, the prophet sold copies of his "Great Book of Writing" for the price of one buckskin or two doeskins each (Mooney 1991, 667). Such methods of disseminating his visions and doctrines enabled the Delaware prophet to spread his influence over a very wide area, and copies of his spiritual map were soon to be found in regions remote from his original territory. The mnemonic functions of hieroglyphic designs were an important adjunct to the oral narrative of the vision and its meaning, allowing the message to be replicated and widely distributed.

The influence of European literacy by no means indicated a tacit approval of white culture in general or even of literacy in particular. Smohalla, the founder of the Shaker Church (not to be confused with the Puritan Shakers of New England), was essentially conservative in his doctrine and, with regard to literacy, does not seem to have used any form of written record in daily religious affairs, relying instead upon the oral tradition—the wisdom of dreams and of Dreamer ceremonies. Yet to convey the idea that he was in control of the natural elements, he made use of an almanac and, with some advice on its use given by a group of surveyors, he was able to predict several eclipses (ibid., 720). He also possessed a blank book, which he filled with characters, some of which resembled letters of the alphabet. This book, he explained, was a record of events and prophecies. Mooney concludes that these characters were probably mnemonic symbols invented for his own use (ibid.). The "transcendental" nature of alphabetic literacy was impressed even upon the conservative members of colonial native society.

Literacy was seen as having functional, not spiritual, value. Its power to communicate over great distances and periods of time was valuable, but for those with attachments to local traditions, its inextricable association with colonial power and the continued vitality of memorization and recitation stood in the way of its veneration as a source of sacred power.

Despite the ineffectiveness of text in capturing the emotional power of visionary experience, some ethnographic records drawing from the memories of spiritual leaders have become standard references, especially for those trying to understand early Plains traditions. John Neihardt's collaboration with Black Elk, an Oglala *wichasha wakan* (holy man), has produced a highly influential vision narrative and spiritual biography. Neihardt freely admits to the fragmentary nature of the reported "power-vision" and to Black Elk's reticence in relating such a sacred matter to a group of listeners that included a stenographer, but Black Elk's impulse to transmit his experience to those who might live beyond the evil days of battle and white men's possession of the land seemed to motivate him to overcome his misgivings: "There is so much to teach you. What I know was given to me for men and it is true and it is beautiful. Soon I shall be under the grass and it will be lost. You were sent to save it, and you must come back so that I can teach you" (Neihardt 1972, xviii).

The resulting story in *Black Elk Speaks*—in which the holy man tells in detail of an important vision he had at the age of nine, the time of intertribal warfare, of greed and destruction by white prospectors and settlers encouraged by government duplicity, warfare against government soldiers, and the spiritual experiences that occurred in this context—has become widely accepted as the central written expression of Plains spirituality. Deloria sees its importance principally as a source of guidance for young Native Americans looking for their own roots in a world of rapid change and conflicting perceptions of the substance of life: "To them it [*Black Elk Speaks*] has become a North American bible of all tribes. They look to it for spiritual guidance, for sociological identity, for political insight, and for affirmation of the continuing substance of Indian tribal life" (1979, xiii); and for non-Indians seeking tribal substance a similar influence has been reported.[5]

There is a tension between written forms of experience and the persistence of oral and nonverbal expression in contemporary native spirituality. If the spoken word is fraught with unpredictable power, writing

5. The recording of Black Elk's autobiography and visions and their reformatting into a new sacred text has some parallel with what Peter van der Veer reports of the impact of Enlightenment-inspired orientalism on modern Indian thought: "By producing critical

can be seen as an even greater source of spiritual compromise. The ethnographic transformation of Native American visionary experience into theology, and of oral narrative into quasi-scriptural text, has produced a literature of ambivalence, a model of ineffable religious encounter conveyed in text without context, a nearly canonized record with no priesthood and no established system of ritual enactment. Such ambiguity has comparatively few implications for those with ties to a native community, who already possess an understanding of the social context of visions and the place of elders as guides and mentors. For others, however, there is a wide field for creativity. Unlike the stable homogenization and canonization of Hindu texts, there are few limits to the creation of new Native American inspirational sources. Personal credentials can be established by replicating and building upon early visionary narratives. The biographical reference point can be shifted, placing emphasis on the neophyte observer as the true source of spiritual growth, with the medicine man as a facilitator. Above all, without a final revelation, there is an irresistible impulse to report or invent new visions and understandings, and for seekers of enlightenment to consume them without the sense that they have achieved a final insight.

Few religious movements in human history have expanded as rapidly as contemporary native spirituality without a clearly defined scriptural foundation. This leaves the field open for sincere and self-interested popularizers (the categories are not mutually exclusive) to write their own versions of the Indian gospel without challenge from an established orthodoxy, with little fear of scrutiny of self-defined qualifications, little fear of censure, no fear of punishment, and a great many potential rewards that stem from authorship of popular publications and leadership of enthusiastic followings.

New Age religiosity develops through the restless proliferation of printed material: spiritual autobiographies, organizational newsletters, and simplified and often fanciful descriptions of tribal religions. The seeker of enlightenment is often socialized in the values and ideas of the "community" or audience in the first instance by selecting and studying

editions of Hindu scriptures they replaced a largely fragmented, oral tradition with an unchanging, homogenized written one. In that way a 'history,' as established by modern science, came to replace a traditional 'past.' They also canonized certain scriptures, such as the *Bhagavad Gita,* which prepared the ground for Mahatma Gandhi to make this Sanskrit work into a fundamental scripture of modern Hinduism" (Veer 1994, 133). Although this "Sanskritization" was not solely the product of orientalist refinement but emerged at least partially through interaction between orientalist and Asian scholars, it resulted in a relatively fixed reinvention of Hindu tradition.

inspirational literature. It is perfectly conceivable that the seeker could be informed in this way without ever meeting a spiritual guide or "co-religionist." Socialization becomes an often private experience.

Many of the issues brought out by critics of the New Age movement stem from an attachment to oral visionary traditions seen to be compromised by their transformation into written form. The New Age movement presents a direct challenge to the attachments of rearticulated native visionary traditions to oral transmission of knowledge in public socialization, private experience, and guidance from elders. In each of these realms, the literary transformation of visionary experience has worked in the opposite direction. Religious instruction can take place privately rather than in a community, visionary experience can be shared with a vast, impersonal audience rather than guarded closely as a source of personal insight and individuality, and self-proclaimed "experts," recognized for literary gifts, are a challenge to the spiritual leadership of elders, recognized for local knowledge and service to a community.

INVENTION AND AUTHENTICITY

Despite the ambiguities and tensions inherent in the transformation of visionary experience to inspirational text, it is still easy to assume that the attention given to native ritual and belief in popular literature and meetings would provide a boost to the morale of native communities. Those who had for so long endured efforts to convert and repress them would now finally be given their due in an enthusiastic appreciation of their heritage. Could this at last be a way to resolve the cultural misunderstandings that have for centuries been part of Indian-white relations?

There would be room for such optimism if popular appreciation were more consistently realistic in its perceptions of native traditions, if more commonly there were nuanced understandings of the complexity, diversity, and dynamics of indigenous ways of life, or if enthusiasm were more often oriented to present realities than to timeless, simplistic distortions from imaginary recreations of the past. Implicit in much of the popular expressions of native spirituality is a form of chronological cultural primitivism, a combination of the ideas that the cultural ideal existed in the past and that it can be salvaged only from remnants of tribal societies in the present. By situating their moral ideal in a culture at the height of its power before Western expansion, the vestiges of which can only be glimpsed though a process of inevitable decline, New Age seekers of enlightenment absolve themselves of responsibility for present conditions and conflicts. The fixation on an Indian golden age as the source of true spiritual power and the present as an unredeemable morass of social pathology and ritual neglect encourages indifference rather than willingness to learn.

One style of what critics might call the literary appropriation of native spirituality takes the form of ethnographic reduction: the simplification and formalization of sophisticated traditions of storytelling, symbol, and ritual to make them more accessible to a wide readership. Perhaps the most influential of these is Hyemeyohsts Storm's *Seven Arrows,* in which Plains spirituality is adjusted to the needs of seekers of enlightenment: simplified in its ritual requirements, romanticized through artistic representation of "shields" and a liberal use of Edward Curtis photographs, and elaborated in the use of the Medicine Wheel as a symbol of great significance with the power to heal and promote personal growth. According to Storm, "The Medicine Wheel is the very Way of Life of the People. It is an Understanding of the Universe. It is the Way given to the Peace Chiefs, our Teachers, and by them to us. The Medicine Wheel is everything of the People" (1972, 1).

Seven Arrows separates Plains spirituality from its context in reservation communities, from the elaborate, sometimes secret knowledge of elders, and from the discipline of the quest for personal visions. In its literary format, the reinterpreted spiritual system was presented as an exotic tribal religion laid bare, accessible to anyone with the ability and inclination to read about it. Its appearance coincided with the resurgence of native ceremonial in the early 1970s, which gave it the status of a source of reference for a newly energized culture. Young non-Indians found in it the key to an alternative, picturesque religion that had once seemed complicated in the turgid prose of ethnographic texts and arcane pronouncements of elders. And, following up on this (re)discovery, some "younger Indians living in isolated urban areas away from the reservation ceremonials . . . believed that it was a true representation of their own tribal religions" (Deloria 1992a, 37).

Another literary genre in the popularization of native traditions is the spiritual autobiography. Such narratives provide indirect access to native spirituality through autobiographical descriptions of encounters with great healers and the numinous experiences the authors had with the elders' guidance. One of the common features of the spiritual autobiography is that it relies heavily on the imagination, on spiritual fantasies that find receptive audiences in those who are unaware of ethnographic charlatanism, who sense similar visionary passions, but to whom such journeys into the unknown would be unthinkable. They are usually written by non-Indians who lack the qualifications to report directly on native herbology, ritual, or mystical lore. These are reported secondhand, through the author's report of an encounter with a great teacher. This teacher is usually one of the last living people to be so well versed in ancient knowledge. The teacher's abilities transcend the mere use of plants and ability to tell stories and myths, and include an astonishing familiarity with the world of Spirit, transcendental skills, and wisdom beyond the ability of an inexperienced onlooker to comprehend. But the powers and teachings of the elder cannot all be revealed at once; the novice must first prove a willingness to learn and be put to the test. The spiritual autobiography is often about this quest for approval and enlightenment, the cultural misunderstandings that arise despite a sincere desire to learn, and the gradual unfolding of higher powers as the teacher perceives that a requisite level of understanding has been acquired.

One of the most influential narratives of this kind is Carlos Castaneda's *The Teachings of Don Juan: A Yaqui Way of Knowledge,* which first appeared in 1968. In this, and in a subsequent series of books, Castaneda describes his search, initially as a graduate student in anthropology at the University of California, for knowledge about native use of hallucinogens. His inquiry leads him to don Juan Matis, a man of unusual expertise in the preparation of hallucinogenic substances and wisdom in guiding the user through his experiences. His account of apprenticeship in the use of peyote, datura, and mushrooms includes descriptions of hallucinogenic experiences and don Juan's tutelage, which gives meaning to the visionary experiences and a glimpse of a very different way of perceiving the universe.

Castaneda's writings do not claim to be founded upon allegory but on ethnographic fact, and on this basis they have been the topic of controversy. Ward Churchill stresses the fraudulent nature of Castaneda's project, undeterred by the fact that Castaneda was awarded a doctorate in anthropology by UCLA for a dissertation based on his *Journey to Ixtlan* manuscript and has received enthusiastic endorsements from scholars and reviewers. "In purest terms, it seems entirely likely that don Juan is and always has been the exclusive product of the over-active imagination of Carlos Castaneda, a product having literally nothing to do with Yaquis, American Indians and, in most instances, with reality of any sort" (1992, 54). He discredits Castaneda's project by pointing to discrepancies between descriptions and realities of the Sonora desert (casual outdoor activities that would have occurred at a time of excruciating heat); the absence of any evidence, whether field notes, tape recordings, or photographs, or even the person of don Juan; the botanical challenge inherent in the concept of "smokable" mushrooms; and the introjection of non-Yaqui characteristics in the profile of "Yaquiness." Taken together, these irregularities bring into question Castaneda's claims of legitimacy in his representation of Yaqui spirituality and indict the scholarly and publishing communities that promoted his seriously flawed body of work.

In 1972 Weston La Barre, one of the foremost experts on the ritual use of peyote and other "hallucinogens," was asked by the *New York Times* to write a review of Castaneda's *A Separate Reality.* In his professional assessment of the book, he found that it fit in not with serious scholarship but with the "plastic flowers of science-writing," and went on to conclude, "The book is pseudo-profound, sophomoric and deeply vulgar. . . . It is frustratingly and tiresomely dull, posturing pseudo-ethnography and, intellectually, kitsch" (cited in La Barre 1989, 272). The review was never published.

SUFFERING AND REDEMPTION

The variety of its belief systems belies an underlying unity to the New Age movement. Every religious system has a perception of evil, an explanation for how it came into creation, and a possibility (not always a certainty) for the believer to escape its power and consequences. For the dissident early Christians, for example, the problem of evil was a central concern that provided a great impetus to heresy. According to Runciman, "The world that they knew, the cruel, luxurious, uncertain world of the Roman Empire, was undoubtedly a wicked place. How had such wickedness come into creation? If God was the Creator, and God was omnipotent and good, why did he permit such things to be?" (1947, 5).

The New Age movement is unusual in that it is largely based upon a secular theodicy. For many leaders of New Age organizations, manifestations of suffering ranging from individual hunger of the soul to global environmental cataclysm are caused by human agency. For many, evil is not to be understood as the design of an inscrutable deity or the collision of opposing spiritual forces, but as a consequence of political and industrial abuse. Greed and powers of technology, seen to be almost beyond the capacity of human beings to control, are destroying the earth, sundering meaningful human relationships, and fueling negative spiritual energy. As many devotees of the New Age see it, before this shadow passes over the entire planet, each one of us can make a difference. By raising our awareness and spiritual energy, showing love toward one another and Mother Earth, a New Age can be brought about, a gentle apocalypse of peace and environmental awareness. "With this graceful kind of life-style," predicts Medicine Eagle, "there will be little disease and illness. Fear and constriction will give way to love and creative expression. A truly golden time will be upon the garden of Earth" (1991, 443).

There is great variety in the New Age's specific formulations of secular conceptions of sin and suffering, and the ways these are combined with spiritual strategies of transcendence and the acquisition of power. A focus on the environment can be found in the teachings of Sun Bear, founder of the Bear Tribe Medicine Society. This organization is one of the most effec-tive venues for the adaptation and communication of native spirituality to an almost exclusively non-native audience, with an apprenticeship pro-gram in Spokane, Washington, and Medicine Wheel Gatherings held in locations throughout the United States. Coordination of an annual calen-dar of ceremonies and workshops and the popularity of his teachings pro-pelled Sun Bear to a strong position of leadership in New Age circles and gave him top billing in AIM's "hit list" of charlatans purporting to be med-icine people (see Churchill 1992, 221–22). Wabun Wind, appointed med-icine chief of the Bear Tribe Medicine Society upon Sun Bear's death in 1992, has struggled to maintain the organization's momentum but reports optimistically on the receptiveness of a new audience to Sun Bear's teach-ings, including the formation of an independent group in Germany call-ing itself the Bear Tribe in Germany (Wind 1996, 14).

Sun Bear's environmentalism begins with the premise of an Earth in crisis and an Earth Mother who must heal herself of sickness caused by human activity. To survive this "earth cleansing," seen already in volcanic eruptions, earthquakes, and changes in weather patterns, humans "would have to reestablish their very personal ties with the natural world" (cited in Albanese 1990, 159). "If people want to find an 'enemy,' they don't have to look far. The enemy is the consciousness of separation that dom-inates most of the world today. It is the consciousness that tells us that we are separate from the Earth, the minerals, the plants, the animals, and that, because we are separate and stronger and 'more intelligent,' we can misuse them in any way that we want to" (Sun Bear 1996, 52).

In the Bear Tribe Medicine Society there are several simple and appeal-ing strategies that can be used to reestablish harmony with the Earth Mother. The Medicine Wheel, a construction of thirty-six stones that sacralizes the place of gathering, is a source of power and personal insight attuned to both external and internal healing; and the "sharing of energy," facilitated by such diverse activities as shamanic ritual, hugging trees (seen as powerful spiritual conductors mediating between heaven and earth), and sexual intercourse, is essential for developing "harmonic merging," an ability to truly know the Earth and sense the coming of upheavals that accompany the Cleansing (Albanese 1990, 160–61).

Clearly, such practices have a potential to reinforce stereotypes and compromise the status of those who continue to see spiritual awareness as a long and sometimes difficult process, as an "ordeal." Those who have perceived the New Age movement as a threat and chosen to respond to it have done so in two principal ways: with ritual secrecy and the exposure of fraudulent practitioners.

Some native organizations have found that by making ritual knowledge and experience inaccessible to those outside a limited group of initiates, they can insulate their ceremonial lives from the simplifications of casual observers. Membership in the Peyote religion of the Native American Church, for example, is restricted by bylaws and articles of incorporation of church organizations. Since virtually all the peyote in the United States grows in the state of Texas, the Native American Church organizations, in order to harvest the cactus for use as a sacrament, must also be registered with the Texas Department of Public Safety. The regulatory scheme of the state of Texas requires harvesters of peyote to be licensed by the state and by the federal Drug Enforcement Agency, and it limits distribution to Native Americans who meet specific requirements.[6] But rather than resist such legal impediments to the distribution of peyote, leaders of the Native American Church support these laws (Government of the United States 1994, 139). How different would the Native American Church be in, say, ten years if membership were open and use of peyote as a sacrament were accessible to anyone? In this instance, the conservative goals of the Native American Church are consistent with government restrictions of the distribution and use of peyote.

Other ceremonial systems have become closed to outsiders, presumably in response to the disruptive effects of professional and amateur

6. Defining Indian membership is not straightforward, as the preamble to hearings on the amendment to the American Indian Religious Freedom Act of 1994 indicates: "The term 'Indian tribe' means any tribe, band, nation, pueblo, or other organized group or community of Indians, including any Alaska Native village . . . which is recognized as eligible for the special programs and services provided by the United States to Indians because of their status as Indians" (Government of the United States 1994, 13).

curiosity. And those who are excluded are sometimes left with a sense of betrayal. William Fenton, for example, is uncharitable toward those he sees as responsible for the new secrecy surrounding the Cayuga long-house ceremonies: "A new generation of younger Iroquois, unsure of their own culture but eager to restore it, while beset by a fallacy that one must have native genes to appreciate Iroquois culture, have closed the longhouse doors to outsiders who might assist them" (1995, ix–x). Under the direction of new organizations with new rules of participation, lead-ership cannot be obtained except through a long apprenticeship, and life-long enlightenment cannot follow from one spontaneous event or vision. Such restrictions to participation in native ritual can be more sympa-thetically understood if we consider the potential appropriations of the New Age movement.

Literate members of native organizations have thus formulated a loose definition of heresy within the practice of native spirituality. The com-bination of the following attributes is usually considered reason for excluding a self-professed native practitioner from native organizations (exclusion may be accompanied by sanction via written articles and leaflets or even active protest at the site of the practitioner's gatherings): the practitioner acquires wealth from spiritual practice, is unable to report an acceptable spiritual genealogy from a recognized elder, and possesses a spiritual eclecticism that combines native practices with other religious elements, such as eastern mysticism and personal innovation. The involvement of New Age leaders in native spirituality has led to a new religious phenomenon in the late twentieth century: oral traditions turning to an educated minority to combat literate heresy.

Native American critics of New Age practices seem to consistently underestimate the appeal of native traditions as they are popularized in literature and ritualized in short-term gatherings. Even if self-styled lead-ers lack instruction and respect, this does not mean that their followers, however naive or misguided, never experience a sincere desire to under-stand or are incapable of deep spiritual emotions. There is, after all, an apocalyptic flavor to some New Age prophecy not altogether unlike the anticipations of the nineteenth-century prophetic movements. The suf-fering and desperation of the original Ghost Dancers cannot be com-pared with the relative affluence of contemporary seekers of enlighten-ment, but occasionally the concern in both systems of belief with imminent, overwhelming, spiritually mediated transformation of the world is fundamentally similar.

Medicine Wheelers and Dealers

Bernard C. Perley

It can be argued that there are benefits to the popularity of native spiritualism, but this popularity is a double-edged sword and the wounds it makes are deep. Two such wounds I wish to address are the profiteering by the purported New Age "native" healers and the insidious proselytizing of native peoples *by* native peoples in the diluted, popularized regurgitations of "authentic" native spiritual practices.

Two scenarios from my experience with New Age native spiritualism come to mind. The first finds me at a public dinner where I was seated across from a "real" medicine woman. During the course of conversation the medicine woman revealed to me that she was of Abenaki ancestry. Her life's travels had taken her to Blackfoot country where, according to her, she was adopted into the Blackfoot tribe. The medicine man of this particular community saw in her the gifts required to be a good healer, a good medicine woman. Thus, her training had begun. At the same dinner, an Anglo-American artist, who was displaying her medicine shields in a local art exhibit, was seated across from me and next to the medicine woman. The artist revealed to me that she received her visionary instructions from the "real" medicine woman seated next to her. I inquired about the symbolism painted on the various shields, but the artist's answers were hesitant and noncommittal. She deferred the questions to her spiritual leader, the medicine woman. When I asked the medicine woman why so many disparate symbols from so many different native belief systems were being employed, she was equally evasive and tried to change the subject. From that point, neither the medicine woman nor the artist would converse with me, despite the fact that they were sitting directly across from me.

A few days later, I learned that the medicine woman was offering healing sessions through native arts and crafts in the local elementary school. The "medicine" mediums were drums and rattles that "spoke with the voice of Mother Earth." The best news of all was that all that healing was offered for only a modest fee. I wondered if the Blackfoot elder who taught the medicine woman was aware of the New Age profiteering she was engaged in based on his teachings. After all, he should be getting a share of the profits.

The second scenario involved another woman from yet another eastern tribe who had learned her craft from yet another western tribe. This "medicine wheel" woman practiced the dissemination of a medicine wheel myth and philosophy, claiming that she had been instructed by her spiritual teacher to spread the word to all those who would learn. To her credit, unlike the above example, this woman refused to accept monetary compensation for her teachings (notable exceptions included workshops she gave at schools, for which an honorarium was paid). Her presentation was very familiar. I had seen most of the same information in publications in the New Age sections found in almost any bookstore. However, there was one aspect of the presentation that caught my attention. She described at length a "precontact" myth that legitimates the wheel and its philosophy. The myth, as I remember it, went something like this: The colors of the medicine wheel correspond to the colors of the four races of humans on this earth. The colors were determined when the Creator, after creating the world and all the creatures and plants on it, decided this wonderful creation needed caretakers. So the Creator invented white people to provide organization and a work ethic. The Creator also invented yellow people to provide wisdom and learning to the world; black people were to provide emotion and compassion, while red people (of course the most blessed of all) were to be the caretakers of Mother Earth.

Being the skeptic that I am, I have a couple of problems with this "precontact" account. First, if this was precontact, how did the wise ones who first transmitted this story know about the "white," "yellow," and "black" peoples? Second, how did those wise ones also know what the stereotypical personalities of these peoples of "other" colors would be? How come there is no evidence, archaeological or historical, of medicine wheels in the local environs? Also, why hasn't the practice and use of medicine wheel spirituality been remembered in anyone's oral history in the local communities?

Although the above questions are sufficient grounds for debate, there are a few more implications of New Age proselytizing in other areas of native social activities that I want to highlight. First, for those who are spiritually challenged, native medicine and healing have a safe but seductive quality that may make them their paradigm of choice. Unfortunately, they usually have to pay a fee for their salvation, while the medicine wheelers and dealers themselves, or spiritual panderers, become "well-healed." Second, not only is the medicine wheel being used by the medicine wheelers and dealers as a paradigm for native spiritual identity and salvation, but these people have also influenced apostles who in turn use the paradigm for organizing social settings, school curriculums, and arguments for land claims. The troublesome aspect of this approach is that it does not appear to matter to people whether such claims or arguments are reasonable as long as they "simulate" an aboriginal stereotype. It would seem that New Age native spiritualism is not rational and will not tolerate reasonable arguments. Any reasonable arguments that question the validity of importing spiritual practices from other regions of the country, such as bringing the medicine wheel into the northeast, will not be entertained. They will most often be dismissed with a disdainful "Ah, you're not a believer" or "They haven't found the evidence yet."

So, all things considered, I thought, "If I can't beat them I might as well join them," and now I want to introduce my own New Age medicine-wheel product line. My favorite idea is for what I will call Medicine Wheel Vision Quest Cigarettes. The marketing slogan will be "Don't think of it as smoking; think of it as smudging." I will point out that the four ingredients—sage, tobacco, cedar, and sweetgrass—correspond to the four directions, while a special fifth ingredient (which will remain undisclosed) contributes to the efficacy of the vision quest. A second product will be a spiritual cleansing bath soap. The soap will take on the shape and colors of the medicine wheel. I'll even include simulated flakes of natural medicines to give the texture of rustic authenticity and naturalness. If people were willing to spend money on a soap called "Irish Spring," won't they be willing to buy a soap called "Indian Summer"? I'll even make it smell like Indian summers (I won't tell you where). So, look for these products in a store near you!

It is still useful to reflect on what Vine Deloria Jr. suggested in 1969, that "Indian people begin to feel that they are merely shadows of a mythical super-Indian" (1969, 82). But he also lamented that it seems "Indians must be redefined in terms that white men will accept, even if that means re-Indianizing them according to a white man's idea of what they were like in the past and should logically become in the future" (ibid., 92). If that was true in 1969, the New Age movement has since then made Native Americans all the more publicly acceptable. It has accomplished this through profit-oriented New Age native spiritualism.

Soap or cigarettes anyone?

CHAPTER 8
Conclusions

The stuff of what we call history grew in a dream, was
remembered, took shape in the intellect, and was born in
action. Everywhere and at all times there have been men and
women who were able to see through the worlds into which
they were born to new kinds of order. Some themselves gave
their dreams form and wrought a change in the way their fel-
lows regarded each other and the world about them. Others
gave their dreams as weapons for disciples to wield.

Kenelm Burridge, *Mambu*

The first three centuries of European exploration, settlement, mercantile
expansion, and conquest in the New World were accompanied by
attempts to transplant European beliefs and practices in a new and usually untested soil. European monotheism was, in essence, universalist
and exclusive, willing to struggle violently in both the Old World and
the New against local versions of the faith in which orthodoxy was compromised by specific idols or witchcraft or creative interpretations of the
origins and nature of good and evil. Truth was transcendent, unique,
authoritative, and universalist, for both the official clerisy and heretical
innovators; above all, it was by virtue of its universalism capable of being
communicated to "savages." The Reformation only reinforced attachments to universal monotheistic Truth by stressing universal access to it;
but at the same time the new vernacular translations of scriptural sources
encouraged fragmentation and interdenominational competition. In the
Americas, this reinforced the humanitarian impulse to convert the heathen; as in the race for colonial supremacy, one had better get there first
and secure a realm of influence before others gained the advantage.
America was Christianized by universalist truth–bearers with initially
regional ambitions who looked forward to the eventual building of a
wider unity of believers.

For many early colonists, the journey to the Americas was a way to leave behind the oppressions of Europe and realize a yearning for truth in the moral order. Early missionaries envisioned a Christian empire, united in its commitment to instructing and exhorting the "savages" to leave behind their "satanic," "uncivilized" state, to achieve redemption through religion and civility. According to Father Le Jeune, who worked among the Hurons in the seventeenth century, "There is no heart so barbarous that it cannot receive Jesus Christ" (Thwaites 1896–1901, 19:27). This, for the time, was a charitable view. It went together with the realization that without the Indians' sincere, personal transformation, the empire could never be realized.

Indigenous peoples often had their own way of expressing the longings, dilemmas, and anxieties that emerged from colonial and nationalist encounters, in visions of moral orders that often included the new religious ideas of the powerful immigrant peoples while explaining new conditions of suffering, holding out hope for a new dispensation, and maintaining essential connections to (re)articulated traditions. These social visions often did not combine well with either Christian evangelical exclusivism or the drive toward linguistic and cultural homogeneity that accompanied nation building. Indigenous spirituality overcame assimilation efforts when its leaders, in addition to defining and maintaining essential practices and methods of teaching, adopted a political approach of vital unrest, reproach, and admonition, when political and spiritual communities made themselves inconvenient and indigestible.

This is the main source of the "Indian problem." The Indians simply could not be made to "leave the blanket" with ordinary inducements and exhortations. Reservations were seen to be a temporary solution, intended to facilitate land surrender and settlement. But the long-term existence of isolated pockets of Indians with rival notions of political loyalty and a disinclination to "improve" their land by labor was widely seen to be inexpedient and unacceptable. Something would have to be done to make them civilized citizens.

It was discovered that Christian missions were one of the most effective tools of assimilation. Universalist monotheism was ideally suited to the assimilationist goals of nationalist particularism. Religion was seen as the best means of teaching the values of citizenship. "Equality" was understood in terms of cultural homogeneity: in the name of equality missionaries enjoined the Indians to leave behind irrational dependency upon unseen spirits and accept the true faith with its individual responsibility for salvation and its attempt to follow the injunction, taken to its extreme in the influential Puritan model of Indian evangelism, that "the hand of the diligent maketh rich" (Proverbs 10:4). Implementing this ideal in reservation communities whose members were deprived of their livelihood but whose attachment to tradition remained largely unshaken proved to be difficult.

The shift in orientation in eighteenth-century European thought, toward ideas of human perfectibility and progress through the advancement of science and reason, did not so much foster pluralism, or recognition of Indian sovereignty and spiritual integrity, as much as develop a Eurocentric vision of human history in which "savages" were but the backward remnants of humanity left out of the rise of civilization. In the nineteenth century this vision gained popularity and practical focus with the development of socioevolutionism and "scientific" racism. So important were these intellectual currents that the "improvement" of Indians by those with philanthropic goals could no longer be left exclusively to Christian missionaries but was seen as the responsibility of non-Christian (though their members professed to Christianity) charitable organizations and of the state. The Indians were not only to be controlled and settled but to take part in civilized life by leaving behind their attachments to "thraldom" and "superstition" and learning a new and better language, religion, and means of livelihood.

In the late nineteenth century another radical but partially obscured shift took place in attempts to achieve spiritual domination over Indians. With state control over far-flung territories complete or nearing completion, with Indians "pacified" and no longer seen as a significant military threat, nationalism emerged as a new belief system intent on acquiring loyalty and conformity within newly prescribed territorial limits. The nascent nationalisms of the United States and Canada were, officially at least, religiously heterodox and particularist: Rival versions of Christianity could be encouraged to coexist. Nationalist loyalty was not understood as pertaining to a global humanity. Within the reach of the state, however, membership and loyalty were demanded. Nationalist particularism was uncomfortable with the rival internal sovereignties of the states' aboriginal inhabitants.

Removing children from the influence of "blanket Indians" proved to be more effective than attempting to educate them while they remained under the influence of their parents and communities. Residential schools in both the United States and Canada were the preferred instrument of communicating the values of religion and citizenship to native children. The French missionary Mother Marie de Saint Joseph, in her Huron seminary, first made the discovery in 1640 that "there is nothing so docile as these children. One can bend them as he will" (Thwaites 1896–1901, 19:39). Docility, of course, was far from the minds of those children in later residential schools who ran away, stole food, started fires, or simply silently detested their routines and curriculums. The experiment of residential education was a failure in large part because it denied children access to meaningful knowledge, heightened the educators' perceptions of Indian inferiority, and subjected children to high risk of abuse in "total institutions."

Paradoxically, for some time the goals of missions and biomedicine were also complementary. The conviction that subscribing to the goals of missions and biomedicine allowed one access to vital knowledge, the perceived need to change human behavior, and tendencies toward cultural intolerance were the bases of a fit between Christian and biomedical evangelism. Largely because of this fit, the normal skepticism of science was overladen with tendencies to disseminate and defend both religious and scientific orthodoxy. The values of the Enlightenment—a growing confidence in scientific rather than Christian universalism—came to hold sway over Indian policy only by the mid-twentieth century. As the missions were gradually divested of access to the powers of the state, formal medicine acquired it. The doctor replaced the priest, not only as the main custodian of social values but as the most important moral visionary, in a historical transition that was much later in coming to geographically and socially isolated native communities than to the centers of administration and technological development.

Negative perceptions of native healing and ceremonialism have varied historically and been expressed differently by distinct categories of social reformers. To missionaries they were at worst "satanic"—the opposite of piously Christian. To medical reformers, and occasionally research-oriented collectors, they were "superstitious"—the opposite of "rational" and biomedically effective. And to government agents, and occasionally leaders of rival native factions, they were "seditious"—acting in opposition to a fragile national unity. In the process of nation building, these perceptions occasionally converged and could be seen together or in close proximity.

It is true that the failure of assimilationist programs has today become widely apparent and that cultural pluralism is with increasing frequency becoming a consideration for policymakers and professionals responsible for native communities. The government of Canada, for example, has made a significant gesture in releasing its "Statement of Reconciliation" expressing regret for the widespread abuse experienced by native students in residential schools and offering a "healing fund" of $245 million for those who continue to suffer emotionally from its effects (Government of Canada 1998). Despite a divided opinion in the native community, this does appear to represent a slackening of the reins of assimilationist intolerance of native cultures in the supposed interests of national unity. The focus in this gesture, however, is on the neglect, violence, and sexual abuse experienced by students of residential schools, not on the broad impact of cultural disparagement and dismantling. Emotional suffering is often assumed to stem from violence to the body, not from assaults upon identity and spirituality. There is, moreover, no firm indication that local healing initiatives will be supported or that the healing fund will be used in the interests of medical pluralism rather than replacing one form of evangelism with another.

It is easy to assume that one effect of evangelical and political repression of ritual is an irreversible loss of spiritual continuity, that as sanctions and force are brought to bear on a people's ceremonial practices they will be reluctantly surrendered, to be replaced by the outsiders' models of virtue and religious observance. This assumption, however, is challenged by numerous examples of resistance and renewal in the history of efforts to assimilate native North Americans. The atrocities of the Spanish could only disrupt, not eliminate, basic attachments to the indigenous ritual calendars, to the gods and spirits controlling the basic elements required for prosperity. Formal repression of and informal attacks on the developing Peyote religion provoked the formation of the Native American Church, the mounting of an organized defense, and, eventually, lobbying in Washington in support of Native American religious freedom. The repression of the Potlatch and its associated ceremonies among the peoples of Canada's Northwest Coast produced a similar defensive reaction in which the law was circumvented or openly flouted in a self-conscious process of resistance that imparted to socially significant acts of giving a new clarity and cohesiveness.

In the age of nation building, in which native peoples suddenly lost land and sovereignty, radical prophecies were occasionally a response to overwhelming oppression and deprivation; but the objectification of ritual practice was more consistently a response to immediate prohibitions, denigration, and assaults on spiritual observance. Practices *became* rituals in response to domination; and through the process of becoming, they were rearticulated, given new importance, adapted to rapidly changing social circumstances, yet anchored to local understandings of ancestral practices. Religious repression, while a catalyst of racism and social injustice, at the same time put a spark to the energies of social renewal.

Does this lead to the repugnant conclusion that the best way to ensure the vitality of ritual is to suppress it (shall we say, with a minimum of violence)? In some specific instances this may indeed have been borne out, certainly enough times to speak to the futility of the goal of assimilation; but looked at from a human rights perspective, this interpretation of the spirit wars of North America is misleading.

Assaults upon religious integrity are not the only outcomes of assimilationist or ethnocidal policies, but they are the most important. Native peoples' cultural continuity was not much compromised by missionary prohibitions against cracking lice between the teeth or learning traffic rules in the residential school of an isolated trading post crisscrossed only by footpaths, but more sweeping religious upheaval was both the cause and symptom of wider social destruction. Those who are spiritually confused, factionalized, or despondent are less able to defend themselves against political and material exploitation; and those recovering from sudden loss of sovereignty or the material bases of their way of life have a keener sense of a need for spiritual beliefs and practices to heal, help them to understand their new circumstances, and provide anchorage to the past. This is the vicious cycle that, despite many good intentions, has made organized intervention in indigenous peoples' beliefs and practices so destructive.

The repression of native North American spirituality can thus inform us more generally about the nature of cultural genocide. This issue is made all the more relevant by the censure of ethnocide and genocide in the draft Declaration on the Rights of Indigenous Peoples. As member states of the United Nations move toward a greater willingness to reconsider their relationships with indigenous peoples, and as the term "cultural genocide" gains wider currency, it becomes important to consider its meaning and implications.

The virulent prejudice inherent in the view that Indians are religiously backward, or worse, inclined toward evil, was in itself an assault upon indigenous spirituality, but one that would probably have had limited effect had it not provided the rationale for the drastic measures taken to enlighten, educate, and reform the Indians. The most inflexible, punitive strategies of conversion or assimilation—using closed communities like the New England praying towns or closed institutions like residential schools—obstructed native strategies of accommodation, attempting to confine the dream of a future moral order to the orthodox visions of the Christian empire or the emerging nation, leaving no room for the "docile" Indians to follow their own exceptional men and women in dreaming, or observing Christianity, or practicing healing. An important aspect of cultural genocide among indigenous peoples has involved instilling in them the values of Christianity while denying them their own style of religious expression, and instilling in them the values of nationalism while denying them the rights of nationhood. The force of the ideas that a universally or nationally valid source of knowledge can guide human behavior, that this faith or system of learning is exclusive of all others, and that human prosperity and salvation depends upon its dissemination, was, among native peoples, an impediment to spiritual and intellectual sovereignty, to the creative adaptation of new ideas in times of tumultuous change.

The meaning of cultural genocide is clarified when we consider what it does, what its consequences are for people. There is a connection between the despondency and despair of those living in indigenous communities who are unable to stem the downward spirals of addiction, family violence, and suicide, between "social pathology" and local histories of rapid social change, institutional dependency, and a loss of autonomy in healing. One of the most volatile cocktails of the colonial encounter combines evangelical convictions of a dominated people's tendency toward religious error with competition between them and the dominant society over resources and sovereignty. Besides the obvious destructive impacts of extractive industry on native peoples living close to the land, instances of "social pathology" can often also be connected to residential school experience, religious factionalism, and interruptions in the process of healing. Cultural genocide does not manifest itself in the purposeful, violent destruction of human lives, but rather in the seemingly inexplicable self-destruction of individuals and communities.

If it is difficult to isolate the social consequences of cultural genocide, it is almost impossible to assign responsibility for it. Obviously some individuals—such as Richard Pratt, the pioneer of Indian residential education; Alice Fletcher, the anthropologist who implemented the division of reservation lands into individual landholdings and the surrender of sacred objects; and William Halliday, the enforcer of the "Potlatch laws"—intended to erase all vestiges of indigenous life, to absorb Indians into mainstream society; but the individual and social histories of cultural conflict and spiritual confusion are numerous and complex. Responsibility for cultural genocide is difficult to assign because of the variety of social forces that contribute to it. Cultural genocide, like the social injustice of racism, is a cumulatively created product of the many.

Clearly, cultural genocide is not the same as purposeful mass killing, although the two, as the Wounded Knee massacre shows, can for brief episodes come together in a one-sided frenzy of violence. The hopelessness and self-destruction we find where economic, political, and spiritual forces have been annexed do not result from malice but from the uncompromising exercise of domination; self-destruction also results from the misguided exercise of philanthropy that, in an error laden with irony, sees domination as a way of encouraging an unrealizable ideal of self-sufficiency. In this way, cultural genocide is not inspired by hate, but by a hateful form of love.

Genocide and cultural genocide share at least one objective: dispossession. The one disposes intentionally and immediately of human life; the other establishes, sometimes unintentionally, a prolonged state of collective suffering. Genocide and cultural genocide share the destruction of human life, the former through organized violence and mass killing, the latter through the slow accretions of hopelessness and self-destruction. A necessary condition of both genocide and cultural genocide is a widespread perception by a dominant society of inferiority and evil in a subject people; but cultural genocide is the response that begins with the goals of improvement and redemption, with a perception of hope in the possibility of separating those who can be reshaped from those who remain intractable—in the possibility of replacing religious waywardness or deficiency with formal training in the virtues of civilization, the benefits of science, the pride of nationhood, and an "education of the heart."

References Cited

Aberle, David
  1991   *The Peyote Religion among the Navaho.* 2nd ed. Norman: University of Oklahoma Press.

Albanese, Catherine
  1990   *Nature Religion in America: From the Algonkian Indians to the New Age.* Chicago: University of Chicago Press.

Anderson, Benedict
  1991   *Imagined Communities: Reflections on the Origin and Spread of Nationalism.* London: Verso.

Arkin, Kimberly
  1998   "Objects, Indians, and Institutions: Alice Fletcher's Anthropology, 1880–1892." Senior thesis, Department of Anthropology, Harvard University.

Augustine
  1972   *Concerning the City of God against the Pagans.* Trans. Henry
  [1467]   Bettenson. New York: Penguin.

Axtell, James
  1981   *The European and the Indian: Essays in the Ethnohistory of Colonial North America.* Oxford: Oxford University Press.
  1988   *After Columbus: Essays in the Ethnohistory of Colonial North America.* Oxford: Oxford University Press.

Barman, Jean, Yvonne Hébert, and Don McCaskill, eds.
  1986   *Indian Education in Canada.* Vol. 1, *The Legacy.* Vancouver: University of British Columbia Press.

Beaver, R. Pierce
  1988   "Protestant Churches and the Indians." In *Handbook of North American Indians,* ed. Wilcomb Washburn. Vol. 4, *History of*

Indian-White Relations. Washington, D.C.: Smithsonian Institution.

Berkhofer, Robert Jr.
1978   *The White Man's Indian: Images of the American Indian from Columbus to the Present.* New York: Vintage Books.

Berlin, Isaiah
1990   *The Crooked Timber of Humanity: Chapters in the History of Ideas.* Ed. Henry Hardy. Princeton: Princeton University Press.

Binford, L. A.
1962   "Archaeology Is Anthropology," *American Antiquity* 28: 217–25.

Boas, Franz
1897   *The Social Organization and the Secret Societies of the Kwakiutl Indians,* 311–738. Washington, D.C.: United States National Museum.

1982   *Race, Language, and Culture.* Chicago: University of Chicago
[1940]   Press.

Bowman, Margaret
1989   "The Reburial of Native American Skeletal Remains: Approaches to the Resolution of a Conflict," *Harvard Environmental Law Review* 13 (1): 147–208.

Bracken, Christopher
1997   *The Potlatch Papers: A Colonial Case History.* Chicago: University of Chicago Press.

Brauer, Jaymie
1992   "Out of the Closet: The Research Value of Human Skeletal Collections," *Museum Anthropology* 16 (2): 35–39.

Brown, Jennifer
1996   "The Track to Heaven: The Hudson Bay Cree Religious Movement of 1842–1843." In *The Native Imprint: The Contributions of First Peoples to Canada's Character,* ed. Olive Patricia Dickason. Vol. 2, *From 1815.* Athabasca, Alta.: Athabasca University Educational Enterprises.

Bruchac, Joseph
1993   *The Native American Sweat Lodge.* Freedom, Calif.: Crossing Press.

Burridge, Kenelm
1960   *Mambu: A Melanesian Millennium.* Princeton: Princeton University Press.

Carter, John
1994   "Museums and Indigenous Peoples in Canada." In *Museums and the Appropriation of Culture.* Ed. Susan Pearce. London: Athlone Press.

Cave, Alfred
1996   *The Pequot War.* Amherst: University of Massachusetts Press.

Christian, William A. Jr.
1981   *Local Religion in Sixteenth-Century Spain.* Princeton: Princeton University Press.

Churchill, Ward
  1992   *Fantasies of the Master Race: Literature, Cinema, and the Colonization of American Indians.* Monroe, Maine: Common Courage Press.
Clark, G. A.
  1996   "NAGPRA and the Demon-Haunted World." Letter, *Society for American Archaeology Bulletin* 14 (5): 3.
Clendinnen, Inga
  1987   *Ambivalent Conquests: Maya and Spaniard in Yucatan, 1517–1570.* Cambridge: Cambridge University Press.
Clifford, James
  1988   *The Predicament of Culture: Twentieth-Century Ethnography, Literature, and Art.* Cambridge, Mass.: Harvard University Press.
Cole, Douglas, and Ira Chaikin
  1990   *An Iron Hand upon the People: The Law against the Potlatch on the Northwest Coast.* Vancouver: Douglas and McIntyre; Seattle: University of Washington Press.
Collier, John
  1952   "The Peyote Cult." Letter, *Science* 115:503–4.
Comrie, Marilyn, and Carol Kimball
  1987   *The Union Baptist Church of Mystic, Connecticut: Its Story.* Mystic, Conn.: Union Baptist Church.
Cordell, Linda S.
  1984   *Prehistory of the Southwest.* New York: Academic Press.
Cornell, Stephen
  1988   *The Return of the Native: American Indian Political Resurgence.* New York: Oxford University Press.
Cronon, William
  1983   *Changes in the Land: Indians, Colonists, and the Ecology of New England.* New York: Hill and Wang.
Crow Dog, Leonard, and Richard Erdoes
  1995   *Crow Dog; Four Generations of Sioux Medicine Men.* New York: HarperCollins Publishers.
Cushing, Frank Hamilton
  1941   *My Adventures in Zuni.* Santa Fe: Peripatetic Press.
DeForest, John
  1852   *History of the Indians of Connecticut from the Earliest Known Period to 1850.* Hartford: Wm. Jas. Hamesley.
Deloria, Vine Jr.
  1969   *Custer Died for Your Sins: An Indian Manifesto.* New York: Avon Books.
  1979   Introduction to *Black Elk Speaks,* by John G. Neihardt. Lincoln: University of Nebraska Press.
  1991   "Commentary: Research, Redskins, and Reality." *American Indian Quarterly* 15 (4): 457–68.
  1992a   *God Is Red: A Native View of Religion.* 2nd ed. Golden, Colo.: North American Press.

1992b   "Indians, Archaeologists, and the Future." *American Antiquity* 57 (4): 595–98.

1994   Foreword to *The Dream Seekers: Native Visionary Traditions of the Great Plains,* by Lee Irwin. Norman: University of Oklahoma Press.

DeMallie, Raymond

1987   "Lakota Belief and Ritual in the Nineteenth Century." In *Sioux Indian Religion.* Ed. Raymond DeMallie and Douglas Parks. Norman: University of Oklahoma Press.

1991   Introduction to *The Ghost-Dance Religion and the Sioux Outbreak of 1890,* by James Mooney. Lincoln: University of Nebraska Press.

DeMallie, Raymond, and Douglas Parks, eds.

1987   *Sioux Indian Religion.* Norman: University of Oklahoma Press.

Densmore, Francis

1928   *Uses of Plants by the Chippewa Indians.* Forty-fourth Annual Report of the Bureau of American Ethnology. Washington: U.S. Government Printing Office.

DePalma, Anthony

1998   "Canada's Indigenous Tribes Receive Formal Apology." *New York Times,* 8 January, p. A3.

Desjarlais, Robert, Leon Eisenberg, Byron Good, and Arthur Kleinman

1995   *World Mental Health: Problems and Priorities in Low-Income Countries.* Oxford: Oxford University Press.

Dorsey, George

1896   "The History of the Study of Anthropology in Harvard University." Harvard University Archives, doc. no. HOC 8896.19, Lamont Library.

Dorsey, George, and H. R. Voth

1901   *The Oraibi Soyal Ceremony.* Publications of the Field Columbian Museum, Anthropological Series, vol. 3, pp. 1–59. Chicago: Field Columbian Museum.

1902   *The Mishongnovi Ceremonies of the Snake and Antelope Fraternities.* Publications of the Field Columbian Museum, Anthropological Series, vol. 3, pp. 159–261. Chicago: Field Columbian Museum.

Dorsey, James Owen

1894   *A Study of Siouan Cults.* Eleventh Annual Report of the Bureau of American Ethnology, 351–544. Washington, D.C.: U.S. Government Printing Office.

Durkheim, Emile

1933   *The Division of Labor in Society.* Trans. George Simpson. New York: Free Press.

Eliot, John

1980   *John Eliot's Indian Dialogues: A Study in Cultural Interaction.*
[1671]   Ed. Henry Bowden and James Ronda. Westport, Conn.: Greenwood Press.

Emerson, Ralph Waldo
    1926   *Emerson's Essays.* New York: Harper and Row.
    1995   *The Heart of Emerson's Journals.* Ed. Bliss Perry. New York:
    [1926]   Dover Publications.
Espinosa, J. Manuel, trans. and ed.
    1988   *The Pueblo Indian Revolt of 1696 and the Franciscan Missions
                in New Mexico: Letters of the Missionaries and Related Docu-
                ments.* Norman: University of Oklahoma Press.
Fee, Elizabeth, and Dorothy Porter
    1992   "Public Health, Preventive Medicine, and Professionalization:
                England and America in the Nineteenth Century." In *Medicine
                in Society: Historical Essays.* Ed. Andrew Wear. Cambridge:
                Cambridge University Press.
Feest, Christian
    1992   "American Indians and Ethnographic Collecting in Europe."
                Museum Anthropology 16 (1): 7–11.
Fenton, William
    1995   Introduction to *Midwinter Rites of the Cayuga Long House,* by
                Frank Speck. Lincoln: University of Nebraska Press.
Fletcher, Alice
    1888   Letter to Frederic Putnam. November 18. Harvard University
                Archives, Putnam Correspondence, Lamont Library.
Fletcher, Alice, and Francis La Flesche
    1992   *The Omaha Tribe.* Lincoln: University of Nebraska Press.
    [1911]
Fred, Randy
    1988   Foreword to *Resistance and Renewal: Surviving the Indian Resi-
                dential School,* by Celia Haig-Brown. Vancouver: Tillacum Library.
Geboe, Charlie
    1997   Unpublished report. Office of the Indian Education Program,
                Bureau of Indian Affairs, Department of the Interior.
Gellner, Ernest
    1981   *Muslim Society.* Cambridge: Cambridge University Press.
Goddard, John
    1991   *Last Stand of the Lubicon Cree.* Vancouver: Douglas and McIntyre.
Goldhagen, Daniel
    1996   *Hitler's Willing Executioners: Ordinary Germans and the Holo-
                caust.* New York: Vintage Books.
Good, Byron
    1994   *Medicine, Rationality, and Experience: An Anthropological Per-
                spective.* Cambridge: Cambridge University Press.
Government of Canada
    1884   *Annual Report of the Department of Indian Affairs for the Year
                Ended 31st December, 1883.* Ottawa: MacLean, Roger, and
                Company.
    1885   *Annual Report of the Department of Indian Affairs for the Year
                Ended 31st December, 1884.* Ottawa: MacLean, Roger, and
                Company.

[1886?]   *The Facts Respecting Indian Administration in the North-West.*
            Ottawa: Department of Indian Affairs.

1977   *Agreement Dated 16th December 1977 between Her Majesty the
            Queen in Right of the Province of Manitoba and the Manitoba
            Hydro-Electric Board and the Northern Flood Committee, Inc.
            and Her Majesty the Queen in Right of Canada as Represented
            by the Minister of Indian Affairs and Northern Development (the
            Northern Flood Agreement).* Unpublished.

1991   *Statistical Profile on Native Mental Health.* Ottawa: Medical Ser-
            vices Branch, Indian and Northern Health Services.

1996   *Report of the Royal Commission on Aboriginal Peoples.* Vol. 1,
            Looking Forward, Looking Back. Minister of Supply and Ser-
            vices. Ottawa: Canada Communication Group Publishing.

1998   *Statement of Reconciliation: Learning from the Past.* Ottawa:
            Department of Indian Affairs and Northern Development.

Government of Québec
1976   *The James Bay and Northern Québec Agreement.* Québec: Édi-
            teur officiel du Québec.

Government of the United States
1868   *Treaty between the United States of America and the Navajo
            Tribe of Indians.* Concluded June 1, 1868, Ratification Advised
            July 25, 1868, Proclaimed August 12, 1868. Washington, D.C.:
            U.S. Government Printing Office.

1872   *Report of the Commissioner of Indian Affairs.* 42nd Congress,
            U.S. doc. 1505. Washington, D.C.: U.S. Government Printing
            Office.

1886   *Report of the Commissioner of Indian Affairs.* Washington, D.C.:
            U.S. Government Printing Office.

1992   *Annual Education Report.* Office of Indian Education Programs,
            Bureau of Indian Affairs. Washington, D.C.: U.S. Government
            Printing Office.

1994   *American Indian Religious Freedom Act Amendments of 1994.*
            Hearing before the Subcommittee on Native American Affairs of
            the Committee on Natural Resources. 103rd Congress. Wash-
            ington, D.C.: U.S. Government Printing Office.

Graham, Lorie
1997   "The Past Never Vanishes: A Contextual Critique of the Exist-
            ing Indian Family Doctrine." Manuscript.

Green, Jesse, ed.
1990   *Cushing at Zuni: The Correspondence and Journals of Frank
            Hamilton Cushing, 1879–1884.* Albuquerque: University of New
            Mexico Press.

Green, Rayna
1989   "'Kill the Indian and Save the Man': Indian Education in the
            United States." In *To Lead and to Serve: American Indian Edu-
            cation at Hampton Institute, 1878–1923.* Ed. Mary Lou Hult-

gren and Paulette Molin. N.p.: Virginia Foundation for the Humanities and Public Policy.

Grimes, Ronald
1986   "Desecration of the Dead: An Inter-religious Controversy." *American Indian Quarterly* 10 (4): 305–18.

Grobsmith, Elizabeth
1994   *Indians in Prison: Incarcerated Native Americans in Nebraska.* Lincoln: University of Nebraska Press.

Gutiérez, Ramon
1991   *When Jesus Came, the Corn Mothers Went Away: Marriage, Sexuality, and Power in New Mexico, 1500–1846.* Stanford: Stanford University Press.

Hackett, Charles, and Charmion Shelby, eds.
1942   *Revolt of the Pueblo Indians of New Mexico and Otermín's Attempted Reconquest, 1680–1682.* Vol. 1. Albuquerque: University of New Mexico Press.

Haig-Brown, Celia
1988   *Resistance and Renewal: Surviving the Indian Residential School.* Vancouver: Tillacum Library.

Hall, Robert
1997   *An Archaeology of the Soul: North American Indian Belief and Ritual.* Urbana: University of Illinois Press.

Handler, Richard
1988   *Nationalism and the Politics of Culture in Quebec.* Madison: University of Wisconsin Press.

Heizer, Robert, and Alan Almquist
1971   *The Other Californians: Prejudice and Discrimination under Spain, Mexico, and the United States to 1920.* Berkeley and Los Angeles: University of California Press.

Herrick, James
1995   *Iroquois Medical Botany.* Ed. Dean Snow. Syracuse: Syracuse University Press.

Hinsley, Curtis
1979   "Anthropology as Science and Politics: The Dilemmas of the Bureau of American Ethnology, 1879 to 1904." In *The Uses of Anthropology.* Ed. Walter Goldschmidt. Washington: Anthropological Association of America.

1983   "Ethnographic Charisma and Scientific Routine: Cushing and Fewkes in the American Southwest, 1879–1893." In *Observers Observed.* Ed. George Stocking. Madison: University of Wisconsin Press.

1992   "Collecting Cultures and Cultures of Collecting: The Lure of the American Southwest, 1880–1915." *Museum Anthropology* 16 (1): 12–20.

1994   *The Smithsonian and the American Indian: Making a Moral Anthropology in Victorian America.* Washington: Smithsonian Institution Press.

Hodge, F. W.
    1931   Letter to Emil W. Haury, October 5. Doc. no. 94–36. Hem-
                menway Collection. Archives of the Peabody Museum, Cam-
                bridge, Mass.
Houk, Rose
    1992   *Anasazi: Prehistoric Cultures of the Southwest.* Tucson: South-
                west Parks and Monuments Association.
Hultgren, Mary Lou, and Paulette Molin
    1989   *To Lead and to Serve: American Indian Education at Hampton
                Institute, 1878–1923.* N.p.: Virginia Foundation for the Human-
                ities and Public Policy.
Hultkrantz, Ake
    1967   *The Religions of the American Indians.* Trans. Monica Setter-
                wall. Berkeley and Los Angeles: University of California Press.
Indigenous Times (Manitoba)
    1998   "MKO Calls for Inquiry," September, p. 10.
Irwin, Lee
    1994   *The Dream Seekers: Native Visionary Traditions of the Great
                Plains.* Norman: University of Oklahoma Press.
James Bay Cree Cultural Education Centre
    1990   *Once Upon This Land: The Legend of Aayaasaau.* Chisasibi,
                Quebec: James Bay Cree Cultural Education Centre.
James, William
    1990   *The Varieties of Religious Experience.* New York: Vintage Books.
    [1902]
Johnston, Basil H.
    1988   *Indian School Days.* Toronto: Key Porter Books.
Jorgensen, Joseph
    1972   *The Sun Dance Religion: Power for the Powerless.* Chicago: Uni-
                versity of Chicago Press.
Kehoe, Alice B.
    1990   "Primal Gaia: Primitivists and Plastic Medicine Men." In *The
                Invented Indian: Cultural Fictions and Government Policies.* Ed.
                James A. Clifton. New Brunswick: Transaction Publishers.
Kessell, John
    1987   *Kiva, Cross, and Crown: The Pecos Indians and New Mexico,
                1540–1840.* Albuquerque: University of New Mexico Press.
Kessell, John, and Rick Hendricks, eds.
    1991   *The Spanish Missions of New Mexico.* Vol. 1, *Before 1680.* New
                York: Garland Publishing.
Kidwell, Clara Sue
    1991   "Aztec and European Medicine in the New World, 1521–1600."
                In *The Anthropology of Medicine: From Culture to Method.* Ed.
                Lola Romanucci-Ross, Daniel Moerman, and Laurence Tancredi.
                2nd ed. New York: Bergin and Garvey.

Kleinman, Arthur
    1995   *Writing at the Margin: Discourse between Anthropology and Medicine.* Berkeley and Los Angeles: University of California Press.
Knaut, Andrew
    1995   *The Pueblo Revolt of 1680: Conquest and Resistance in Seventeenth-Century New Mexico.* Norman: University of Oklahoma Press.
Kunitz, Stephen, and Jerrold Levy
    1994   *Drinking Careers: A Twenty-Five-Year Study of Three Navajo Populations.* New Haven: Yale University Press.
La Barre, Weston
    1989   *The Peyote Cult.* 5th ed. Norman: University of Oklahoma Press.
Lafitau, Joseph-François
    1983   *Moeurs des sauvages américains comparées aux moeurs des pre-*
    [1724]   *miers temps.* Vol. 2. Paris: François Maspero.
LaFramboise, Teresa
    1988   "American Indian Mental Health Policy." *American Psychologist* 43 (5): 388–97.
Lamar, Howard, and Sam Truett
    1996   "The Greater Southwest and California from the Beginning of European Settlement to the 1880s." In *The Cambridge History of the Native Peoples of the Americas.* Ed. Bruce Trigger and Wilcomb Washburn. Vol. 1, pt. 2. Cambridge: Cambridge University Press.
Lavallée, Claudette
    1988   "Evaluation of the Bush Kit Program." Unpublished report. Département de santé communautaire, Hôpital Général de Montréal.
    1991   "Faisabilité d'inclure des éléments de medicine traditionelle dans le programme bush-kit." Unpublished report. Département de santé communautaire, Hôpital Général de Montréal.
Lazarus, Edward
    1991   *Black Hills, White Justice: The Sioux Nation versus the United States, 1775 to the Present.* New York: HarperCollins.
Legters, Lyman
    1992   "The American Genocide." In *Native Americans and Public Policy.* Ed. Fremont Lyden and Lyman Legters. Pittsburgh: University of Pittsburgh Press.
Lindholm, Charles
    1990   *Charisma.* Cambridge, Mass.: Blackwell.
Locke, John
    1996   *Some Thoughts Concerning Education and of the Conduct of the*
    [1693,   *Understanding.* Ed. Ruth Grant and Nathan Tarcov. Indianapo-
    1706]   lis: Hackett Publishing Company.

Loesch, Martin
1996   "The First Americans and the 'Free' Exercise of Religion." In
          Native American Cultural and Religious Freedoms. Ed. John
          Wunder. New York: Garland Publishing.
Lovejoy, Arthur, and George Boas
1965   *Primitivism and Related Ideas in Antiquity.* New York: Octagon
          Books.
Macdonald, John A.
1884   "Report of the Superintendent General of Indian Affairs." In
          Annual Report of the Department of Indian Affairs, by the
          Dominion of Canada. Ottawa: MacLean, Roger, and Company.
Macfarlane, Alan
1970   *Witchcraft in Tudor and Stuart England: A Regional and Com-
          parative Study.* Prospect Heights, Ill.: Waveland Press.
MacGregor, Roy
1989   *Chief: The Fearless Vision of Billy Diamond.* Toronto: Penguin
          Books.
Mancall, Peter
1995   *Deadly Medicine: Indians and Alcohol in Early America.* Ithaca:
          Cornell University Press.
Manitoba Keewatinowi Okimakanak Nations
1998   "MKO Calls for Public Inquiry into Former Manitoba Sanato-
          riums" (Thompson, Manitoba), 1 (11): 1.
Manson, Spero, James Shore, and Joseph Bloom
1985   "The Depressive Experience in Native American Communities: A
          Challenge for Psychiatric Theory and Diagnosis." In *Culture and
          Depression: Studies in the Anthropology and Cross-Cultural Psy-
          chiatry of Affect and Disorder.* Ed. Arthur Kleinman and Byron
          Good. Berkeley and Los Angeles: University of California Press.
Mark, Joan
1988   *A Stranger in Her Native Land.* Lincoln: University of Nebraska
          Press.
Maybury-Lewis, David
1997   *Indigenous Peoples, Ethnic Groups, and the State.* Needham
          Heights, Mass.: Allyn and Bacon.
McBride, Kevin
1990   "The Historical Archaeology of the Mashantucket Pequots,
          1637–1900: A Preliminary Analysis." In *The Pequots in South-
          ern New England: The Fall and Rise of an American Indian
          Nation.* Ed. Laurence M. Hauptman and James Wherry. Nor-
          man: University of Oklahoma Press.
McGarry, John, and Brendan O'Leary, eds.
1993   *The Politics of Ethnic Conflict Regulation.* New York: Routledge.
McIlwraith, T. F.
1992   *The Bella Coola Indians.* Toronto: University of Toronto Press.
[1948]

McLaughlin, Daniel

1992 *When Literacy Empowers: Navajo Language in Print.* Albuquerque: University of New Mexico Press.

McLean, Scott

1980 Introduction to *The Real Work: Interviews and Talks, 1964–1979,* by Gary Snyder. New York: New Directions Publishing.

Medicine Eagle, Brooke

1991 *Buffalo Woman Comes Singing.* New York: Ballantine Books.

Mennonite Central Committee

1975 Report of the Panel of Public Enquiry into Northern Hydro Development. Appendix B. Transcript of Hearings Convened at Holy Rosary Church, Winnipeg. Unpublished report.

Miller, J. R.

1996 *Shingwauk's Vision: A History of Native Residential Schools.* Toronto: University of Toronto Press.

Moerman, Daniel

1991 "Poisoned Apples and Honeysuckles: The Medicinal Plants of Native America." In *The Anthropology of Medicine.* Ed. Lola Romanucci-Ross, Daniel Moerman, and Laurence Tancredi. 2nd ed. New York: Bergin and Garvey.

Montesquieu, Charles de Secondat

1989 *The Spirit of the Laws.* Trans. and ed. Anne Cohler, Basia Miller,
[1748] and Harold Stone. Cambridge: Cambridge University Press.

Mooney, James

1991 *The Ghost Dance Religion and the Sioux Outbreak of 1890.*
[1896] Lincoln: University of Nebraska Press.

1897 "The Kiowa Peyote Rite." *Der Urquell* 1:329–33.

Moore, Martin

1842 *Memoir of Eliot, Apostle to the North American Indians.* Boston: Seth Goldsmith and Crocker and Brewster.

Moore, Richard

1975 Letter to Stephen Williams, June 1. Peabody Museum, Cambridge, Mass.

Morgan, Lewis Henry

1962 *League of the Iroquois.* New York: Citadel Press.
[1851]

1974 *Ancient Society, or Researches into the Lines of Human Progress*
[1877] *from Savagery through Barbarism to Civilization.* Gloucester, Mass.: Peter Smith.

Nabokov, Peter

1992 *Native American Testimony: A Chronicle of Indian-White Relations from Prophecy to the Present, 1492–1992.* New York: Penguin Books.

Neihardt, John

1979 *Black Elk Speaks: Being the Life Story of a Holy Man of the*
[1932] *Ogalala Sioux.* Lincoln: University of Nebraska Press.

Niezen, Ronald

1993   "Power and Dignity: The Social Consequences of Hydro-Electric
            Development for the James Bay Cree." *Canadian Review of Soci-
            ology and Anthropology* 30:510–29.

1997   "Healing and Conversion: Medical Evangelism in James Bay
            Cree Society." *Ethnohistory* 44 (3): 463–91.

1998   *Defending the Land: Sovereignty and Forest Life in James Bay
            Cree Society.* Needham Heights, Mass.: Allyn and Bacon.

Nishnawbe-Aski Nation

1991   "Agenda for First Nations and Inuit Mental Health." Unpub-
            lished report.

1996   "Nishnawbe-Aski Nation Youth Forum on Suicide." Unpub-
            lished report.

O'Connor, Bonnie Blair

1995   *Healing Traditions: Alternative Medicine and the Health Pro-
            fessions.* Philadelphia: University of Pennsylvania Press.

O'Nell, Theresa

1996   *Disciplined Hearts: History, Identity, and Depression in an Amer-
            ican Indian Community.* Berkeley and Los Angeles: University of
            California Press.

Parezo, Nancy J.

1985   "Cushing as Part of the Team: The Collecting Activities of the
            Smithsonian Institution." *American Ethnologist* 12 (4): 763–75.

Peabody Museum

1884   *Annual Report.* Cambridge, Mass.

1890   *Annual Report.* Cambridge, Mass.

Pratt, Richard Henry

1964   *Battlefield and Classroom: Four Decades with the American
            Indian, 1867–1904.* Ed. Robert Utley. Lincoln: University of
            Nebraska Press.

Prucha, Francis Paul

1979   *The Churches and the Indian Schools, 1888–1912.* Lincoln: Uni-
            versity of Nebraska Press.

1994   *American Indian Treaties: The History of a Political Anomaly.*
            Berkeley and Los Angeles: University of California Press.

Prucha, Francis Paul, ed.

1973   *Americanizing the American Indians.* Cambridge, Mass.: Har-
            vard University Press.

Radin, Paul

1933   *The Method and Theory of Ethnology.* New York: McGraw-Hill.

1945   *The Road of Life and Death.* New York: Pantheon Books.

Reff, Daniel

1995   "The 'Predicament of Culture' and Spanish Missionary Accounts
            of the Tepehuan and Pueblo Revolts." *Ethnohistory* 42 (1): 63–90.

Religious Tract Society

[183?]   *Missionary Records: North America.* London: J. Rider.

Reyhner, Jon

1990   *Teaching American Indian Students.* Norman: University of Oklahoma Press.

Riddington, Robin

1988   "A Tree That Stands Burning: Reclaiming a Point of View as from the Center." Manuscript, University of British Columbia.

1992   Introduction to *The Omaha Tribe,* by Alice Fletcher and Francis La Flesche. Lincoln: University of Nebraska Press.

Ronda, James

1977   "'We Are Well as We Are': An Indian Critique of Seventeenth-Century Christian Missions." *William and Mary Quarterly* 34 (1): 66–82.

Rousseau, Jean-Jacques

1966   *Émile ou de l'éducation.* Paris: Garnier-Flammarion.
[1759]

Runciman, Steven.

1947   *The Medieval Manichee; A Study of the Christian Dualist Heresy.* Cambridge: Cambridge University Press.

Russel, Howard S.

1980   *Indian New England before the Mayflower.* Hanover: University Press of New England.

Russell, Bertrand

1976   *Unpopular Essays.* London: Unwin Paperbacks.

Sagan, Carl

1996   *The Demon-Haunted World: Science as a Candle in the Dark.* New York: Ballantine Books.

Said, Edward

1978   *Orientalism.* New York: Vintage Books.

Salisbury, Neal

1974   "Red Puritans: The 'Praying Indians' of Massachusetts Bay and John Eliot." *William and Mary Quarterly* 31 (1): 27–54.

1982   *Manitou and Providence: Indians, Europeans, and the Making of New England, 1500–1643.* Oxford: Oxford University Press.

1987   "Social Relationships on a Moving Frontier: Natives and Settlers in Southern New England, 1638–1675." *Man in the Northeast* 33:89–99.

1990   "Indians and Colonists in Southern New England after the Pequot War: An Uneasy Balance." In *The Pequots in Southern New England: The Fall and Rise of an American Indian Nation.* Ed. Laurence Hauptman and James Wherry. Norman: University of Oklahoma Press.

1996   "Native People and European Settlers in Eastern North America, 1600–1783." In *The Cambridge History of the Native Peoples of the Americas.* Ed. Bruce Trigger and Wilcomb Washburn. Vol. 1, pt. 1. Cambridge: Cambridge University Press.

Sando, Joe
    1979   "The Pueblo Revolt." In *Handbook of North American Indians,
                Southwest. Ed. Alfonso Ortiz. Vol. 9. Washington: Smithsonian
                Institution.
Sarfaty, Galit
    1997   "Bridging the Great Divide: Repatriation as a Springboard for
                Cooperation between Native Americans and Anthropologists."
                Manuscript.
Saum, Jeremy
    1995   "The Control of Culture: The Smithsonian National Museum of
                the American Indian." Senior thesis, Committee on Degrees in
                Social Studies, Harvard University.
Schiffer, Michael B.
    1976   *Behavioral Archaeology*. New York: Academic Press.
Schindlbeck, Markus
    1993   "The Art of Collecting: Interactions between Collectors and the
                People They Visit." *Zeitschrift für Ethnologie* 118:57–67.
Schoolcraft, Henry Rowe
    1846   *Plan for the Investigation of American Ethnology: To Include the
                Facts Derived from Other Parts of the Globe and the Eventual
                Formation of a Museum of Antiquities and the Peculiar Fabrics
                of Nations; and also the Collection of a Library of the Philology
                of the World, Manuscript and Printed*. New York: Edward O.
                Jenkins.
    1851–60   *Historical and Statistical Information Respecting the History,
                Condition, and Prospects of the Indian Tribes of the United
                States*. 6 vols. Philadelphia: J. B. Lippincott.
Shkilnyk, Anastasia
    1985   *A Poison Stronger Than Love: The Destruction of an Ojibwa
                Community*. New Haven: Yale University Press.
Simmons, William
    1983   "Red Yankees: Narragansett Conversion in the Great Awaken-
                ing." *American Ethnologist* 10 (2): 253–71.
Simmons, William, and Cheryl Simmons, eds.
    1982   *Old Light on Separate Ways: The Narragansett Diary of Joseph
                Fish, 1765–1776*. Hanover, N.H.: University Press of New
                England.
Slotkin, J. S.
    1956   *The Peyote Religion: A Study in Indian-White Relations*. Glencoe:
                Free Press.
Smith, Huston, and Reuben Snake, eds.
    1996   *One Nation under God: The Triumph of the Native American
                Church*. Santa Fe: Clear Light Publishers.
Snyder, Gary
    1974   *Turtle Island*. New York: New Directions Publishing.
    1980   *The Real Work: Interviews and Talks, 1964–1979*. New York:
                New Directions Publishing.

1990   *The Practice of the Wild.* San Francisco: North Point Press.

Speck, Frank

  1928   *Native Tribes and Dialects of Connecticut: A Mohegan-Pequot Diary.* 43rd Annual Report of the Bureau of American Ethnology. Washington, D.C.: U.S. Government Printing Office.

  1977   *Naskapi: The Savage Hunters of the Labrador Peninsula.* Norman: University of Oklahoma Press.

Spicer, Edward

  1962   *Cycles of Conquest: The Impact of Spain, Mexico, and the United States on the Indians of the Southwest, 1533–1960.* Tucson: University of Arizona Press.

Standing Bear, Luther

  1928   *My People the Sioux.* Boston: Houghton Mifflin Company.

Starr, Paul

  1982   *The Social Transformation of American Medicine.* New York: Basic Books.

Steward, Julian

  1955   *Theory of Culture Change.* University of Illinois Press.

Stewart, Omer

  1948   *Ute Peyotism: A Study of a Cultural Complex.* University of Colorado Studies, Series in Anthropology, no. 1. Boulder: University of Colorado Press.

Stiffarm, Lenore, and Phil Lane Jr.

  1992   "The Demography of Native North America: A Question of American Indian Survival." In *The State of Native America: Genocide, Colonization, and Resistance.* Ed. M. Annette Jaimes. Boston: South End Press.

Stocking, George

  1987   *Victorian Anthropology.* New York: Free Press.

  1988   "Bones, Bodies, Behavior." In *Bones, Bodies, Behavior: Essays on Biological Anthropology.* Ed. George Stocking. Madison: University of Wisconsin Press.

Storm, Hyemeyohsts

  1972   *Seven Arrows.* New York: Ballantine Books.

Sturtevant, William

  1991   "New National Museum of the American Indian Collections Policy Statement: A Critical Analysis." *Museum Anthropology* 15 (2): 29–30.

Stutwinii

  1992   Foreword to *The Bella Coola Indians,* by T. F. McIlwraith. Toronto: University of Toronto Press.

Sun Bear

  1996   "The Rainbow Path." *Wildfire* 7 (1): 52–53.

Swan, James

  1868   *The Indians of Cape Flattery, at the Entrance to the Strait of Fuca, Washington Territory.* Smithsonian Contributions to Knowledge. Philadelphia: Collins, Printer.

Szasz, Margaret

1977   *Education and the American Indian: The Road to Self-Determi-
            nation since 1928.* 2nd ed. Albuquerque: University of New Mex-
            ico Press.

1988   *Indian Education in the American Colonies, 1607–1783.* Albu-
            querque: University of New Mexico Press.

Taylor, Colin

1988   "The Indian Hobbyist Movement in Europe." In *Handbook of
            North American Indians,* ed. Wilcomb Washburn. Vol. 4, *History
            of Indian-White Relations.* Washington: Smithsonian Institution.

Thomas, David Hurst

1991   "Repatriation: The Bitter End or a Fresh Beginning?" *Museum
            Anthropology* 15 (1): 10.

Thomas, Keith

1971   *Religion and the Decline of Magic.* New York: Penguin Books.

Thompson, Hildegard

1975   *The Navajos' Long Walk for Education: A History of Navajo
            Education.* Tsaile, Ariz.: Navajo Community College Press.

Thoreau, Henry David

1981   *Walden and Other Writings.* New York: Bantam Books.
[1854]

Thornton, Russell

1987   *American Indian Holocaust and Survival: A Population History
            since 1492.* Norman: University of Oklahoma Press.

Thwaites, Reuben Gold, ed.

1896–   *The Jesuit Relations and Allied Documents.* 73 vols. Cleveland:
1901   Burrows Brothers.

Titley, E. Brian

1986   *A Narrow Vision: Duncan Campbell Scott and the Administra-
            tion of Indian Affairs in Canada.* Vancouver: University of British
            Columbia Press.

Tocqueville, Alexis de

1966   *Democracy in America.* Trans. J. P. Mayer. New York: Harper
[1848]   and Row.

Todorov, Tzvetan

1984   *The Conquest of America.* Trans. Richard Howard. New York:
            Harper and Row.

Trautmann, Thomas

1987   *Lewis Henry Morgan and the Invention of Kinship.* Berkeley and
            Los Angeles: University of California Press.

Trigger, Bruce

1985   *Natives and Newcomers: Canada's "Heroic Age" Reconsidered.*
            Kingston and Montreal: McGill-Queen's University Press.

Turner, Bryan S., with Colin Samson

1995   *Medical Power and Social Knowledge.* 2nd ed. London: Sage.

Ubelaker, Douglas
    1988   "North American Indian Population Size, A.D. 1500 to 1985." *American Journal of Physical Anthropology* 77:289–94.

Underhill, Ruth
    1965   *Red Man's Religion.* Chicago: University of Chicago Press.

United Nations
    1995   *Draft United Nations Declaration on the Rights of Indigenous Peoples.* United Nations doc. E/CN.4/1995/2.

United States Congress
    1974   *First Annual Report to the Congress of the United States from the National Advisory Council on Indian Education.* Pt. 1. Washington, D.C.: U.S. Government Printing Office.

    1987   *National American Indian Museum Act (Part 1): Joint Hearing before the Select Committee on Indian Affairs and the Committee on Rules and Administration.* 100th Cong., 1st sess., 12 November.

    1990   *Indian Adolescent Mental Health.* Office of Technology Assessment. Washington, D.C.: U.S. Government Printing Office.

    1991   Native American Graves Protection and Repatriation Act (Public Law 101–601, November 16, 1990). Reprinted in *Museum Anthropology* 15 (1): 11–14.

Veer, Peter van der
    1994   *Religious Nationalism: Hindus and Muslims in India.* Berkeley and Los Angeles: University of California Press.

Vico, Giambattista
    1968   *The New Science of Giambattista Vico.* Trans. Thomas Bergin
    [1744]   and Max Fisch. Ithaca: Cornell University Press.

Vizenor, Gerald
    1986   "Bone Courts: The Rights and Narrative Representation of Tribal Bones." *American Indian Quarterly* 10 (4): 319–31.

Vogel, Virgil J.
    1970   *American Indian Medicine.* Norman: University of Oklahoma Press.

von Gernet, Alexander
    1994   "Saving the Souls: Reincarnation Beliefs of the Seventeenth-Century Huron." In *Amerindian Rebirth: Reincarnation Beliefs among North American Indians and Inuit.* Ed. Antonia Mills and Richard Slobodin. Toronto: University of Toronto Press.

Voth, H. R.
    1901   *The Oraibi Powamu Ceremony.* Publications of the Field Columbian Museum. Anthropological Series, vol. 3, pp. 60–158. Chicago: n.p.

    1903   *The Oraibi Summer Snake Ceremony.* Publications of the Field Columbian Museum. Anthropological Series, vol. 3, pp. 262–358. Chicago: n.p.

Walker, Phillip, and Travis Hudson
    1993   *Chumash Healing: Changing Health and Medical Practices in an
                American Indian Society.* Banning, Calif.: Malki Museum Press.
Wallace, Anthony F. C.
    1969   *The Death and Rebirth of the Seneca.* New York: Vintage Books.
Washington, Booker T.
    1965   *Up from Slavery: An Autobiography.* New York: Dodd, Mead,
                and Company.
Waugh, Earle H.
    1996   *Dissonant Worlds: Roger Vandersteene among the Cree.* Water-
                loo: Wilfrid Laurier University Press.
Wax, Murray, Rosalie Wax, and Robert Dumont Jr.
    1989   *Formal Education in an American Indian Community: Poor Soci-
                ety and the Failure of Minority Education.* 1964. Reprint,
                Prospect Heights, Ill.: Waveland Press.
Weber, Max
    1948   *From Max Weber: Essays in Sociology.* Ed. and trans. H. H.
                Gerth and C. Wright Mills. London: Routledge and Kegan Paul.
Weil, Simone
    1996   *The Need for Roots: Prelude to a Declaration of Duties towards
    [1949]   Mankind.* Trans. A. F. Wills. New York: Routledge.
White, Leslie A.
    1964   *The World of the Keresan Pueblo Indians in Primitive Views of
                the World.* Ed. S. Diamond. New York: Columbia University
                Press.
Wilcox, U. Vincent
    1978   "The Museum of the American Indian, Heye Foundation."
                American Indian Art Magazine 3 (2): 40–49, 78–81.
Willey, G. R., and J. Sabloff
    1993   *A History of American Archaeology.* New York: W. H. Freeman
                and Co.
Wind, Wabun
    1996   "A Conversation with Wabun Wind." *Wildfire* 7 (1): 12–18.
Worl, Rosita
    1998   "Tlingit *At.oow*: Tangible and Intangible Property." Ph.D. diss.,
                Department of Anthropology, Harvard University.
Yemma, John
    1997   "Sunflowers, or Something More?" *Boston Globe Magazine*
                (September 12).
York, Geoffrey
    1989   *The Dispossessed: Life and Death in Native Canada.* Toronto:
                Lester and Orpen Dennys.
Young, T. Kue
    1988   *Health Care and Cultural Change: The Indian Experience in the
                Central Subarctic.* Toronto: University of Toronto Press.

Index

Abenaki, 217
Aberle, David, 142–43, 147
Abishabis, 206
acculturation, 7–8
Acoma, and Pueblo Revolt, 18
Aenons, and Huron epidemics, 28
agriculture, 4, 11, 54, 71, 151, 181, 188
Aiguillon, Duchess d', 29
Ainu, xv
Alaska Native Claims Settlement Act, 85
Albanese, Catherine, 202
Alberni Indian Residential School, 76–77, 84
Alcanfor Pueblo, 17
alcohol, use of, 3, 82, 115, 116, 120, 122, 177
Algonquin, 32, 181
allotment, 176–78
Ambrose, Saint, 13
American Civil Liberties Union, 145
American Horse, Robert, 62
American Indian Movement (AIM), 185, 194, 214
American Indian Policy Review Commission, 70
American Indian Religious Freedom Act, 146–47, 155, 215n
American Indian Religious Freedom Coalition, 152
American Missionary Association, 59
Anadarko School, 90
Anasazi, 181
Anderson, Benedict, 5
Anderson, W. W., 67

Anglican Church, 53, 109; and St. Peter's school, 74, 78, 81
anthropology: and archaeology, 6, 163–64, 183–85, 190–93; Boasian or "American school" of, 169–70; and collecting, 6, 161–93; and ethnography, xiv, 162–74, 208–9; and evolutionism, 51–52; and osteology, 183–85, 188–89, 191; and repatriation, 185–93. *See also* museums
Antilla, 16
anti-Semitism, 79
Apaches, 18
Apes, William, 43
Apodaca, Raymond, 152
Aquinas, Saint Thomas, 13
Arapahoe, 56, 131–32
Arawaks, 18n
archaeology, 6, 163–64, 183–85, 190–93
Armstrong, Samuel, 59, 60
Army School of Instruction for Cavalry Recruits, 60
assimilation, xvi, 1–2, 6, 8, 46, 52–54, 67–70, 76, 80, 91, 96, 111, 122, 146, 162, 176, 222, 224–26; and biomedicine, 111; and education, 67–70, 84
Association of American Indian Affairs, 90
astrology, 40
Athabaskans, 102n, 124
Augustine, Saint, 13
August Meeting, 44
Axtell, James, 27, 108
Aztec, 16

Text:	10/13 Sabon
Display:	Sabon
Composition:	Impressions Book and Journal Services, Inc.
Printing and binding:	Edwards Bros.